Xamarin.Forms Solutions

Gerald Versluis

Steven Thewissen

Foreword by David Ortinau

Xamarin.Forms Solutions

Gerald Versluis
Hulsberg, The Netherlands

Steven Thewissen
Hulsberg, Limburg, The Netherlands

ISBN-13 (pbk): 978-1-4842-4133-2
https://doi.org/10.1007/978-1-4842-4134-9

ISBN-13 (electronic): 978-1-4842-4134-9

Library of Congress Control Number: 2018964067

Managing Director, Apress Media LLC: Welmoed Spahr
Acquisitions Editor: Jonathan Gennick
Development Editor: Laura Berendson
Coordinating Editor: Jill Balzano

Cover image designed by Freepik (www.freepik.com)

Distributed to the book trade worldwide by Springer Science+Business Media New York, 233 Spring Street, 6th Floor, New York, NY 10013. Phone 1-800-SPRINGER, fax (201) 348-4505, e-mail orders-ny@springer-sbm.com, or visit www.springeronline.com. Apress Media, LLC is a California LLC and the sole member (owner) is Springer Science + Business Media Finance Inc (SSBM Finance Inc). SSBM Finance Inc is a **Delaware** corporation.

For information on translations, please e-mail rights@apress.com, or visit http://www.apress.com/rights-permissions.

Apress titles may be purchased in bulk for academic, corporate, or promotional use. eBook versions and licenses are also available for most titles. For more information, reference our Print and eBook Bulk Sales web page at http://www.apress.com/bulk-sales.

Any source code or other supplementary material referenced by the author in this book is available to readers on GitHub via the book's product page, located at www.apress.com/9781484241332. For more detailed information, please visit http://www.apress.com/source-code.

Printed on acid-free paper

Table of Contents

About the Authors

Gerald Versluis is a developer and Microsoft MVP from the Netherlands with years of experience working with Xamarin, Azure, ASP.NET, and other .NET technologies. He has been involved in numerous projects, in various roles. A great number of his projects are Xamarin apps. Not only does Gerald like to code, but he is keen on spreading his knowledge as well as gaining some in the bargain. He speaks, provides training sessions, and writes blogs and articles in his spare time.

Steven Thewissen is a developer and Microsoft MVP from the Netherlands focusing on Xamarin, Azure, and other .NET technologies. He started working with Xamarin in 2014, and has been in love with it ever since. Steven shares his knowledge by regularly writing blogs about topics that interest him. He loves to push the boundaries of what's graphically possible with Xamarin.Forms due to his interest in UI design. He loves to create kick-ass user interfaces to accompany his mobile apps.

About the Technical Reviewer

Pieter Nijs is a Belgian .NET architect with a passion for mobile and cloud development. He has played a key role in several projects, ranging from large consumer-facing telecom and media apps to smaller LOB applications. As he is primarily interested in the Microsoft stack. His interest and expertise translate to technologies like .NET, C#, Xaml, Xamarin, UWP, Azure, Visual Studio, TFS, VSTS, and more. Both at work as well as in his spare time, Pieter is constantly working and playing with these and other new technologies. He likes to tell everybody about the things he does, sharing his knowledge. You can find him speaking at conferences, giving trainings, and blogging at blog.pieeatingninjas.be. In 2017, Pieter received a Microsoft MVP Windows Development Award for sharing his passion and expertise with the community.

Acknowledgments

We would like to take some time to thank all of the people who made it possible for us to write this book.

First and foremost, our loving spouses Nadia and Laurie. Without them keeping the little munchkins out of our hair so we had the time to write, we would not be where we are today. They were just as important in completing this book as we were.

Also, our strict but very fair technical reviewer, Pieter. We know you have put in a lot of time to check and recheck every word, even in the code blocks. What really stood out to us is that you did not just point out mistakes and errors, but you also gave positive notes on the parts you liked. Thank you for taking the effort to make this book better.

A proper book cannot do without a wonderful foreword. For that, we were honored to have none other than David Ortinau write that for us. We are thankful that you could find time for us in your busy schedule to read our drafts. It really is the icing on the cake to have your foreword in this book.

From Apress, we would like to thank the entire publishing team, but Jill and Jonathan in particular. They have been there to guide us through this entire process and have been looking out for us along the way.

Foreword by David Ortinau

I love working with teams to build mobile apps, and to help make the whole process better. Working with Microsoft on Xamarin and mobile developer tools is the perfect fit for me. The work keeps me up at night laboring to solve some nagging issue blocking a customer, and it gets me up early in the morning to push forward. Day in and day out, that work ends up being a lot of screen time!

A few years back, I started venturing into the great outdoors where I could for a brief time leave all my work behind. I recall my first time hiking on a single-track trail only 1.5 miles from the nearest road, house, or human; a wave of panic came over me. I looked at my phone and prayed to see bars. Phew, I was okay. But what if I sprained my ankle? What if I ran out of water? What if I saw a bobcat? (I live in Missouri —that's about as dangerous as it gets at the foothills of the Ozark Mountains.)

I realized if I was going to spend more time in the woods and get farther and farther from civilization, I needed to know what to do in emergency situations and how to sustain myself. As my goals went from two miles to 10 to eventually 50 miles, the planning and the knowledge I needed to be successful grew and grew.

The first book I picked up was a survival handbook with practical advice such as how to escape a mountain lion, and not so practical advice such as how to survive jumping from a building into a dumpster. I talked to others whom I met out on the trails, I read a lot of blogs, and I watched a lot of YouTube. I learned valuable lessons all along the way.

A while later, I did see a coyote and it was enormous! I quickly texted my hiking friend who had hiked part of the Appalachian Trail the previous year about what to do, and he replied: "Back away slowly, makes some noise so he knows you're there, and just keep moving. Make a lot of noise if comes toward you." Phew! Good advice, and the coyote went bounding away.

Perhaps for you the questions are more like: "How do I make my Entry field look and work like this design?" or "How do I do barcode scanning in Xamarin.Forms?" or any number of other common questions. As I look at his book, I see a great success guide for mobile developers. It will answer many of your questions and help you like those survival guides have helped me.

Steven is a long-time Xamarin developer and community advocate known for blogging about how to make beautiful apps with Xamarin.Forms. Gerald is a recognized Microsoft MVP and an active contributor to Xamarin.Forms. Steven and Gerald should be on the top of anyone's list to call when that "coyote" surprises you in the middle of your day.

If you heed the guidance in this book, you'll not only survive your project, but you'll thrive! As you master the fundamental lessons, the book becomes a great resource to grab code samples from that help solve the common challenges along your way to building and shipping better and bigger apps more quickly.

—David Ortinau

Introduction

First of all, we would like to thank you for acquiring this book. Hopefully you will enjoy reading it as much as we enjoyed writing it.

This book is all about Xamarin.Forms. We have tried to provide you with a very complete reference on this matter. Whether you are a starting developer or a more seasoned one, this book should hold useful information for anyone.

We will start you off by going over the basic fundamentals of Xamarin.Forms. You will learn about renderers, which are at the heart of Forms. These renderers perform the translation between abstract controls and the native controls. You also have the possibility to hook into that and write so-called custom renderers. You will also learn how to leverage platform-specific code in a shared code context. This is accomplished with the `DependencyService` that is built-in right into Xamarin.Forms. This and much more is just in the first chapter.

From there, we will target the user interface. Contrary to popular belief, you can create beautiful UIs in Xamarin.Forms. We will provide you with all the information and tools to do that for yourself. We will see what options there are to create layouts and how the elements work in-depth. Of course, data is something you cannot do without, so we will show you how you can influence the way your interface looks based on that data. Other things that you will learn are working with animations and custom fonts and how to create reusable controls that you can not only share within your project, but even across projects!

In the remaining chapters you will find all kinds of solutions for various scenarios. All of them conveniently categorized into a couple of chapters. As already mentioned: we can't do without data. Therefore, a good understanding of how to get that data into our app and update it through data-binding is crucial. We learn how to show data, how to transform data through value converters, and how to show repeatable data in the `ListView` control.

To retrieve this data, a network connection is very important. Because of that, we have also included a whole chapter full of solutions that cover network and security. It teaches you how to connect to a backend and how to save code while doing so. We learn how to check our connectivity, cache data so we don't impose unnecessary costs on our users, save data in a secure place, and deal with an unstable network.

Toward the end of this book you will encounter more common real-life scenarios. Think about showing a PDF file and scanning or generating barcodes but also how to version your app and collect crash reports and analytics from your app when it is released. To top it off, there are some advanced topics. Xamarin.Forms app can be a bit bulkier in file size than true native apps. You will learn how to shave off some of that extra size. Also, with the transition from PCL libraries to .NET Standard, you might want to look into converting your shared code in that area. We will teach you how to do just that and much, much more.

It would be impossible to cover everything about everything, but with this book in hand, we hope to provide you with a solid base. Based on our years of hands-on experience, we have tried to identify the most frequently asked questions and capture the solutions in this book. Hopefully we will be able to transfer all this knowledge to you through the means of this book and enable you to do amazing things and build great apps.

CHAPTER 1

Fundamentals

In this chapter, we look at some Xamarin.Forms fundamentals. The concepts explained here will be used throughout this book, so it is important that you have an understanding of how these fundamentals work. If you already have some knowledge of Forms and more specifically, custom renderers, the DependencyService, the MessagingCenter, behaviors and effects, then it is probably safe to skip this chapter. If not, please keep reading.

Custom Renderers

At the heart of Xamarin.Forms are the renderers. Xamarin.Forms is a library that allows you to define the user interface (UI) as an abstract layer as opposed to implementing a UI per platform. To make this work, Xamarin has provided a set of so-called renderers that will take these abstract controls and translate them into the native counterparts for you.

Built-in Renderers

For example, if you define a (Xamarin.Forms) `Button` at runtime, this will be translated to a `UIButton` and `Android.Widget.Button` for iOS and Android, respectively. All the properties you have set on the Forms button will be mapped by the renderer to the native equivalent of that property. Or, if a similar property is not available, code is injected to simulate the intended behavior.

A schematic overview of this process is shown in Figure 1-1.

© Gerald Versluis and Steven Thewissen 2019

G. Versluis and S. Thewissen, *Xamarin.Forms Solutions*, https://doi.org/10.1007/978-1-4842-4134-9_1

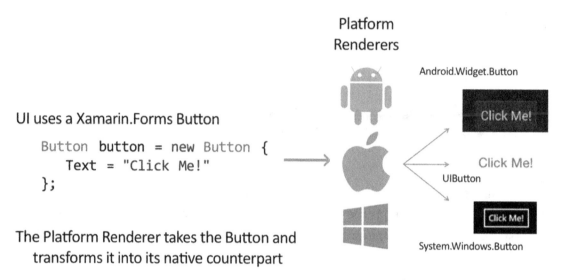

UI uses a Xamarin.Forms Button

```
Button button = new Button {
    Text = "Click Me!"
};
```

The Platform Renderer takes the Button and
transforms it into its native counterpart

Figure 1-1. Schematic overview of a renderer in Xamarin.Forms

You might be wondering why a custom renderer would be needed at all. The
team at Xamarin has mostly focused on implementing the most basic properties of
each control. More specifically the properties that are supported by all the platforms
that were supported by Xamarin.Forms at that time. But the platform-specific
controls usually have more properties and capabilities that you might want to use
but aren't supported by Xamarin.Forms right now. To make the platform-specific
properties available to you, you can write your own renderer, typically referred to as
a *custom renderer*.

So, if the default renderer, implemented by Xamarin, doesn't cut it for you,
you can always choose to implement your own. I wouldn't recommend writing
it from scratch, but if that is what you want, it is possible. Creating a full custom
renderer on your own can be done by inheriting from the `ViewRenderer`. When you
do implement your own renderer from scratch, you are responsible for creating a
platform control from start to finish. That means translate the abstract Xamarin.
Forms control into the control that belongs on the targeted platform. This includes
setting all the necessary properties.

Instead, typically you would inherit the default renderer and just tweak the bits that
are relevant to you. That way, you can normally use 99% of the code that the Xamarin
team wrote for you and you just have to set that one property that you would want to
change. To explain the basics, let's look at an example in the next section.

Implementing a Custom Renderer

Let's say that we want to customize a Xamarin.Forms Entry. In Figure 1-2, you can see how the entry control is rendered for each specific platform if we are creating an app for iOS, Android, and Windows.

At the top level, we define an Entry either in XAML or code. Whenever this code is executed, through reflection Xamarin.Forms will go through the associated renderer for this control and instantiate a new control. The newly created control is the platform-specific equivalent of the Entry.

In the case of the entry control, the renderer is named EntryRenderer. This is the typical naming convention: *<control name>*Renderer. There are some exceptions to this. For a full list of renderers and when to use which, refer to the documentation page: https://docs.microsoft.com/en-us/xamarin/xamarin-forms/app-fundamentals/custom-renderer/renderers.

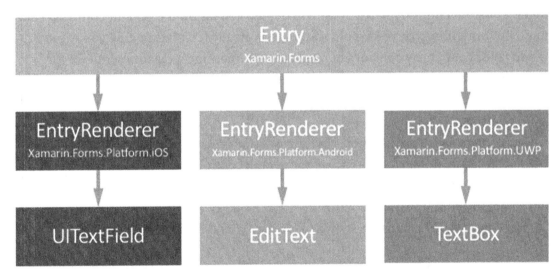

Figure 1-2. *Default path for rendering an Entry*

Imagine that we want to change something in the default behavior of the Forms renderer. For instance, we want to change the background color for this control. Note that this is possible with Forms out of the box, but for this example we will do it with our own renderer.

Creating a custom renderer takes roughly three steps:

1. Create a custom control—This needs to be created in the shared Xamarin.Forms project. Typically you would want to create an inheritance of the control that you want to create a renderer for. We will see why in a minute.

2. Use the control in your app—This also happens in the shared Forms project. You can use your control from either XAML or code, use it anywhere in your screens and layout.

3. Create a custom renderer for your control—Finally, you have to implement the custom renderer in each platform that you want to add something custom. Implementing it for each platform is not absolutely necessary. We will see this a little later.

The first step isn't absolutely necessary, but I would recommend it. If you do not create a custom control, the renderer will be invoked for *all* the default controls. That could be something that you would want, but typically it isn't. Imagine you want to add color your `Entry` control's border. By implementing a custom renderer for the `Entry`, all entries in your project will have a colored border. By sub-classing the `Entry` into `MyEntry` and applying the renderer to that, you can apply the color to only those controls.

Let's proceed with the first step, creating a custom control. This does not have to be too hard; it can be just an inheritance of the default control without adding anything new. At least, if in the future your requirements change, you have the possibility to still add something to your custom control.

The entry for this example is shown in Listing 1-1 and is called `MyEntry`.

Listing 1-1. The Custom Entry to Which We Will Apply the Custom Renderer

```
public class MyEntry : Entry
{
}
```

We have now simply created a new type with the sole purpose of not rendering all entry controls, but only the ones of the `MyEntry` type.

For the second step, we need to implement this control somewhere in our app. Since we do not have one sample app that we will work with in this book, refer to Listing 1-2 for a sample code snippet.

Listing 1-2. A Basic Page in XAML Using the MyEntry Control

```xml
<?xml version="1.0" encoding="utf-8"?>
<ContentPage xmlns="http://xamarin.com/schemas/2014/forms"
             xmlns:x="http://schemas.microsoft.com/winfx/2009/xaml"
             xmlns:local="clr-namespace:SolutionsSampleApp"
             x:Class="SolutionsSampleApp.MainPage">
    <local:MyEntry Text="Welcome to Xamarin Forms!"
    VerticalOptions="Center" HorizontalOptions="Center" />
</ContentPage>
```

The code in Listing 1-2 is *XAML* (Extensible Application Markup Language). With this XML-like syntax you can define your UI design. For this book, we assume that you already have worked with Xamarin.Forms before and that you know what XAML is. If not, refer to this link for more information: `https://docs.microsoft.com/en-us/xamarin/xamarin-forms/xaml/xaml-basics/`.

Note   Throughout the course of this book, we will be defining the UI in XAML. Everything that can be done in XAML can also be done in code. Whether you want to use XAML or code is mostly a matter of taste.

There are two things notable in the code in Listing 1-2. First, make sure that you included a new namespace declaration in the root of the page. In Listing 1-2, it is this line: `xmlns:local="clr-namespace:SolutionsSampleApp"`. This is similar to adding a `using` statement in your class. Now, the local prefix is available to declare controls in the namespace that is associated to it. You will see this prefixing of tags more often in the remainder of this book, now you know that this is because of a namespace declaration. This is what the `<local:MyEntry />` tag does. It defines a new control, our custom control, and takes it from the namespace that we have abbreviated as `local`. Since our `MyEntry` control is just an inheritance of the `Entry` control, all properties of the `Entry` are also available in our control.

Now that we have our own custom control and consumed it in our app, it is time for the final step: create the custom renderer for it. The renderer classes are to be created for each platform that we want to support. But note that you are not required to implement a custom renderer for each platform if you decide to implement it for one platform.

For example, if you want to implement something specific to iOS, you can create a renderer for iOS only. On Android (or any other platform), the default renderer will stay in effect and nothing will change there.

To create a custom renderer, create a new class in the targeted platform project. In this example, I will name it MyEntryRenderer. Let's first focus on iOS. The full implementation can be seen in Listing 1-3.

Listing 1-3. The Implemented iOS Custom Renderer

```
public class MyEntryRenderer : EntryRenderer
{
    protected override void OnElementChanged (ElementChangedEventArgs<Entry> e)
    {
        base.OnElementChanged (e);

        if (Control != null)
        {
            // Platform native control is created here, have at it
            Control.BackgroundColor = UIColor.FromRGB (42, 42, 42);
            Control.BorderStyle = UITextBorderStyle.Line;
        }
    }
}
```

On the first line, you can see how we inherit from the default renderer, EntryRenderer. This is the renderer implemented by the Xamarin team. From that renderer, we override the OnElementChanged method. This pattern is what you will see for the most custom renderers.

The ElementChangedEventArgs contains a couple of properties that will tell you something about the lifecycle of the rendered control. During runtime, the OnElementChanged method can be called a couple of times. Here is a list of important properties and an explanation of what they tell you.

- OldElement—This can be null when a control is created. When it is not null, a control is being destroyed and you should unsubscribe from events and clean up any other resources.

- NewElement—This can also be null whenever a control is being destroyed. When it is not null, a control is being created and you should initialize it as needed.

Both OldElement and NewElement will contain a reference to the Xamarin.Forms variant of the control. In case of this example, it would be an Entry.

Inside a renderer, there are a couple of notable properties. I will explain them next.

- Control—This property contains a reference to the *native* control. In our example, when the renderer is initialized, it will contain a typed reference to a UITextField.

- Element—This will hold a reference to the Xamarin.Forms control. So, in our case that would be the Entry.

All these properties and objects together should give you enough information to understand the lifecycle of a control. Basically, you can use the boilerplate code, as seen in Listing 1-4.

Listing 1-4. Boilerplate for Any Custom Renderer

```
protected override void OnElementChanged (ElementChangedEventArgs<ControlType> e)
{
    base.OnElementChanged (e);

    if (Control == null)
    {
        // Instantiate the native control and assign it to the Control
        property
    }

    if (e.OldElement != null)
    {
        // Unsubscribe from event handlers and clean up any resources
    }
```

```
    if (e.NewElement != null)
    {
        // Configure the control and subscribe to event handlers
    }
}
```

Typically, you are probably only interested whenever the `Control` property is not null. That is, when the platform control is created and you can do your custom magic.

There is one very important piece of code missing to make this work. We have to register this renderer as the renderer for our `MyEntry` control. This is done through an attribute on the namespace level. To match our example, this would look like the code in Listing 1-5.

Listing 1-5. Register the Custom Renderer with the Runtime

```
[assembly: ExportRenderer (typeof(MyEntry), typeof(MyEntryRenderer))]
namespace CustomRenderer.iOS
{
    public class MyEntryRenderer : EntryRenderer
    {
        // Code from Listing 1-3
    }
}
```

The important line is at the top. With the `ExportRenderer` attribute, we register with this attribute we inform Xamarin that we want to use this type of renderer when it needs to render a view of type `MyEntry`. It takes two parameters—the type of the control that we want to render and the type of the renderer we want to use for it. Failing to add this attribute will result in the default renderer taking over and your renderer having no effect at all.

When we now run this code, the entry on iOS will have a background color.

At this stage, we don't have a custom renderer for the other platforms. As `MyEntry` inherits from `Entry`, Xamarin will use the default `EntryRenderer` to render this control on the other platforms. Hence there will be no custom background or anything—a native control will be rendered as if it were a standard `Entry`.

If we also want to give this control a background color on Android, we need to create a custom renderer in our Android project. Listing 1-6 shows the code that we need to implement for Android to give our MyEntry object a red background color.

Listing 1-6. Implementation of the Custom Renderer on Android

```
[assembly: ExportRenderer(typeof(MyEntry), typeof(MyEntryRenderer))]
namespace CustomRenderer.Android
{
    public class MyEntryRenderer : EntryRenderer
    {
        public MyEntryRenderer(Context context) : base(context)
        {
        }

        protected override void OnElementChanged(ElementChangedEventArgs
        <Entry> e)
        {
            base.OnElementChanged(e);

            if (Control != null)
            {
                Control.SetBackgroundColor (global::Android.Graphics.Color.Red);
            }
        }
    }
}
```

You can see the concept is mostly the same. Only the code to set the background color on an Android control is different. As we learned earlier, the Control property contains a reference to the native control, in this case of type EditText. Since the renderers are implemented in the platform-specific projects, we can access the native APIs directly and set the background on the Android natives EditText. This really is how Xamarin.Forms works, inside these renderers—either made by you or the Xamarin team—the translation happens from the Forms control to its native counterpart.

Figure 1-3 shows a schematic overview of how all the components are arranged.

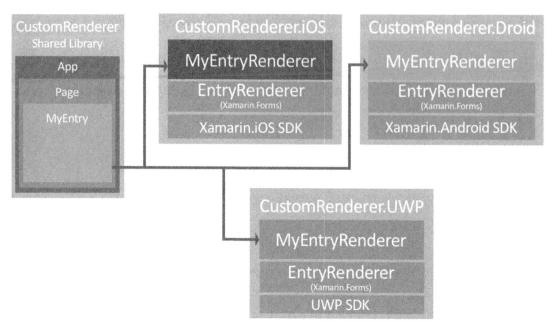

Figure 1-3. *The situation after implementing a custom renderer on each platform*

While UWP is depicted in Figure 1-3, we will not show you this example in code. It is mostly the same as the other examples or Android and iOS you saw earlier.

Tip   For more information on how to create custom renderers, take a look at the documentation at `https://docs.microsoft.com/en-us/xamarin/ xamarin-forms/app-fundamentals/custom-renderer/`.

Effects

Somewhat relatable to the custom renderers are *effects*. With effects, you do not need to subclass a whole renderer, instead you can write just enough code to customize the control a little bit.

Effects Versus Custom Renderers

Of course, then the question arises: when do you use an effect and when do you use a custom renderer? The short answer is that it's totally up to you. There are however a few differences between renderers and effects. While effects can be reused more easily, custom renderers offer more flexibility in terms of what you can achieve with them.

In the official documentation, this list can be found on when to choose effects over custom renderers:

- An effect is recommended when changing the properties of a platform-specific control will achieve the desired result.

- A custom renderer is required when there's a need to override methods of a platform-specific control.

- A custom renderer is required when there's a need to replace the platform-specific control that implements a Xamarin.Forms control.

All documentation on effects can be found at `https://docs.microsoft.com/en-us/xamarin/xamarin-forms/app-fundamentals/effects/introduction`.

Implementing an Effect

To create our own effect, we need to create a subclass of the `PlatformEffect` class. Each platform has its own `PlatformEffect` class and has three important properties:

- `Container`—Holds a reference to the parent the control is added to.

- `Control`—References the platform-specific control.

- `Element`—Contains a reference to the Xamarin.Forms control.

These properties are not typed and will contain references to high-level objects. You can see these objects per platform underneath:

- *iOS*—`UIView` both for `Container` and `Control`

- *Android*—`ViewGroup` (`Container`) or `View` (`Control`)

- *UWP*—`FrameworkElement` for `Container` and `Control`

The `Container` and `Control` properties are implemented as high-level properties so that they can be applied to all elements. You can strongly type the `Container` and `Control` properties by inheriting from the generic `PlatformEffect<TContainer, TControl>` class. For instance, on iOS if you know the `Container` should be a `UIView` and the `Control` should be a `UILabel`, you can declare your effect like this:

```
public class YourCustomEffect : PlatformEffect<UIView, UILabel>
```

Therefore, it is important to know for which control you are creating an effect so you can strongly type it or cast it to the right type yourself.

In addition to these properties, there are two methods that need to be overridden when creating an effect.

- `OnAttached`—This method is called when the effect is attached to the Forms control. In here you need to implement your custom styling, hooking up events, etc. You also need to take into account any error handling for when the effect fails to attach.

- `OnDetached`—Basically, this is the opposite of the attached method. You need to clean up any resources and unhook events, etc.

The `PlatformEffect` class also has a `OnElementPropertyChanged` method that can be overridden. This method is invoked whenever a property on the element changes. Please note that this method can be called many times potentially.

In order to implement an effect, we need to take five steps:

1. Create a new class that inherits from `PlatformEffect` in the platform project.

2. Override the `OnAttached` method to apply our new effect.

3. Override the `OnDetached` method and implement code to clean up after our effect, which is not always required.

4. Add a `ResolutionGroupName` attribute as part of the unique identifier of this effect. Think of this as the namespace for a class.

5. Add a `ExportEffect` attribute to register the effect with the runtime, equal to the way we register the custom renderer.

If we wanted to achieve the same result as with the custom renderer from the previous part of this chapter, we have to implement an effect like in Listing 1-7.

Listing 1-7. Implementing an Effect to Set the Background Color

```
[assembly:ResolutionGroupName ("com.MyApp")]
[assembly:ExportEffect (typeof(BackgroundColorEffect),
nameof(BackgroundColorEffect))]
namespace MyApp.iOS
{
    public class BackgroundColorEffect : PlatformEffect
    {
        protected override void OnAttached ()
        {
            try
            {
                Control.BackgroundColor = UIColor.FromRGB (42, 42, 42);
            }
            catch (Exception ex)
            {
                Console.WriteLine ("Cannot set property on attached
                control. Error: ", ex.Message);
            }
        }

        protected override void OnDetached ()
        {
            // No need to do anything in this example
        }
    }
}
```

This code shows you an example of how we can implement this effect for iOS.
It shows a couple of similarities with the custom renderer. An effect also needs to be
implemented at platform project level. Also, just like with the renderers, you will have
to register the effect with an attribute. In the code from Listing 1-7, you can see it being
done with the ExportEffect attribute above the namespace declaration. The additional
ResolutionGroupName attribute is needed to be able to uniquely identify the effects
in your project. The ResolutionGroupName together with the class name will make for

the fully qualified name. We will see this in a little bit. Also, you just need to set the ResolutionGroupName once per project. It will carry over to all other effects defined in the project.

For completeness, we implement the same effect on Android. You can see it in Listing 1-8.

Listing 1-8. Implementing the BackgroundEffect on Android .

```
[assembly:ResolutionGroupName ("com.MyApp")]
[assembly:ExportEffect (typeof(FocusEffect), "FocusEffect")]
namespace MyApp.Droid
{
    public class BackgroundColorEffect: PlatformEffect
    {
        protected override void OnAttached ()
        {
            try
            {
                Control.SetBackgroundColor (Android.Graphics.Color.Red);
            } catch (Exception ex) {
                Console.WriteLine ("Cannot set property on attached
                control. Error: ", ex.Message);
            }
        }

        protected override void OnDetached ()
        {
        }
    }
}
```

You can see the gist of the code is the same, but here you can also use the platform-specific APIs just like with renderers. This is because we are implementing the effects in the platform code.

Consuming an effect is a bit harder than with a custom renderer. The biggest difference here is that you have to keep in mind that each control will have its own instance of the effect, whereas a custom renderer will be used for all the controls going through. This also means that you don't need to create your own inheritance of a control; you can just attach the effect to one instance of a regular control.

To be able to consume an effect in XAML, you need to create a subclass of the `RoutingEffect` class in your shared library. The class itself doesn't really do that much except for pointing to the right implementation on the platform. Listing 1-9 shows the `RoutingEffect` for our example `BackgroundColorEffect`.

Listing 1-9. RoutingEffect in Shared Code To Be Able to Consume Our Effect in XAML

```
public class BackgroundColorEffect : RoutingEffect
{
    public BackgroundColorEffect () : base ("com.MyApp.
    BackgroundColorEffect")
    {
    }
}
```

Notice how the effect in our shared code is named exactly the same as the effect in the platform project. Although this is not absolutely necessary, it helps identifying them easily. The real identification of the effect happens on this line:

```
public BackgroundColorEffect () : base ("com.MyApp.BackgroundColorEffect")
```

In the base call you have to specify the value from the `ResolutionGroupName` and the class name combined. From that, Xamarin.Forms will know which effect to route to.

With this in place we are now ready to use the effect in our XAML. This is shown in Listing 1-10.

Listing 1-10. Consuming the Effect in XAML

```
<?xml version="1.0" encoding="utf-8"?>
<ContentPage xmlns="http://xamarin.com/schemas/2014/forms"
             xmlns:x="http://schemas.microsoft.com/winfx/2009/xaml"
             xmlns:local="clr-namespace:SolutionsSampleApp.Effects"
             x:Class="SolutionsSampleApp.MainPage">
    <Entry Text="Welcome to Xamarin Forms!" VerticalOptions="Center"
    HorizontalOptions="Center">
        <Entry.Effects>
            <local:BackgroundColorEffect />
        </Entry.Effects>
```

```
    </Entry>
</ContentPage>
```

Our sample effect is pretty simple. It just changes the background color whenever it is attached. Before, I told you that effects are better suited for reusability. We could easily extend our effect with a property that takes a color and we would then be able to apply that color as the background color for instance. Because each control will have its own instance of the effect, we can also specify a different color for each control. To achieve this, we can add a property on our RoutingEffect, which is in the shared code. In Listing 1-11 you see the same effect as in Listing 1-9, but now we have added an extra property that takes in a Xamarin.Forms.Color.

Listing 1-11. Adding a Color to Our Effect So We Can Set Different Colors

```
public class BackgroundColorEffect : RoutingEffect
{
    public Color BackgroundColor { get; set; }

    public BackgroundColorEffect () : base ("com.MyApp.
    BackgroundColorEffect")
    {
    }
}
```

In the implementation on the platform, you will now have access to this property. The one thing you do need to do is translate the Xamarin.Forms.Color to the equivalent on that platform. In Listing 1-12, you see the implementation on iOS. This is basically the same one as we saw in Listing 1-7, but now uses our BackgroundColor property.

Listing 1-12. Effect with Dynamic Color

```
[assembly:ResolutionGroupName ("com.MyApp")]
[assembly:ExportEffect (typeof(BackgroundColorEffect),
nameof(BackgroundColorEffect))]
namespace MyApp.iOS
{
    public class BackgroundColorEffect : PlatformEffect
    {
```

```
protected override void OnAttached ()
{
    try
    {
        var effect = (BackgroundColorEffect)Element.Effects.
        FirstOrDefault (e => e is BackgroundColorEffect);

        if (effect != null)
        {
            Control.BackgroundColor = effect.BackgroundColor.
            ToUIColor();
        }
    }
    catch (Exception ex)
    {
        Console.WriteLine ("Cannot set property on attached
        control. Error: ", ex.Message);
    }
}

protected override void OnDetached ()
{
    // No need to do anything in this example
}
    }
}
```

In this code, you can see something funny going on while assigning the effect variable. A control can have multiple effects, so we need to find the right effect, cast it, and extract the value for our background color. After doing that, we can assign this color as we did before. Luckily, the Xamarin team has already provided us with helper extension methods to translate a Forms color into a platform color. I will skip over the Android counterpart for brevity. The extraction of the color from the RoutingEffect will be the same, only the translation of the color will happen through another extension method (ToAndroid()).

To specify a color, you just assign a value to it. Based on the code in Listing 1-10, we can now change the effect line in XAML like this:

```
<local:BackgroundColorEffect BackgroundColor="Red" />
```

And in code you can now simply set this property just as well. You can see this in the code example of Listing 1-13.

Consuming the effect when creating a control in code is much easier. It does not require you to have a separate RoutingEffect in place. This is due to the fact that we can just resolve the effect by the unique identifier directly. In Listing 1-13, you can see the same Entry from our XAML code being created in code.

Listing 1-13. Consuming the Effect When Creating a Control from Code

```
public MainPage()
{
    var entry = new Entry
    {
        Text = "Welcome to Xamarin Forms!"
    };

    // Add the effect by resolving it yourself...
    entry.Effects.Add (Effect.Resolve ("com.MyApp.BackgroundColorEffect"));

    // ... Or by using the RoutingEffect
    var effect = new BackgroundColorEffect();
    effect.BackgroundColor = Xamarin.Forms.Color.Red;

    entry.Effects.Add (effect);
}
```

This concludes creating and consuming effects in Xamarin.Forms.

MessagingCenter

One of the core functionalities of Xamarin.Forms is the *MessagingCenter*. Although I would recommend using it as a last resort, it does have its use. The MessagingCenter helps you keep your code decoupled. Sometimes you will find yourself in a position that requires you create a reference between certain code, but by doing so, you have to compromise on reusability, maintainability, and probably a whole lot of other *-ilities*.

How MessagingCenter Works

To overcome these kinds of situations, you can use the MessagingCenter. The MessagingCenter is a simple messaging service that allows you to subscribe to a certain message. The sender and receiver do not need to know each other besides a simple message contract. As I have mentioned, this is also not ideal since your code will become less readable.

To implement the MessagingCenter, you basically need to do two things:

- *Subscribe:* From the point in code where you want to execute logic based on a received message, you need to subscribe to said message.

- *Send:* Whenever you need to trigger logic, you need to send a message. Any subscribers will then receive the message and act accordingly. When sending a message, you have no knowledge whatsoever about the number of subscribers. This could just as well be zero.

To access the service, you can call upon a static class called MessagingCenter, which has basically three, self-describing methods: Subscribe, Unsubscribe, and Send.

Using MessagingCenter

Using the service is very easy. From some point in your code where you want to execute logic based on a trigger, subscribe to a message as shown in Listing 1-14.

Listing 1-14. Subscribing to a Simple String Message

```
MessagingCenter.Subscribe<MainPage> (this, "YourMessageName", (sender) => {
    // do something whenever the "YourMessageName" message is received
    Console.WriteLine("YourMessageName was received!");
});
```

When we want to trigger the logic inside of our subscription, we can send this message from somewhere else in our code, like in Listing 1-15.

Listing 1-15. Sending a Message Through the MessagingCenter

```
MessagingCenter.Send<MainPage>(this, "YourMessageName");
```

The key thing in this example it the "YourMessageName" string. This binds the two together and acts as a contract. This is very useful if you just want this mechanism in place as some kind of event.

However, you might want to send some extra data with you message. Think of them as your event arguments. This is also possible. Have a look at Listing 1-16, where we see a more extensive example.

Listing 1-16. Receiving a Message with Arguments

```
MessagingCenter.Subscribe<MainPage, string> (this, "YourMessageName",
(sender, arg) => {
    // ... Your logic here
});
```

With this code we again subscribe to a message with the name "YourMessageName" but notice how we also stated a string type between the angle brackets after Subscribe. This indicates that we expect an argument to come along with our message. In the handler, you will notice that I have added another parameter, args. Because we indicated that this has to be of type string, this is strongly typed.

When we want to send a message that is received by this subscriber, we need to do that a little differently as well. Check out the code in Listing 1-17.

Listing 1-17. Sending a Message with Arguments

```
MessagingCenter.Send<MainPage, string> (this, "YourMessageName", "Your
parameter value");
```

You will notice in this code that we also added the second type between the angle brackets. Also, after specifying the message name, we now also need to add the arguments' value. In this case, of type string.

Note   Even though the message names can be the same, the full signature of the Send and Subscribe calls needs to match. For example, the Subscribe from Listing 1-14 will not be invoked by the Send of Listing 1-17 and vice versa.

If, for some reason, you want to stop listening for messages, you can manually unsubscribe. This is done by calling the Unsubscribe method. Just like the Send and Subscribe messages, you will need to match the exact signature. An example can be seen in Listing 1-18.

Listing 1-18. Unsubscribing from Message As Seen in Listing 1-16

```
MessagingCenter.Unsubscribe<MainPage, string> (this, "YourMessageName");
```

The MessagingCenter included by Xamarin.Forms makes it easy to reduce coupling in your code where needed. As mentioned, I do use it as a last resort; usually there is another way to achieve your desired functionality. While sending a message can be very powerful, using it too much can really eat into your readability.

A real-life example would be a case where you need to update values in multiple parts of your app. You can subscribe to a message from multiple places and thus execute code in multiple places when a message is received. Another use case could be if some background process is done, it can send a message and you can then inform the user in your UI.

If you want to learn even more about the MessagingCenter, have a look at this official documentation: https://docs.microsoft.com/en-us/xamarin/xamarin-forms/app-fundamentals/messaging-center.

DependencyService

While Xamarin.Forms is designed to help you overcome writing different code for different platforms, there are limits to what is implemented. Each platform will have features unique to that platform that cannot be leveraged on any of the other platforms. Also, the team at Xamarin has implemented a lot of basic functionality, but not for everything.

To enable the developer to write native code in a shared manner, Xamarin.Forms introduces DependencyService. This component is in essence a dependency resolver. To implement platform-specific code through DependencyService, you basically need to take four steps:

1. *Create an interface*—At the shared code level you will have to define an interface that is the contract for each implementation.

2. *Implement*—For each platform that you support, implement the interface. You must implement it for each platform that you target.

3.   *Register the implementation*—Similar to the custom renderers and effects, you need to register this implementation with the runtime.

4.   *Call DependencyService*—Consume the new functionality from your shared code.

Note   Instead of an interface you can also use an abstract class. While an interface should be sufficient in most cases, an abstract class certainly has it uses. For instance, if only one method needs a platform-specific implementation, you could implement it through an abstract class and just mark that one method as abstract. You can then inherit the abstract class and implement only the abstract method as needed. In this section, we stick with the interface, but keep in mind that you can substitute this with an abstract class.

Figure 1-4 shows how all the elements work together.

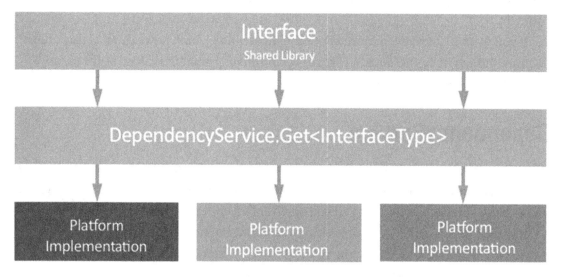

Figure 1-4. *Schematic overview of the DependencyService workings*

Using the DependencyService

We will now look at how to implement this in code. As we have just learned, a good start would be to create an interface. In Listing 1-19, you can see an interface definition that we will use to implement text-to-speech functionality.

Text-to-speech is something that is available on all platforms but isn't implemented as an abstraction by Xamarin.Forms. By the means of the DependencyService, we will do this ourselves.

Listing 1-19. Interface Definition for Text-To-Speech

```
public interface ITextToSpeech {
    void Speak (string text);
}
```

This interface should be defined in the shared project. The implementations will go into the platform-specific platforms. Let's look at the implementation for iOS. The full code for this is in Listing 1-20.

Listing 1-20.   iOS Implementation of the Text-To-Speech Functionality

```
[assembly: Dependency (typeof (TextToSpeech_iOS))]

namespace SolutionsSampleApp.iOS
{
    public class TextToSpeech_iOS : ITextToSpeech
    {
        public void Speak (string text)
        {
            var speechSynthesizer = new AVSpeechSynthesizer ();

            var speechUtterance = new AVSpeechUtterance (text) {
                Rate = AVSpeechUtterance.MaximumSpeechRate/4,
                Voice = AVSpeechSynthesisVoice.FromLanguage ("en-US"),
                Volume = 0.5f,
                PitchMultiplier = 1.0f
            };

            speechSynthesizer.SpeakUtterance (speechUtterance);
        }
    }
}
```

Note that the implementation has an attribute to register it with the runtime, the Xamarin.Forms.DependencyAttribute. There is another Dependency attribute in .NET as well, so make sure you pick the right one. This attribute has one mandatory parameter that takes in a type. This should be the type of the platform-specific implementation of this class. You only need to specify the platform-specific class, since it will always implement an interface or inherit from an abstract class, that class can be inferred for when you want to resolve it.

The actual code is not really relevant at this point, the thing that should be mentioned here is that you should see some iOS specific types pointing out that we're working in a platform-specific project.

For brevity I will skip over the actual implementations of the other platforms. They will look very similar, the only thing different will be the implementation of the Speak method.

Note   On UWP when using Universal Windows Platform .NET Native Compilation, registration needs to be done differently. In the App.xaml.cs file, you will need to register each class in the DependencyService through a separate line of code instead of through the attribute. In our example, it would look like this:

```
Xamarin.Forms.Forms.Init(e, assembliesToInclude);

// Register your DependencyService

Xamarin.Forms.DependencyService.Register<TextToSpeechImplemen
tation>();
```

The last step is to call the DependencyService and execute our just implemented functionality. Of course, this is done through our shared code. Xamarin.Forms includes a static class called DependencyService that can be used to locate the implementation of our text-to-speech platform-specific implementation.

To let our app say something, we can simply do this:

```
DependencyService.Get<ITextToSpeech>().Speak("Hello from Xamarin.Forms");
```

This call will locate the right implementation and invoke the Speak method on it. When an implementation could not be found, the Get<T> method will return null, so you might want to implement checks for that as well.

Note   You will need to implement the platform-specific code for each platform that you want to support. If, for some reason, you should only implement it for one platform, you can wrap it in a check to see on what platform the app is running.

This will look like:

```
if (Device.RuntimePlatform == Device.iOS)
DependencyService.Get<ITextToSpeech>().Speak("Hello from Xamarin.Forms");
```

This will cause the code only to be executed on iOS.

DependencyFetchTarget

While retrieving the implementation of a class through the DependencyService, you have the option to get a global copy or a new instance. A global copy in this case, meaning a singleton instance. You can do this by providing an extra parameter to the Get method of the DependencyFetchTarget enum type. The Get method has a default parameter value that defaults to DependencyFetchTarget.GlobalInstance. So, by default, a class registered in the DependencyService will be retrieved as a singleton.

By specifying the DependencyFetchTarget.NewInstance as a value, you will retrieve a new instance of the class.

For more information on the DependencyService, see the full documentation at https://docs.microsoft.com/en-us/xamarin/xamarin-forms/app-fundamentals/dependency-service/introduction.

Behaviors

With *behaviors,* you are able to enrich a user-control's functionality without having to subclass it. This can be useful whenever you want to add or change only a small bit.

Instead of needing to subclass the targeted control, you can write a behavior and attach that to the control. In Xamarin.Forms there are two types of behaviors:

- Xamarin.Forms behaviors
- Attached behaviors

Both can do pretty much the same; the way to implement them is different. Also, both of them can be set up in a way so that they are reusable, even across different applications. One example of a behavior that is used often is for *commanding*. There are lots of controls that expose *events*. With events, you are able to act on certain actions that the user invokes on a control. For instance, the click on a button has a backing event of whenever an item is selected in a picker.

The downside of events is that they are always used from the code-behind of your page. If you want to use an architectural pattern like MVVM, which is pretty common in Xamarin.Forms apps, using events is something you typically want to avoid. To convert events to a command, you can use a behavior. Note that there are multiple plugins out there that do this. Unless you have some specific requirements, I would recommend using a plugin that does the hard work for you. Still, to be aware of what is going on, it might be nice to see how it works on the inside. You can look at the specific event to command behavior at this sample repository by Xamarin: `https://github.com/xamarin/xamarin-forms-samples/tree/master/Behaviors/EventToCommandBehavior`.

If you would rather use a plugin for it like I have mentioned, look at the Xamarin. Forms Community Toolkit plugin. You can find all the info on their project page at `https://github.com/xamarin/XamarinCommunityToolkit`.

Other examples of behaviors could be input validation, limiting the length of an input, restricting the character use, or controlling animations.

Through a simple example, I will show you how to implement a Xamarin.Forms behavior and an attached behavior.

Xamarin.Forms Behaviors

Implementing a Xamarin.Forms behavior is done through inheriting from the `Behavior` class. It can be strongly typed by inheriting from the `Behavior<T>` class, where `T` is the type of the control you want the behavior to apply to.

The lifecycle of a Xamarin.Forms behavior is very similar to that of an `Effect`, which we have seen earlier. For a behavior, we have the `OnAttachedTo` and `OnDetachingFrom` events that we need to override in order to instantiate and destruct our behavior. The boilerplate code for a behavior then looks like the code in Listing 1-21.

Listing 1-21. Boilerplate Code for a Xamarin.Forms Behavior

```
public class CustomBehavior : Behavior<View>
{
    protected override void OnAttachedTo (View bindable)
    {
        base.OnAttachedTo (bindable);
        // Perform setup
    }

    protected override void OnDetachingFrom (View bindable)
    {
        base.OnDetachingFrom (bindable);
        // Perform cleanup
    }

    // Behavior implementation
}
```

To stick with a simple example, let's see how we could use a Xamarin.Forms behavior to create an Entry that only accepts numeric values. To do this, we hook into the TextChanged event of the entry. When this event is fired, we evaluated whether or not the new value is numeric and, if not, we will make the color in the entry red. The implementation code can be seen in Listing 1-22.

Listing 1-22. Implementation of a Numeric Validation with a Xamarin.Forms Behavior

```
public class NumericValidationBehavior : Behavior<Entry>
{
    protected override void OnAttachedTo(Entry entry)
    {
        entry.TextChanged += OnEntryTextChanged;
        base.OnAttachedTo(entry);
    }
```

```
    protected override void OnDetachingFrom(Entry entry)
    {
        entry.TextChanged -= OnEntryTextChanged;
        base.OnDetachingFrom(entry);
    }

    private void OnEntryTextChanged(object sender, TextChangedEventArgs args)
    {
        bool isValid = double.TryParse (args.NewTextValue, out double result);
        ((Entry)sender).TextColor = isValid ? Color.Default : Color.Red;
    }
}
```

To attach this behavior to an actual Entry, we can simply add it to the Behaviors property of said entry. In Listing 1-23, you can see how to do this both from XAML as well as in code.

Listing 1-23. Adding a Behavior to a Control

```
<Entry Placeholder="Enter a number">
    <Entry.Behaviors>
        <local:NumericValidationBehavior />
    </Entry.Behaviors>
</Entry>

var entry = new Entry { Placeholder = "Enter a number" };
entry.Behaviors.Add (new NumericValidationBehavior ());
```

Note that when you are writing a strongly-typed behavior, you can only attach it to that specific type of control. Failing to do so will result in a runtime exception being thrown.

You can reuse this behavior by applying it to multiple entries, or maybe even create your own custom inheritance of an entry control with this behavior attached by default. By implementing the behavior for higher level control or by not applying strong typing, you can make it available to all kinds of controls that share a certain property of event.

> **Tip**   Since a lot of behaviors focus on pretty common concepts, a group of people in the community have collected a number of them in a handy NuGet package. By the name of Xamarin Community Toolkit, they have hosted the project on GitHub: `https://github.com/xamarin/XamarinCommunityToolkit`. It includes behaviors (and effects, animations, and converters for that matter) for validations and commanding.

Attached Behaviors

So-called *attached behaviors* are static classes with one or more properties that can be attached to a control. The attached properties are a special implementation of the *bindable property*. So, it might be good to explain the bindable property first. A bindable property is a property that you can bind to. This means it does not have a hardcoded value, but you *bind* it to a property in your code-behind or view model. That way you can update your controls, without having to actually reference the controls itself. You only need to update the property on your view model. The Xamarin Binding Engine will update the value of the `BindableProperty` of the control to which the property on your view model is bound. This can also work the other way around, depending on the binding mode. Chapter 3 has more on data-binding.

Now that we know what bindable properties are, let's go back to the attached properties. Basically, these properties are defined in one (static) class and are attached to another class, a control.

This might sound a little abstract, but we already know at least two attached properties if you have worked with a `Grid`. On all the controls that you put inside a grid can specify the `Grid.Row` and `Grid.Column` property. The Xamarin team could've chosen to add a `Row` and `Column` property to every control that can be put inside a grid. Of course, this would be far from ideal, but most of the time they probably wouldn't be in a grid and you would be stuck with a couple of useless properties. Instead, what the people at Xamarin did was add the attached properties to the `BindableObject` class. The `Grid`, in its turn, can now read the values of these attached properties from each of its children and determine how and where to show them.

So, why not put it as a "regular" bindable property on the BindableObject? If tomorrow a new container control (equivalent to the grid) is launched, there is no need to update the BindableObject class; the new control can just introduce new attached properties that it can query. This way, there is no impact on existing base objects, and no gazillion (layout-)properties on a base object where only a few are used in a particular occurrence.

The way we interact with the control and the behavior is by the propertyChanged event handler. Whenever a property on the control this behavior is attached to changes, the attached behavior will get notified. An example will speak more than a thousand words, so let's see how we can implement the same numeric validation from the Xamarin.Forms behavior, but this time with an attached behavior. Observe the code rewritten to an attached behavior in Listing 1-24.

Listing 1-24. Numeric Validation with an Attached Behavior

```
public static class NumericValidationBehavior
{
    public static readonly BindableProperty AttachBehaviorProperty =
        BindableProperty.CreateAttached (
            "AttachBehavior", typeof(bool),
            typeof(NumericValidationBehavior),
            false, propertyChanged:OnAttachBehaviorChanged);

    public static bool GetAttachBehavior (BindableObject view)
    {
        return (bool)view.GetValue (AttachBehaviorProperty);
    }

    public static void SetAttachBehavior (BindableObject view, bool value)
    {
        view.SetValue (AttachBehaviorProperty, value);
    }
```

```
private static void OnAttachBehaviorChanged (BindableObject view,
object oldValue, object newValue)
{
    var entry = view as Entry;
    if (entry == null) {
        return;
    }

    bool attachBehavior = (bool)newValue;
    if (attachBehavior) {
        entry.TextChanged += OnEntryTextChanged;
    } else {
        entry.TextChanged -= OnEntryTextChanged;
    }
}

private static void OnEntryTextChanged (object sender,
TextChangedEventArgs args)
{
    double result;
    bool isValid = double.TryParse (args.NewTextValue, out result);
    ((Entry)sender).TextColor = isValid ? Color.Default : Color.Red;
}
}
```

In this code, note that GetAttachBehavior and SetAttachBehavior can vary by name. These methods should be named by a certain convention. Notice that in the BindableProperty.CreateAttached method right above it, as the first parameter we give the behavior a name, this is critical for the naming of your methods. The convention needs the be Get or Set, followed by the behavior name. In this case, the behavior name is AttachBehavior. So the methods are named GetAttachBehavior and SetAttachBehavior. If the behavior was named MyAwesomeBehavior, the methods would be named GetMyAwesomeBehavior and SetMyAwesomeBehavior. Also, and this might be redundant, but the return value specified in the BindableProperty.CreateAttached method must be the same as the return type of the getter and setter.

The least interesting logic is going on at the bottom. This validation logic is identical to the logic we have used in our Xamarin.Forms behavior. Actually, the most important part is all the way at the top. This `public static readonly BindableProperty AttachBehaviorProperty` property defines the name of the property we can attach to a control and is used to tie it to the logic that is executed.

When we look at how the `AttachBehaviorProperty` is defined through a `BindableProperty.CreateAttached`, you will notice that we need to specify the type of our property (a `bool` in this case). Hooking up the property changed event happens with this little piece of code: `propertyChanged:OnAttachBehaviorChanged`. With this we refer to the `OnAttachBehaviorChanged` method and mark this for invocation whenever a value of a property changes. Of course, the implementation of the `OnAttachBehaviorChanged` method needs to adhere to a certain signature. Because of that, we can gain information about the control invoking this event and information about the old and new value. Since these behaviors are not strongly-typed you, as the developer, will need to verify the right types and take care of error handling.

Attached behaviors can also be consumed both in XAML and in code. In Listing 1-25, you can see how to do this for both.

Listing 1-25. Consuming an Attached Behavior in XAML and Code

```
<Entry Placeholder="Enter a number" local:NumericValidationBehavior.
AttachBehavior="true" />
```

```
var entry = new Entry { Placeholder = "Enter a number" };
NumericValidationBehavior.SetAttachBehavior (entry, true);
```

The attached behavior we have created now just takes in a Boolean value to enable of disable it. You could of course take another approach to just enable it when you attach the behavior. You can then use an attached property to influence the workings of your behavior. For instance, set a maximum value on our entry, so the maximum numeric value could be set. Also, you are not limited to just one property, add as much as you like. So, you could both use the Boolean from this example and add a numeric property to specify the maximum value.

The obvious question now is: when do you use a Xamarin.Forms behavior and when do you use an attached behavior? Since you can achieve pretty much the same functionality both ways, the answer is that it's mostly up to you. It is a bit a matter of taste. Forms behaviors can be strongly-typed, which is an advantage in my opinion, so I like to go with these. Also, there is a little less overhead, because a Forms behavior doesn't get invoked with each property change. But in the end, it is up to you!

Summary

In this chapter we saw some of the fundamentals of working with Xamarin.Forms. It is important to have a basic understanding of these concepts as they might be used or referred to throughout the rest of this book.

With custom renderers you can create your own implementation of renderers that are normally defined by the Xamarin team. If you want to leverage a functionality that isn't in the default Xamarin.Forms toolkit (yet), you can access it through a renderer. You don't like how a certain control or page looks? Render it your own way!

A little less rigorous than a custom renderer is an effect. With an effect you can just tweak your control a little bit. At the end of the day, a renderer and an effect can do the same thing, an effect just feels a little more lightweight since you don't have to inherit a whole class.

Another thing we learned in this chapter is how to work with the DependencyService and the MessagingCenter. The DependencyService is a service locator that can be used to reach platform-specific functionality that isn't available in the Xamarin.Forms abstraction. Through a simple contract in the form of an interface or by the use of an abstract class, we can still call platform-specific code in our platform projects where the contracts are implemented.

The MessagingCenter can be used to keep our code loosely-coupled. You might find yourself in a situation where you have to create a reference to a piece of code that just doesn't feel right. To still be able to reach that code, you have a simple message bus at your disposal with the MessagingCenter.

Lastly, we looked at behaviors. With both Xamarin.Forms behaviors and attached behaviors we can achieve the same functionality, although logistics are a bit different. With both we can influence the functionality of a control by invoking logic when events are fired. This way we can implement commanding, to make out controls more suitable for the MVVM pattern or implement things like entry validation.

In the next chapters, you will find all kinds of solutions for common scenarios that you will encounter in Xamarin.Forms. Through our, the authors, combined experience of over a decade, we want you to benefit from that. Where we might have to have spent precious time finding these answers to our questions, we want to provide you with this handbook, so you won't have to. The concepts in this chapter are part of the Xamarin. Forms fundamentals and you will probably recognize some of these patterns in the solutions to come.

CHAPTER 2

User Interface

The smartphone has invaded our lives. Whether we are working out, reading emails, checking up on our social media, or doing our banking. A huge part of all of these different kinds of activities we perform on our smartphones is the experience these apps give us through their user interface. A good user interface aims to meet the users' needs and makes their experience pleasant and satisfying.

In Chapter 1 we talked about how the Xamarin.Forms user interface is an abstraction layer on top of the different platforms it supports. We also talked about creating our user interface in either XAML or code. In this chapter, we will look into some of the common concepts we will have to know about when creating our own user interface.

This chapter will also look into some of the more advanced user interface concepts, such as working with the existing Xamarin.Forms animations and creating your own animations. Working with custom fonts is also something we will need to do frequently, which is why it is also covered in this chapter.

Code sharing and reuse is an important concept in Xamarin.Forms. That's why we will also dive into creating reusable controls with custom bindings. To end this chapter, we will cover the basics of gestures, because navigating through the app using intuitive gestures is becoming more and more commonplace.

Exploring the Layout Options

Structuring and positioning our information on the screen is one of the harder tasks of creating a good-looking user interface. Luckily, Xamarin.Forms provides some out-of-the-box controls that we can use to better structure our data. We will start this chapter by covering a lot of these controls in depth, giving you the tools that you need to be able to choose the right control for the job.

© Gerald Versluis and Steven Thewissen 2019
G. Versluis and S. Thewissen, *Xamarin.Forms Solutions*, https://doi.org/10.1007/978-1-4842-4134-9_2

Using the Right Layout Controls

Since each layout control works in its own way, it is important to understand what each of them does and how they might benefit our user interface design. We can combine all of these layouts in all sorts of different combinations to achieve the look and feel we're after. A comparison of all the different available layout types is shown in Figure 2-1. We will describe most of these types in more detail in this chapter.

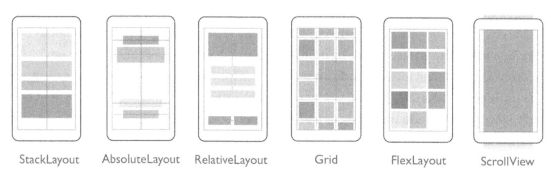

StackLayout   AbsoluteLayout   RelativeLayout   Grid   FlexLayout   ScrollView

Figure 2-1. *The different types of layouts available in Xamarin Forms*

StackLayout

The StackLayout is one of the simplest layout controls to work with. It simply stacks all its children in either a horizontal or a vertical fashion. The StackLayout enables us to create a very simple linear layout, but also enables us to create a more complex layout by nesting other layout controls within it.

Each StackLayout applies a small margin between each of its child controls, which is controlled by the Spacing property. The default value for this property is six device-independent units. The sample in Listing 2-1 shows how to create a StackLayout.

Listing 2-1. A Simple StackLayout That Stacks All of Its Children Vertically

```
<StackLayout Spacing="3" VerticalOptions="Center"
HorizontalOptions="Center" Orientation="Vertical">
        <Label Text="The First Element" />
        <Label Text="The Second Element" />
        <Label Text="The Third Element" />
        <Label Text="The Fourth Element" />
        <Label Text="Just Another Element" />
</StackLayout>
```

The result of the sample shown in Listing 2-1 is shown in Figure 2-2.

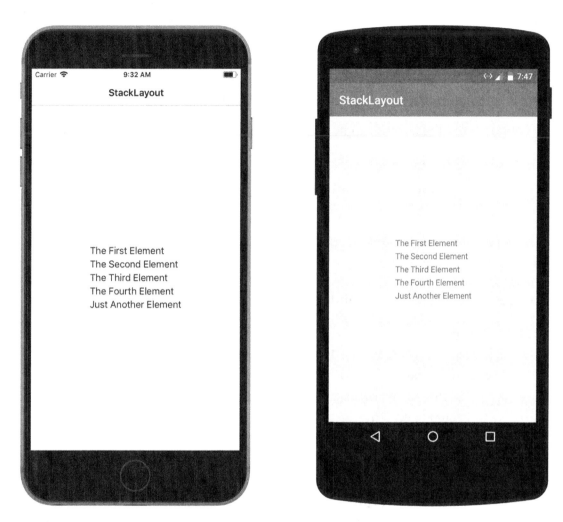

Figure 2-2. *Using a StackLayout on iOS and Android*

RelativeLayout

The RelativeLayout is used to position and size items relative to its parent layout or to another layout. To define the behavior of a view in a RelativeLayout we can use constraints. Each view can be constrained using the XConstraint and the YConstraint, which enable us to constrain the view's position on either the X-axis (horizontally) or the Y-axis (vertically), or both. We can also constrain our view using `WidthConstraint` and `HeightConstraint` to constrain the size of the view. A constraint consists of a few properties that we can use to influence how an element is positioned:

- *Type*—Defines if the constraint is relative to the parent view or another view

- *Property*—The property used as the base for the constraint.

- *Factor*—The factor to apply to the property value.

- *Constant*—The offset of the value.

- *ElementName*—The name of the view this constraint is relative to (if not the parent).

When defining a constraint in XAML, we can combine all of these properties into a single attached property. The sample shown in Listing 2-2 shows how to do this.

Listing 2-2. Setting Up Constraints on a RelativeLayout

```
<RelativeLayout>
    <StackLayout HeightRequest="100" WidthRequest="100" BackgroundColor="Red"
        RelativeLayout.XConstraint=
            "{ConstraintExpression Type=RelativeToParent,
            Property=Width,
            Factor=0.5,
            Constant=-10}"
        RelativeLayout.YConstraint =
            "{ConstraintExpression Type=RelativeToParent,
            Property=Height,
            Factor=0.5,
            Constant=-10}">
    </StackLayout>
</RelativeLayout>
```

When looking at this sample we can see a few things are going on here. The first thing that we see is that we are constraining our `StackLayout` using the `XConstraint` and the `YConstraint` attached properties.

To create a constraint, we use a `ConstraintExpression`, which is an object containing all of the properties we need to define it. In this example the constraint is based on the width and height of the parent container. We constrain the `StackLayout` in the example in such a way that it is positioned at half (0.5) the height and width of its parent container. The X and Y values of the layout are then decreased by 10 device-independent units due to the defined `Constant` value. Figure 2-3 shows how this sample looks on a device. Keep in mind that the default anchor point of a view is in its top-left corner, which is why that is the point that the positioning is applied to.

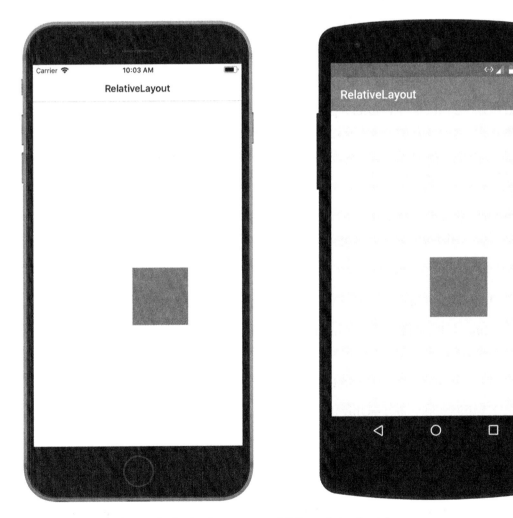

Figure 2-3. *Using a RelativeLayout on IOS and Android*

AbsoluteLayout

The AbsoluteLayout control can be used to position and size elements proportional to its own size and position. The way it works is similar to the absolute positioning of elements in HTML/CSS. The AbsoluteLayout makes it easy to position elements flush to one side of the screen or to center elements.

The way we can anchor elements is at the core of the AbsoluteLayout. The default anchor of an element within a view is always at the top-left corner of its container. To position elements within an AbsoluteLayout, we can use the following four values:

- *X*—The horizontal position of the anchor.

- *Y*—The vertical position of the anchor.

- *Width*—The width of the view.

- *Height*—The height of the view.

Each of these values has either a proportional value or an absolute value. A proportional value ranges from 0 to 1 and sizes the view within its parent. Applying a proportional width value of 0.5 to a control that is contained in a layout control that is 500 device-independent units wide, results in a control that is 250 device-independent units wide.

To provide these values, they need to be wrapped in a Rectangle object. Each label has a LayoutBounds and a LayoutFlags attached property. The LayoutBounds attached property accepts this Rectangle object to allow you to define the X, Y, width, and height.

The following options are available for the LayoutFlags property:

- *None*—All values are interpreted as absolute. This is the default behavior.

- *All*—All values are interpreted as proportional.

- *WidthProportional*—Only the width is interpreted as proportional, while the other values are interpreted as absolute.

- *HeightProportional*—Only the height is interpreted as proportional, while the other values are interpreted as absolute.

- *XProportional*—Only the X value is interpreted as proportional, while the other values are interpreted as absolute.

- *YProportional*—Only the Y value is interpreted as proportional, while the other values are interpreted as absolute.

- *PositionProportional*—Only the X and Y values are interpreted as proportional, while the other values are interpreted as absolute.

- *SizeProportional*—Only the width and height are interpreted as proportional, while the other values are interpreted as absolute.

So how would we combine these two properties to position our view? Listing 2-3 shows five Labels positioned in an AbsoluteLayout using LayoutBounds and LayoutFlags where applicable.

Listing 2-3. Using the AbsoluteLayout and Defining its Bounds in XAML

```
<AbsoluteLayout>
    <Label BackgroundColor="Red" Text="Fixed"
        AbsoluteLayout.LayoutBounds="120,110,150,130" />
    <Label BackgroundColor="Red" Text="Center bottom"
        AbsoluteLayout.LayoutBounds=".5,1,.5,.1"
        AbsoluteLayout.LayoutFlags="All" />
    <Label BackgroundColor="Red" Text="Right center"
        AbsoluteLayout.LayoutBounds="1,.5, 25, 100"
        AbsoluteLayout.LayoutFlags="PositionProportional" />
    <Label BackgroundColor="Red" Text="Left center"
        AbsoluteLayout.LayoutBounds="0,.5,25,100"
        AbsoluteLayout.LayoutFlags="PositionProportional" />
    <Label BackgroundColor="Red" Text="Center top"
        AbsoluteLayout.LayoutBounds=".5,0,100,25"
        AbsoluteLayout.LayoutFlags="PositionProportional" />
</AbsoluteLayout>
```

This code sample results in a screen looking like the ones shown in Figure 2-4. We can see that each Label has a specific position within the AbsoluteLayout.

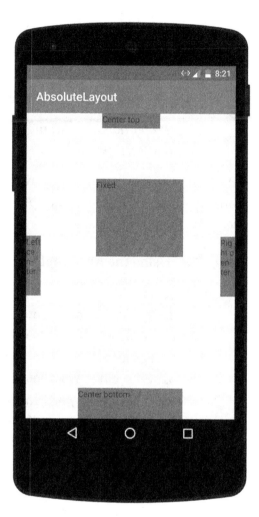

Figure 2-4. *Using an AbsoluteLayout on IOS and Android*

Grid

A Grid layout is essentially a table with rows and columns. However, the grid's main purpose is not to display tabular data. The rows and columns of the Grid control exist purely to structure other controls on the page and do not have any styling properties of their own except for a height and a width.

Setting up a Grid is done by defining both rows and columns through RowDefinitions and ColumnDefinitions, respectively. These objects define the size of the rows and columns and can be set to one of three values:

- *An absolute value*—The row or column will be this fixed value in size.

- *Proportional*—By using an asterisk (*), we can proportionally size rows and columns.

- *Auto*—This automatically sizes the row or column depending on its contents.

The sample in Listing 2-4 shows a simple Grid setup that explores all of these options.

Listing 2-4. Creating a Grid Using All Its Unit Types in XAML

```
<Grid>
    <Grid.RowDefinitions>
        <RowDefinition Height="3*" />
        <RowDefinition Height="*" />
        <RowDefinition Height="150" />
    </Grid.RowDefinitions>
    <Grid.ColumnDefinitions>
        <ColumnDefinition Width="Auto" />
        <ColumnDefinition Width="*" />
    </Grid.ColumnDefinitions>
</Grid>
```

This Grid contains three rows, where the last row is exactly 150 device-independent units high. The remaining height is divided equally between the other two rows where the first row is three times bigger than the middle row. It also features two columns where the first column is sized to fit its contents and the rest of the available width is taken by the second column.

To place controls into a specific row or column, we need to add them as children of the Grid first. In XAML we can then use the attached properties Grid.Row and Grid. Column to define in which row and column a control should be placed. Keep in mind that these values are a zero-based numbering sequence, meaning that the first row and column is identified by a value of 0. Additional options such as Grid.RowSpan and Grid.

ColumnSpan allow us to place a control across multiple rows or columns at once. Using the RowSpacing and ColumnSpacing properties on the Grid, we can define a constant amount of space between each row and column. Listing 2-5 shows an example of how to use these additional properties.

Listing 2-5. Using the Additional Grid Options in XAML

```xaml
<Grid Padding="10" RowSpacing="10" ColumnSpacing="10">
    <Grid.RowDefinitions>
        <RowDefinition Height="3*" />
        <RowDefinition Height="*" />
        <RowDefinition Height="150" />
    </Grid.RowDefinitions>
    <Grid.ColumnDefinitions>
        <ColumnDefinition Width="Auto" />
        <ColumnDefinition Width="*" />
    </Grid.ColumnDefinitions>
    <Label Grid.Row="0" Grid.Column="0" Text="1" WidthRequest="50"
        BackgroundColor="LightGray" HorizontalTextAlignment="Center"
        VerticalTextAlignment="Center" />
    <Label Grid.Row="1" Grid.Column="0" Text="2" BackgroundColor="LightGray"
        HorizontalTextAlignment="Center" VerticalTextAlignment="Center" />
    <Label Grid.Row="2" Grid.Column="0" Grid.ColumnSpan="2" Text="3"
        BackgroundColor="LightGray" HorizontalTextAlignment="Center"
        VerticalTextAlignment="Center" />
    <Label Grid.Row="0" Grid.Column="1" Grid.RowSpan="2" Text="4"
        BackgroundColor="LightGray" HorizontalTextAlignment="Center"
        VerticalTextAlignment="Center" />
</Grid>
```

The result of this example is shown in Figure 2-5.

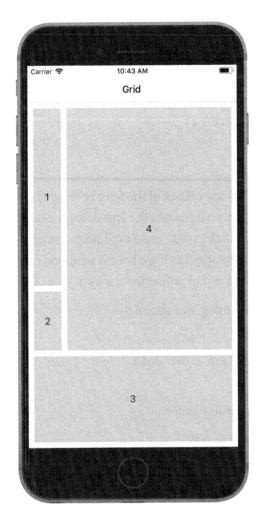
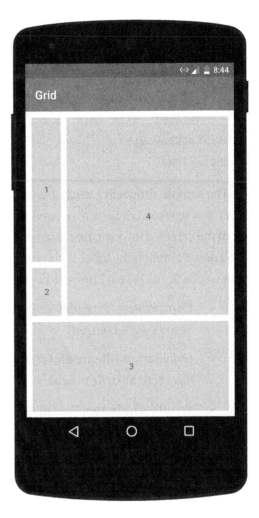

Figure 2-5. *Using a Grid on IOS and Android*

ScrollView

We will inevitably come across a scenario where the content we're trying to show on the screen exceeds the amount of available space. This is where the ScrollView comes into play. As the name suggests, we can use it to ensure that content that doesn't fit the screen can be scrolled to, so users with smaller device resolutions can also use the app. A ScrollView can also be used to move up content automatically when the keyboard is shown. See Listing 2-6.

Listing 2-6. Defining a ScrollView in XAML

```
<ScrollView>
    <StackLayout>
        <BoxView BackgroundColor="Yellow" HeightRequest="1600" />
        <Label Text="This is offscreen somewhere" />
    </StackLayout>
</ScrollView>
```

The sample shown in Listing 2-6 uses the scrolling capabilities of the ScrollView. The BoxView is way too tall for any normal screen resolution, so it pushes the Label down and out of the screen. However, because we wrapped the StackLayout in a ScrollView we can scroll down to reach the label. This would not have been possible if we hadn't wrapped our content in a ScrollView. The ScrollView has a few additional properties for us to use:

- *ContentSize*—Provides a Size object representing the size of the ScrollView's content.

- *Orientation*—Represents the scrolling direction, either Both, Horizontal or Vertical.

- *ScrollX*—Indicates the current horizontal scroll position.

- *ScrollY*—Indicates the current vertical scroll position.

- *HorizontalScrollBarVisibility*—Defines whether or not to show the horizontal scroll bar.

- *VerticalScrollBarVisibility*—Defines whether or not to show the vertical scroll bar.

The ScrollView also provides us with a few additional interesting options. We can use its ScrollToAsync method to scroll to a specific child view or to specific coordinates of the ScrollView. This method also accepts a boolean value indicating whether or not the scrolling movement should be smoothly animated or instant. Finally, when scrolling to a particular child view, we can use the ScrollToPosition enumeration:

- *Start*—Scrolls the child view to the start of the visible portion of the ScrollView.

- *End*—Scrolls the child view to the end of the visible portion of the ScrollView.

- *Center*—Scrolls the child view to the center of the visible portion of the `ScrollView`.

- *MakeVisible*—Scrolls the child view so that it's visible within the view.

If we want to know when a user has scrolled within our `ScrollView` we can handle the `Scrolled` event. It is important to note that this event will only be raised when scrolling has finished. The event handler takes `ScrolledEventArgs`, which has `ScrollX` and `ScrollY` properties that indicate the final position of the `ScrollView` after scrolling has finished.

Determining the Right Alignment and Expansion

Every Xamarin.Forms view has the ability to be aligned both horizontally and vertically. To do so we use the `HorizontalOptions` and `VerticalOptions` properties. Each of the possible options has a different effect on the alignment and expansion of a view. The available options are defined in the `LayoutOptions` structure. The default option for both `HorizontalOptions` and `VerticalOptions` is `Fill`. Valid values are:

- `Start`
- `Center`
- `End`
- `Fill`
- `StartAndExpand`
- `CenterAndExpand`
- `EndAndExpand`
- `FillAndExpand`

Alignment

The alignment of a control determines how the view is positioned within its parent layout. This applies only if the parent layout has available space for the control to be positioned in. The `Start`, `Center`, `End`, and `Fill` values can be used to define the alignment of a view.

- When aligning horizontally, `Start` puts the element at the left side. For vertical alignment, the element is positioned at the top of its parent.

- When aligning horizontally, End puts the element at the right side. For vertical alignment, the element is positioned at the bottom of its parent.

- The Center value centers the element both horizontally and vertically.

- The Fill value ensures that the element fills the entire width of its parent when applied horizontally. For vertical alignment, the element will fill the entire height of its parent.

A sample of all the alignment options is shown in Figure 2-6.

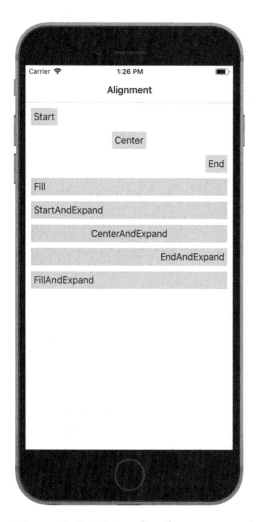
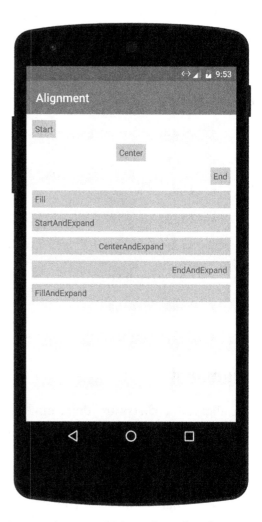

Figure 2-6. *Using the alignment and expansion options on iOS and Android*

Expansion

The expansion of a control defines whether or not the control should consume additional space, if it's available, in the parent controls. To provide this kind of behavior, all of the available LayoutOptions values have a variation that is suffixed with AndExpand. When defining StartAndExpand, CenterAndExpand, EndAndExpand, or FillAndExpand, the element will take up any unused space available after it has been aligned. There are a few additional things we need to consider when it comes to expansion:

- The unused space is shared equally by all child elements that have expansion enabled.

- When there is no unused space available, the expansion options have no effect.

- When using Fill, any value that we provide as the width or height of the view will be overridden.

A sample of all the expansion options is also shown in Figure 2-6.

Margin and Padding

Defining a margin or padding on a view allows us to influence how that view is rendered on the screen. These two properties are related:

- *Margin* defines the amount of space between an element and its adjacent elements. A margin can be applied to all of the different Layout classes and View classes provided by Xamarin.Forms.

- *Padding* defines the amount of space between an element and its child elements. Setting a padding separates a control from its content. A padding can be applied to all of the different Layout classes provided by Xamarin.Forms.

When specifying a margin and/or a padding, we need to consider that these values are added to the height and/or width of the control we're applying them to. For example, when giving an element a margin of 20 device-independent units and a padding of 30 device-independent units, the distance between that element and other elements is at least 50 device-independent units.

Specifying Thickness Values

Both margin and padding are expressed using a *Thickness* structure. When it comes to creating an instance of a thickness, there are three ways we could do it:

- *Use a single value*—This means that the value we provide will be applied to all four sides of the element (left, top, right, and bottom). This means that specifying a padding of 20 device-independent units increases the width and height of the element by 40 device-independent units.

- *Use two values*—Instantiating a Thickness using two values means that the first of these is applied horizontally (left and right) and the second value is applied vertically (top and bottom).

- *Use four values*—Using all four values allows us to differentiate between the left, top, right, and bottom side of an element, giving us the most control over where the element and its children are positioned.

The sample shown in Listing 2-7 touches on all three of these options.

Listing 2-7. Applying a Padding and a Margin in XAML Using the Thickness Structure

```
<StackLayout Padding="0,20,0,0">
    <Label Text="The same all around" Margin="20" />
    <Label Text="Horizontal and vertical" Margin="5,10" />
    <Label Text="Left, Top, Right, Bottom" Margin="0,5,10,15" />
</StackLayout>
```

Introducing the FlexLayout

The FlexLayout is a special kind of layout control introduced in Xamarin.Forms 3.0. It works similar to how a StackLayout works, displaying its child controls across either a horizontal or vertical cross axis depending on the Direction property. However, when there are too many child controls to fit on the screen, it is capable of wrapping them, creating a flexible box layout. It also supports a variety of options when it comes to aligning and spacing its child controls.

Because of its flexibility the FlexLayout can be used as a drop-in replacement for the StackLayout. However, the FlexLayout gives us some more options out-of-the-box. Let's take a look at the example in Listing 2-8, the result of which is shown in Figure 2-7.

Listing 2-8. A Simple FlexLayout Defined in XAML, Acting Similar to a StackLayout

```
<FlexLayout Direction="Column" AlignItems="Center"
    JustifyContent="SpaceEvenly">
    <Label Text="The first label" />
    <Button Text="Just a button" />
    <Label Text="The second Label" />
</FlexLayout>
```

The Direction property that we have set to Column causes all of the children to be arranged in a single column, similar to a vertically oriented StackLayout. The AlignItems property is set to Center, meaning all of the children are centered horizontally. This is a huge improvement over the StackLayout, where we would need to set this for each child element individually. Lastly, we've set the JustifyContent property to SpaceEvenly. This causes all the elements to space evenly across the available height. This is similar to setting the VerticalOptions property on each individual child element, but a lot easier to achieve using a FlexLayout.

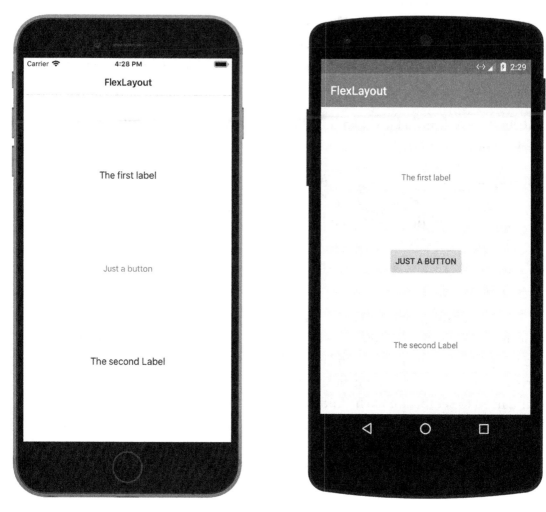

Figure 2-7. *A FlexLayout acting as a vertically oriented StackLayout*

Due to the amount of properties available in the FlexLayout, we should dive a bit deeper into what they are and how we can use them to create the layout we want. Some of these properties function as attached properties, meaning they can be set on child elements to determine how they should interact with the FlexLayout.

Direction

The `Direction` property is an enumeration of type `FlexDirection` and can contain one of the following four values:

- *Column*—Stacks items vertically, starting at the top, similar to a vertically oriented `StackLayout`.

- *Row*—Default, stacks items horizontally, starting at the left side, similar to a horizontally oriented `StackLayout`.

- *ColumnReverse*—Stacks items vertically but in reverse order, starting at the bottom.

- *RowReverse*—Stacks items horizontally but in reverse order, starting at the right side.

All of these options are shown in Figure 2-8 (from left to right, top to bottom) in the order they are listed.

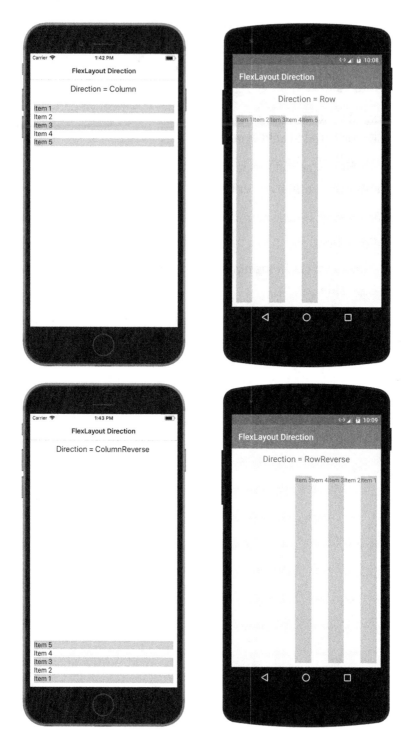

Figure 2-8. *The options of the Direction property illustrated*

Wrap

The `Wrap` property is an enumeration of type `FlexWrap` and can contain one of the following three values:

- *NoWrap*—Default, no wrapping at all, meaning that the items are resized to fit the screen. This behavior can be influenced by using the `Shrink` property.

- *Wrap*—Wraps the items, meaning that when an item doesn't fit the screen, it is moved to the next row or column depending on the `Direction` property.

- *Reverse*—Identical to the `Wrap` option, but the items are ordered in reverse.

All of these options are shown in Figure 2-9 (from left to right) in the order they are listed.

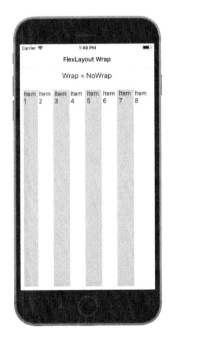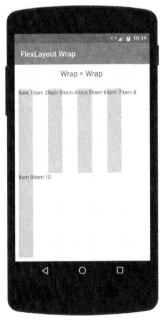

Figure 2-9. *The options of the Wrap property illustrated*

JustifyContent

The JustifyContent property is an enumeration of type FlexJustify and can contain one of the following six values:

- *Start*—Default, aligns the items to the left side of the screen.

- *Center*—Aligns the items to the center of the screen.

- *End* —Aligns the items to the right side of the screen.

- *SpaceBetween*—Divides the leftover space equally between all the items.

- *SpaceAround*—Divides the leftover space equally around all the items.

- *SpaceEvenly*—Divides the leftover space equally between the items, before the first item and after the last item.

All of these options are shown in Figure 2-10 to illustrate their behavior.

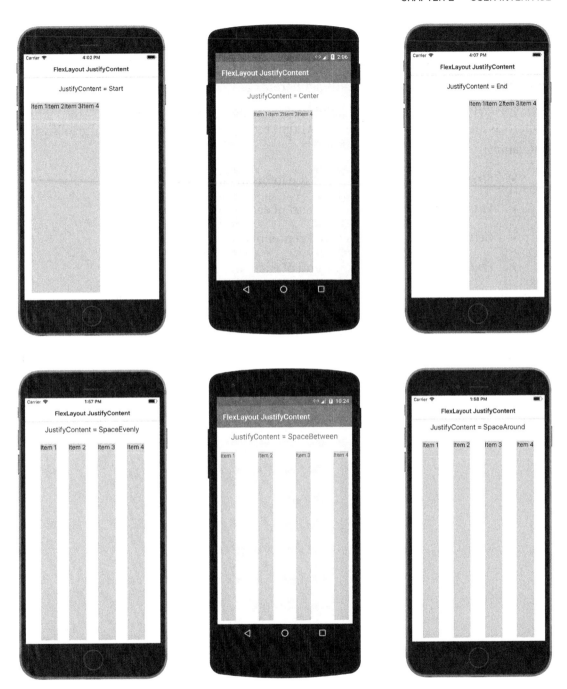

Figure 2-10. *The available options for the JustifyContent property illustrated*

AlignItems

This property, along with `AlignContent`, determines how children are aligned on the cross axis. When a specific item needs a different value, we can use the `AlignSelf` attached property to override the value that's set through this property. The `AlignItems` property is an enumeration of type `FlexAlignItems` and can contain one of the following four values:

- *Stretch*—The default, stretches the items to fill the screen.
- *Start*—Aligns the items at the start of each row or column.
- *Center*—Aligns the items at the center of each row or column.
- *End*—Aligns the items at the end of each row or column.

All of these options are shown in Figure 2-11 to illustrate their behavior.

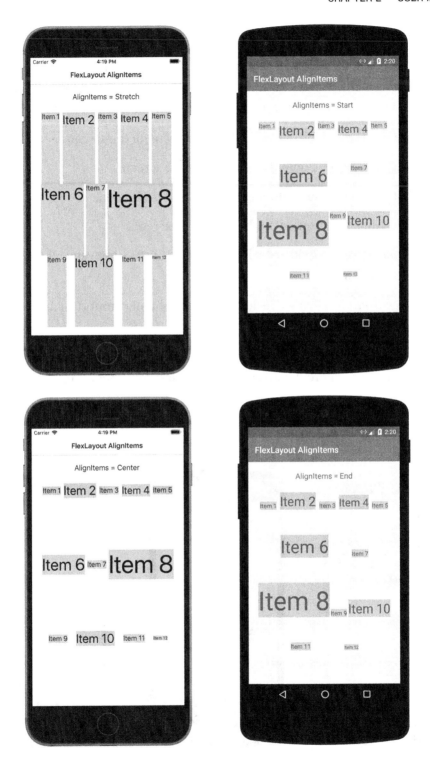

Figure 2-11. *The available options for the AlignItems property illustrated*

AlignContent

Similar to `AlignItems`, the `AlignContent` property also aligns items on the cross axis but instead of aligning items, it aligns the entire row or column. The `AlignContent` property is an enumeration of type `FlexAlignContent` and can contain one of the following seven values:

- *Stretch*—The default, stretches the content to fill the screen.

- *Start*—Aligns the content at the start of the screen.

- Center—Aligns the content in the center of the screen.

- *End*—Aligns the content at the end of the screen.

- *SpaceBetween*—Divides the leftover space equally between all the rows or columns.

- *SpaceAround*—Divides the leftover space equally around all the rows or columns.

- *SpaceEvenly*—Divides the leftover space equally between each row or column and before the first and after the last row or column.

The result of applying the `Start`, `Center`, and `End` values is shown in Figure 2-12 to illustrate their behavior.

Figure 2-12. *A few of the available options for the AlignContent property illustrated*

The result of applying the SpaceBetween, SpaceAround, and SpaceEvenly values are shown in Figure 2-13 to illustrate their behavior.

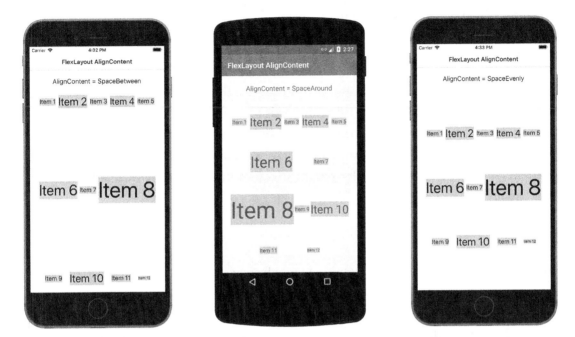

Figure 2-13. *More of the available options for the AlignContent property illustrated*

AlignSelf

The AlignSelf attached property is an enumeration of type FlexAlignSelf and can contain one of the following five values:

- *Auto*—The default, inherits the value set in the AlignItems property on the FlexLayout.

- *Stretch*—Stretches the item to fill the screen.

- *Start*—Aligns the item at the start of each row or column.

- *Center*—Aligns the item at the center of each row or column.

- *End*—Aligns the item at the end of each row or column.

Because this property is an attached property we can add it to any child element of the FlexLayout. This property allows us to override the value we specified in the AlignItems property on the FlexLayout for specific elements, giving us a higher degree of control over the alignment of items.

Order

The Order attached property allows us to influence the order in which items in the FlexLayout are arranged. When no order is specified, each control gets added to the FlexLayout in the order it is added to the Children property of the FlexLayout. By specifying the Order property, we can override its position. Child elements without a specified order get arranged in the order they were added to the FlexLayout.

Basis

The Basis attached property indicates how much space is allocated to the child of the FlexLayout it is applied to. Using the Basis property, we can specify the amount of space an element takes up across the main orientation axis of the FlexLayout. This property is of type FlexBasis, which is a structure allowing us to specify the size we want in either device-independent units or as a percentage of the available size. The default value is FlexBasis.Auto, which means that the requested width or height for the child control is used. Listing 2-9 shows an example of setting the Basis property.

Listing 2-9. Setting the Basis Property Using Device-Independent Units or a Percentage

```
<FlexLayout>
    <Label Text="Test DIP" FlexLayout.Basis="40" />
    <Label Text="Test Percentage" FlexLayout.Basis="25%" />
</FlexLayout>
```

The sample shown in Figure 2-14 shows a few different options set for the Basis property. If the Basis is set at 100%, the child takes the full height of the FlexLayout. In this situation it will also wrap to the next column and occupy the entire height of that column. This behavior is also illustrated in Figure 2-14, where the screenshot on the left shows two Label elements with the Basis set to an absolute value in device-independent units.

The screenshot on the right shows the same sample but with the `Basis` property set to 100%. Notice that the `Label` elements show up as if they're ordered in a `Row` fashion, but the `Direction` property is actually set to `Column`.

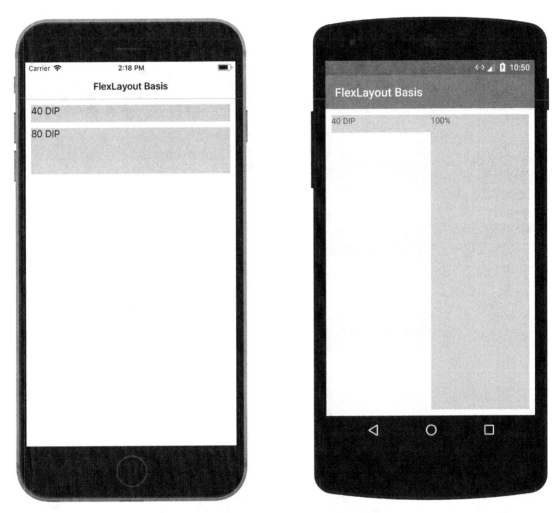

Figure 2-14. *Using the Basis property to scale child elements*

Grow

The `Grow` property is a float value greater than or equal to 0, which is important when we're using the `NoWrap` value for the `Wrap` property. Normally, when the width or height of a child elements is less than the available space, the child element is resized to fit the screen. By specifying a positive value for the `Grow` property, we can prioritize which controls should take up the available space in the `FlexLayout`.

Setting the Grow value to a positive value indicates that the given element should take up all of the remaining space along the main axis. When multiple elements have a positive Grow value set the remaining space will be shared between these elements. The value for the Grow property defines how these elements should be sized proportionally to each other. Figure 2-15 shows an example of using the Grow property.

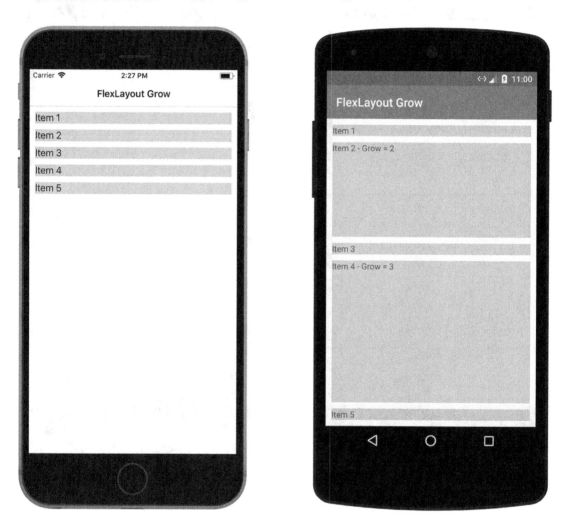

Figure 2-15. *Using the Grow property to prioritize controls when NoWrap is used*

In this example, the labels in the screenshot on the left side have no Grow value set. In the screenshot on the right side, the second item has a Grow value of 2 and the fourth item has a Grow value of 3. This means that these two items will take up all the remaining space and divide it equally between them in a 2:3 ratio.

Shrink

The Shrink property is a float value greater than 0, which is important when we're using the NoWrap value for the Wrap property. It is the exact opposite of the Grow property, which means that when the width or height of a child element is greater than the available space, the child element is resized to fit the screen. By specifying a value for the Shrink property, we can prioritize which controls should be displayed at their full size.

Setting the Shrink value to 0 means that the element will be shown at its full size, if possible. The default value is 1, so setting a value greater than 1 means that that element will be shrunk down even more compared to the others. We can also use both Grow and Shrink to accommodate situations where the size of an element may vary between being too small to fit the screen or too large to fit the screen. Figure 2-16 shows an example of using the Shrink property.

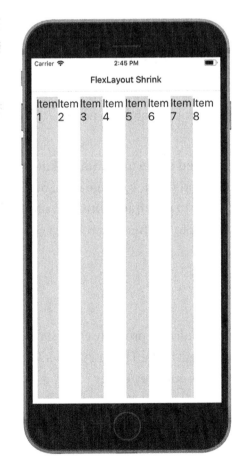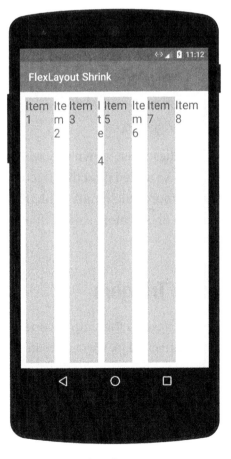

Figure 2-16. *Using the Shrink property to prioritize controls when NoWrap is used*

In the sample on the left, each label has the same default `Shrink` value of 1. This means that all items are resized equally to fit the screen. In the sample on the right the second and sixth item have a `Shrink` value of 4, while the fourth item has a `Shrink` value of 6. As you can see, this changes the way each of these items are resized compared to the other items.

Changing Our UI Based on Data

We may come across a scenario where we need to change the appearance of controls based on events or changes in the data. There are a few different ways to achieve this, but the simplest option is using triggers in Xamarin.Forms. There are four types of triggers:

- *Property triggers*—Fire when a property on a control is set to a specific value.

- *Data triggers*—Fire when a data binding of a property changes.

- *Event triggers*—Fire when an event triggers on a control.

- *Multi triggers*—Allow for multiple trigger conditions before an action is triggered.

Each of these has its own use, which will be explained in the upcoming sections. Triggers can be added directly to a control, or we can add them to a page-level or app-level resource dictionary, which applies the trigger to multiple controls at once. A trigger has one or more setters that define what needs to happen when a trigger is fired.

Property Triggers

This type of trigger is the simplest one available. It responds to a property change on the control it is attached to. We can create a trigger by adding it to the `Triggers` collection of the control. One or more setters define the actions that should be taken.

Listing 2-10. Adding a Property Trigger to an Entry to Change its Style

```
<Entry>
    <Entry.Triggers>
        <Trigger TargetType="Entry" Property="IsFocused" Value="True">
            <Setter Property="BackgroundColor" Value="#ffffcc" />
        </Trigger>
    </Entry.Triggers>
</Entry>
```

The sample in Listing 2-10 shows an `Entry` control that has a property trigger added to its `Triggers` collection. The property that should be monitored for changes is the `IsFocused` property and when its value becomes true, we use a setter to set the background color of the control to a shade of yellow. We can add multiple setters in the same trigger, so for example if we want to change the border color as well, we can simply add a new setter to the trigger.

Data Triggers

A data trigger uses data binding to determine whether or not it should be fired and thus calling its setters. It looks very similar to a property trigger, with one important change being that it doesn't use a `Property` attribute, but a `Binding` attribute.

Listing 2-11. Adding a Data Trigger to an Entry to Change its Style

```
<Entry Text="{Binding MyIntegerValue}">
    <Entry.Triggers>
        <DataTrigger TargetType="Entry" Binding="{Binding MyIntegerValue}"
        Value="0">
            <Setter Property="BackgroundColor" Value="#ccffff" />
        </DataTrigger>
    </Entry.Triggers>
</Entry>
```

The example in Listing 2-11 uses the data binding syntax `{Binding MyIntegerValue}`, which is how we refer to a property in the binding context of the control we are defining our trigger on. More information on data binding can be found in Chapter 3. When the integer value of the data binding is equal to zero, the trigger is activated. The background color of the Entry control should become light blue if the trigger is successfully fired.

Event Triggers

An event trigger works on each event exposed by the control. For example, a button's Clicked event can be used to fire an event trigger. The sample in Listing 2-12 shows how to implement the event trigger in XAML.

Listing 2-12. Adding an Event Trigger to a Button and Using a TriggerAction

```
<ContentPage xmlns="http://xamarin.com/schemas/2014/forms"
             xmlns:x="http://schemas.microsoft.com/winfx/2009/xaml"
             xmlns:local="clr-namespace:TriggerSample">
    <Entry>
        <Entry.Triggers>
            <EventTrigger Event="TextChanged">
                <local:ValidationTriggerAction />
            </EventTrigger>
        </Entry.Triggers>
    </Entry >
</ContentPage>
```

Because the event trigger itself is a fairly simple concept to grasp, we decided to shake things up a bit by introducing the concept of a trigger action instead of using the setters we've used in the previous examples. The local namespace prefix is defined in the ContentPage declaration, which means we can use any control or class declared in this namespace on our XAML page. In this example, we've created a custom TriggerAction in this namespace. Let's take a look at how to implement this.

To create a trigger action, we create a new class and make it inherit from TriggerAction<T>, where T is the type of the control it will be applied to. The only thing left to do after this is overriding the Invoke method, which is called whenever trigger criteria are met.

Listing 2-13. A Trigger Action That Changes the Text Color When It Is Not a Valid Double

```
public class ValidationTriggerAction : TriggerAction<Entry>
{
    protected override void Invoke (Entry entry)
    {
        bool isValid = Double.TryParse (entry.Text, out double result);
        entry.TextColor = isValid ? Color.Black : Color.Red;
    }
}
```

The sample in Listing 2-13 shows a trigger action that changes the text color of an Entry when the user input is not a numerical value. The trigger action provides us with an instance of the control it is applied to through a parameter of the Invoke method. We can use that instance to set properties depending on conditions of our choosing. Trigger actions can be applied to any type of trigger described in this chapter.

Multi Triggers

A multi trigger is very similar to the other types of triggers mentioned in this chapter. What makes them special is the ability to define multiple conditions that all need to be true for the trigger to fire. Using a multi trigger, we could define a trigger that takes input from multiple controls at once, as is shown in Listing 2-14.

Listing 2-14. A Multi Trigger Taking Input from Multiple Controls on the Page

```
<StackLayout>
    <Entry x:Name="EmailEntry" Text="{Binding MyEmail}" />
    <Entry x:Name="PhoneEntry" Text="{Binding MyPhone}" />
    <Button>
        <Button.Triggers>
            <MultiTrigger TargetType="Button">
                <MultiTrigger.Conditions>
                    <BindingCondition Binding="{Binding Source={x:Reference
                    EmailEntry}, Path=Text.Length}" Value="0" />
```

```
                    <BindingCondition Binding="{Binding Source={x:Reference
                        PhoneEntry}, Path=Text.Length}" Value="0" />
                </MultiTrigger.Conditions>
                <Setter Property="IsEnabled" Value="False" />
            </MultiTrigger>
        </Button.Triggers>
    </Button>
</StackLayout>
```

This sample shows a multi trigger that uses two `Entry` controls on the page to determine whether or not the `Button` is enabled. In this example we're using the `BindingCondition` to bind to properties of different controls on the page. Another option would be to use the `PropertyCondition` to reference a property of the current control.

Using Triggers with Style

At the start of this section, we mentioned that we can also add triggers to a page-level or app-level resource dictionary, which enables us to reuse them throughout our application. To do so we can create a `Style` out of them, which we put in the page-level or app-level resource dictionary. An example of this is shown in Listing 2-15.

Listing 2-15. Adding a Trigger Through a Style

```
<ContentPage.Resources>
    <ResourceDictionary>
        <Style TargetType="Entry">
            <Style.Triggers>
                <Trigger TargetType="Entry" Property="IsFocused"
                Value="True">
                    <Setter Property="BackgroundColor" Value="#ccffff" />
                </Trigger>
            </Style.Triggers>
        </Style>
    </ResourceDictionary>
</ContentPage.Resources>
```

This sample shows how we can add a trigger to each Entry on the current page. This trigger makes sure that when an Entry is focused it will receive a gray background color. By putting this style declaration in the app-level resource dictionary, we can apply it to each Entry control throughout our entire app.

Using EnterActions and ExitActions

So far, we've looked at triggers that set a certain property but there are other ways to handle a trigger event. We can also use the EnterActions and ExitActions collections of a trigger by providing them with implementations of TriggerAction<T>, as we've seen in Listing 2-13. One particular case where this works very well is when creating animations to be triggered when a certain property changes value.

Listing 2-16. Running an Animation When a Trigger Condition Is Fired

```
<ContentPage xmlns="http://xamarin.com/schemas/2014/forms"
             xmlns:x="http://schemas.microsoft.com/winfx/2009/xaml"
             xmlns:local="clr-namespace:TriggerSample">
    <Entry Placeholder="Emailaddress">
        <Entry.Triggers>
            <Trigger TargetType="Entry" Property="Entry.IsFocused"
            Value="True">
                <Trigger.EnterActions>
                    <local:FadeTriggerAction StartsFrom="0" />
                </Trigger.EnterActions>
                <Trigger.ExitActions>
                    <local:FadeTriggerAction StartsFrom="1" />
                </Trigger.ExitActions>
            </Trigger>
        </Entry.Triggers>
    </Entry>
</ContentPage>
```

The sample in Listing 2-16 shows that we can add multiple EnterActions and ExitActions to our trigger. We could even provide additional setters as well. In this example we use the FadeTriggerAction from Listing 2-17 to animate changing the background color of the Entry control when the control is focused.

Listing 2-17. The Trigger Action That Animates the Background Color on Focus

```
public class FadeTriggerAction : TriggerAction<VisualElement>
{
    public FadeTriggerAction() {}

    public int StartsFrom { set; get; }

    protected override void Invoke (VisualElement element)
    {
        element.Animate("FadeOnFocus", new Animation( (d)=>{
            var val = StartsFrom == 1 ? d : 1-d;
            element.BackgroundColor = Color.FromRgb(1, val, 1);
        }),
        length: 1000,
        easing: Easing.Linear);
    }
}
```

Do keep in mind that some rules apply to using EnterActions and ExitActions. For instance, this type of behavior is not applicable to event triggers since they aren't linked to a specific property. It is also important to note that a setter doesn't wait for EnterActions and ExitActions to be completed. These two mechanisms behave completely independent from one another.

Working with Animations

In the previous section, we saw a little bit of animation magic going on and we can achieve quite a few cool animations from within Xamarin Forms. That means we don't even have to write any platform specific code for it! When using an app on a daily basis we may not even notice them anymore, but animations are everywhere in mobile apps. It could be a small animation like a heart icon that pulses when we click a "Like" button, but these simple animations can add a lot of character to our app.

Adding Simple Animations

Animations in Xamarin.Forms are implemented as extension methods on the View class. This means we can apply them to any class inheriting from View, which basically any UI element available in Xamarin.Forms. Each animation method implements a single type of animation. These animation methods are asynchronous, which means we should call them with the await operator to be able to determine whether they have completed. By omitting the await operator we can make multiple animations run concurrently, because we won't be waiting for each animation to finish. Both of these scenarios can be used to create complex animations by combining them.

The sample images in this section show the before and after scenario of each of the animations we will cover on different platforms to illustrate that the animation works exactly the same on both.

Translation

The translate animation allows us to move a view horizontally and/or vertically across the screen. This could be used to move a view off screen or onto the screen or for a vertical bounce animation. To use a translation animation, we need to call the TranslateTo method. The first two parameters are the X and Y coordinates that we want to translate the view to. Negative values will translate the view to the left and upward, whereas positive values move the view to the right and downward. The third parameter is the duration of the animation in milliseconds. The sample in Listing 2-18 shows how to translate a view and Figure 2-17 shows the result.

Listing 2-18. Translating a View on the Screen Using the TranslateTo Method

```
public async Task PerformTranslation(View view)
{
    await view.TranslateTo(100, 100, 1000);
}
```

Figure 2-17. *The result of translating a view using an animation*

One thing that's important to note is that when we initially position an interactive element such as a button off screen and then translate it onto the screen, the part of the element that handles the input remains off screen and the user can't interact with it. That means we can press the button, but nothing will happen. In such scenarios it's recommended to initially position the view where it needs to be after the animation has completed and perform any translations we need to do to move it off screen when the screen loads.

Scaling

We can scale a view to increase or decrease its size through the ScaleTo extension method. This method takes the current Scale factor and multiplies that with a given value. Providing a value of 2 means that the element will scale to 2x its original default scale size of 1. The second parameter is the duration of the animation in milliseconds. A sample of scaling is shown in Listing 2-19. Figure 2-18 shows the result.

Listing 2-19. Scaling an Image on the Screen Using the ScaleTo Method

```
public async Task ScaleElement(Image image)
{
    // Default value of the Scale property is 1.
    // Sets the value of Scale to current value * 2.
    await image.ScaleTo(2, 1000);

    // Sets the value of Scale to 5 (2+3).
    await image.RelScaleTo(3, 1000);
}
```

Figure 2-18. *The result of scaling an image using an animation*

Another scaling method we can use is the RelScaleTo method. This relative scaling method takes the current Scale property value before the start of the animation and adds the value provided to the method to the current value of the Scale property. We can use the relative scaling to *increment* the Scale value instead of *multiplying* it like the ScaleTo method does. A sample of this is shown in Listing 2-19.

Rotation

To rotate an element in place we can use a rotation animation. This rotation takes place over a given angle with a maximum of 360 degrees. To do so, the RotateTo method takes the current Rotation angle and rotates to the given angle in the provided animation duration. This means that when the element is currently rotated 20 degrees and you supply a rotation angle of 90 degrees the element will only rotate 70 degrees. The code in Listing 2-20 illustrates how to use the `RotateTo` method. This animation takes 1,000 milliseconds to complete. Figure 2-19 shows the result.

Listing 2-20. Rotating an Image on the Screen Using the RotateTo Method

```
public async Task RotateImage(Image image)
{
    await image.RotateTo(45, 1000);
}
```

Figure 2-19. *The result of rotating an image using an animation*

But what if we don't want to have to take the current rotation of an element into account? To rotate an element a given angle from its starting position, we can use the RelRotateTo method. This relative rotation takes the current Rotation property of an element and rotates that using the rotation angle supplied, ensuring that the element is always rotated the given amount from its starting position.

Fading

When we want to fade an element in or out we can use the FadeTo method to influence its Opacity value. An opacity of 0 means an element is completely invisible, whereas an opacity of 1 represents a fully visible element. The FadeTo method takes a parameter representing the desired Opacity and uses it to animate toward that value from its current opacity. As with most animation methods, the final parameter of this method represents the duration of the animation in milliseconds. Listing 2-21 shows the code and Figure 2-20 shows the result.

Listing 2-21. Fading an Image on the Screen Using the FadeTo Method

```
public async Task FadeImage(Image image)
{
    await image.FadeTo(0.3, 1000);
}
```

 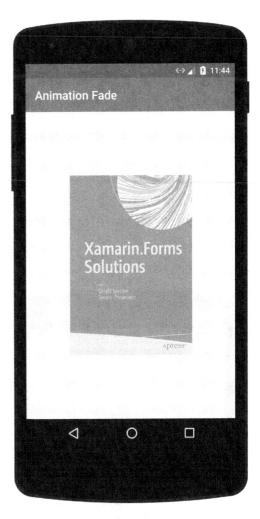

Figure 2-20. *The result of fading an image using an animation*

Working with Anchors

Both the ScaleTo and the RotateTo methods can be influenced by setting their anchors. These are represented by the AnchorX and AnchorY properties of the element we're animating. By default, these are set to the center point of the view we're scaling or rotating. By setting anchor points we can animate a view based on the position of other elements instead of its own. The sample in Listing 2-22 rotates the image around the top-left corner of the screen located at the coordinate value (0, 0). Consider that the values for these properties are relative. This means that a value of 0 is at the start of the axis and a value of 1 is at the end of the axis. The default value (0.5) for an anchor is at the center.

If we want to rotate around the top-right corner of the screen, we would set our anchor values to 0 (AnchorX) and 1 (AnchorY), respectively (see Listing 2-22). Figure 2-21 shows the result.

Listing 2-22. Changing the Anchor of an Animation

```
public async Task RotateImage(Image image)
{
    image.AnchorX = 0;
    image.AnchorY = 0;
    await image.RotateTo(40, 1000);
}
```

Figure 2-21. *Changing the anchor of a rotation animation*

Cancelling an Animation

When there is an active animation, it can be cancelled using the ViewExtensions. CancelAnimations method. This static method cancels all animations running on the view that is passed in as a parameter. The sample in Listing 2-23 cancels all of the running animations on an image.

Listing 2-23. Cancelling an Animation on a Specific View

```
public void CancelAnimation(Image image)
{
    ViewExtensions.CancelAnimations(image);
}
```

Combining Animations

So far, we've only looked at creating a single animation. The animation methods can also be combined to create a sequence of animations, which is also known as a *compound animation*. To do so, we can use the await operator, which triggers the next animation as soon as the current animation is completed, thus creating a sequential animation. The sample in Listing 2-24 moves an image around on the screen in four seconds, ending in such a way that it ends up in its starting position at the end of the animation.

Listing 2-24. A Compound Animation Triggers Multiple Animations in Sequence

```
public async Task CompoundAnimation(Image image)
{
    await image.TranslateTo(-10, 0, 1000);
    await image.TranslateTo(0, -10, 1000);
    await image.TranslateTo(10, 0, 1000);
    await image.TranslateTo(0, 10, 1000);
}
```

Another option we have to combine animations is to create a composite animation. The main difference between a compound and a composite animation is that the latter lets you create animations that run simultaneously. This is done by omitting the await operator for animations that should run simultaneously.

Listing 2-25. A Composite Animation Can Run Animations Simultaneously

```
public async Task CompositeAnimation(Image image)
{
    image.RotateTo (360, 4000);
    await image.TranslateTo(-10, 0, 1000);
    await image.TranslateTo(0, -10, 1000);
    await image.TranslateTo(10, 0, 1000);
    await image.TranslateTo(0, 10, 1000);
}
```

The sample in Listing 2-25 shows the same compound animations we saw in Listing 2-24, but we added a rotation component, which lasts the same amount of time as the translation animations. By omitting the `await` operator the rotation animation is treated as a "fire-and-forget" animation with code immediately continuing with the translation animations. We can create all sorts of complex animations by playing with the timing of each animation and by either using the `await` operator or not.

Another option we could use is to combine animations using their individual `Task` objects and await them in bulk using some of the `Task` methods available to use. The sample shown in Listing 2-26 illustrates this.

Listing 2-26. Using the Task Object to Create a Composite Animation

```
public async Task CompositeAnimation()
{
    var rotateAnimation = image.RotateTo(360, 4000);
    var translateAnimation = image.TranslateTo(-100, 0, 3000);

    await Task.WhenAll(rotateAnimation, translateAnimation);

    image.TranslateTo(10, 0, 1000);
    image.TranslateTo(0, 10, 1000);
}
```

We create two animations that are started simultaneously using the `WhenAll` method of the `Task` object. This starts all of the tasks and only continues when all of them have completed. The two additional translate animations then run simultaneously as well because they are not awaited.

Working with Easing

Each animation we create supports a concept called *easing*. This is a representation of how an animation speeds up and slows down during its lifetime. There is a list of predefined easing functions available in Xamarin.Forms allowing us to create different kinds of animations by playing around with their easing value. The following easing functions are available by default:

- *BounceIn*—Bounces the animation at the beginning.

- *BounceOut*—Bounces the animation at the end.

- *CubicIn*—Slowly increases the speed of the animation.

- *CubicInOut*—Increases the speed of the animation at the beginning, and decreases the speed of the animation at the end.

- *CubicOut*—Quickly decreases the speed of the animation.

- *Linear*—The default value, uses a constant animation speed.

- *SinIn*—Smoothly increases the speed of the animation.

- *SinInOut*—Smoothly increases the speed of the animation at the beginning and smoothly decreases the speed of the animation at the end.

- *SinOut*—Smoothly decreases the speed of the animation.

- *SpringIn*—Speeds up the animation very quickly toward the end.

- *SpringOut*—Speeds down the animation quickly toward the end.

The In and Out suffixes indicate which part of the animation is affected by the given easing function. Using an easing function is as simple as providing it as an additional parameter to our animation method, as the sample in Listing 2-27 shows.

Listing 2-27. Using Easing.CubicOut When Rotating an Image

```
public async Task RotateImage(Image image)
{
    await image.RotateTo(90, 1000, Easing.CubicOut);
}
```

In addition to all of the existing easing functions, we can also create our own. To do so Xamarin.Forms includes an `Easing` class, which allows us to specify a transfer function that controls how our animation speeds up or slows down as it's running.

Working with Custom Animations

All of the existing animations in Xamarin.Forms are created using one or multiple instances of the `Animation` class. To create our own custom animations, we can use this class to animate properties that aren't animated by the existing extension methods.

Creating an Animation

When creating a custom animation there are a few parameters we need to pass into an instance of an `Animation` type object: a start and end value of the property being animated and a callback method that sets this property. Running the actual animation requires us to call the `Commit` method on our custom `Animation` object.

Listing 2-28. A Custom Animation Being Created in Code

```
public void CustomAnimation(Image image)
{
    var animation = new Animation (v => image.Scale = v, 1, 2);
    animation.Commit (this, "ScaleIt", 100, 2000, Easing.Linear, (v, c) =>
    image.Scale = 1, () => true);
}
```

In the example shown in Listing 2-28, we create an animation that animates the `Scale` property of the image parameter from 1 to 2. The `Commit` method requires some additional clarification due to the number of parameters it accepts. The following values need to be passed in:

- The first argument represents the *owner* of the animation. We can pass in the view that is being animated or the page on which the view resides.

- The second argument is the *name* of the animation. This name is combined with the owner to identify the animation throughout the app, for example when the animation needs to be cancelled or to check whether or not it's currently running.

- The third argument is the *rate* of the animation, which is the number of milliseconds between each call to the callback method defined in the animation's constructor.

- The fourth argument represents the *length* of the animation in milliseconds.

- The fifth argument is the *easing* function we want to apply to the animation.

- The sixth argument is a callback that is executed when the animation has *finished*. The first parameter of this callback represents the final value of the property we're animating whereas the second parameter is a `boolean` value indicating whether or not the animation was cancelled. This callback can also be defined in the `Animation` constructor, but when both are defined only the one from the `Commit` method will be executed.

- The seventh and last argument is a callback indicating whether or not the animation should be *repeated*. Returning true from this callback means that the animation is repeated.

The end result of the code shown in Listing 2-28 is an animation that scales an image to twice its original size over 2,000 milliseconds (2 seconds). Because the repeat callback always returns true, this animation is repeated indefinitely.

Cancelling an Animation

Earlier on in this chapter we created a custom animation and we learned that each animation is uniquely identified by the combination of its owner and its name. To cancel a custom animation, we need to call the `AbortAnimation` method on its owner, in this case the current page (represented by the `this` keyword). We also need to provide the name of the animation that we specified when we created it. The sample shown in Listing 2-29 shows how to cancel the custom animation we created in Listing 2-28.

Listing 2-29. Cancelling the Custom Animation We Created Earlier in this Chapter

```
public void CancelAnimation()
{
    this.AbortAnimation("ScaleIt");
}
```

Using Child Animations

The Animation class also supports the use of child animations. This means we can add multiple animations to one parent animation to create a series of animations that we can treat as a single unit. An example of this kind of animation is shown in Listing 2-30.

Listing 2-30. Creating a Custom Animation Using Multiple Child Animations

```
public void UseChildAnimations(Image image)
{
    var parentAnimation = new Animation();
    var increaseSize = new Animation(v => image.Scale = v, 1, 2);
    var decreaseSize = new Animation(v => image.Scale = v, 2, 1);
    var rotate = new Animation (v => image.Rotation = v, 0, 360);

    parentAnimation.Add(0, 0.5, increaseSize);
    parentAnimation.Add(0.5, 1, decreaseSize);
    parentAnimation.Add(0, 1, rotate);

    parentAnimation.Commit(this, "ChildAnimations", length: 2000);
}
```

In this sample we create an empty parent animation that will act as the container for all our child animations. We then add three animations to it—a scale animation increasing the size of the image, a scale animation decreasing the size of the image, and a rotation animation. The first two parameters of the Add method represent the relative placement of that child animation in the parent animation using a value from 0 to 1. The example shown here contains an animation that scale the image up during the first half of the animation, scales it back down in the second half and rotates the image 360 degrees for the entire duration of the animation. When committing this animation, we define its total runtime as 2,000 milliseconds (2 seconds).

Using child animations differs from directly using an `Animation` object in a few ways:

- The finished callback method on a child animation indicates whether or not the child animation is finished. The finished callback method for the `Commit` method indicates whether or not the entire animation is finished.

- When we're using child animations and we return true from the repeat callback method the animation will not repeat, but it will continue to run without updating its values.

- When including an easing function in the `Commit` method of the parent animation, and the easing function returns a value greater than 1 the animation will be stopped. When returning a value less than 0 it will be changed to 0. When we want to use an easing function that goes below 0 or above 1, we need to use it in our child animations instead of the `Commit` method.

Creating a Custom Animation Extension Method

In the beginning of this section on animations, we discussed the built-in animation extension methods such as `TranslateTo` and `ScaleTo`. These are all extensions methods available in the `ViewExtensions` class. We also learned about creating custom animations using the `Animation` class. Putting these two techniques together allows us to create our own extension methods containing any custom animation we can come up with. The sample shown in Listing 2-31 is an extension method we can use to create the illusion that a view is being flipped.

Listing 2-31. Creating an Extension Method to Animate a VisualElement

```
public static class Extensions
{
    public static void Flip(this VisualElement self, uint length = 250,
    Easing easing = null)
    {
        var animation = new Animation();

        animation.WithConcurrent((f) => self.Opacity = f, 0.5, 1);
```

```
    animation.WithConcurrent((f) => self.RotationY = f, 90, 0, Xamarin.
    Forms.Easing.Linear);

    self.Animate("Flip", animation, 16, length, easing);
  }
}
```

In this sample we use the `Animate` method, which exists in the `AnimationExtensions` class. This class provides methods that give developers more control over how animations occur and uses callbacks for handling completions or repeating animations. The flip animation shown here is rather simple, but when creating more complex animations, the `Animate` extension method offers you a lot of control.

Using Custom Fonts

Typography is one of the most important aspects of a design. In a mobile app we don't have all the fonts in the world at our disposal, so we might want to add our own custom font. Or perhaps the app just looks so much better when everything is in Comic Sans MS. Either way, when it comes to branding our app, using a custom font can go a long way.

Adding a Custom Font in iOS

To add a custom font, we first need a font file (.TTF generally works well). Add this font file to a newly created `Fonts` folder that resides in the `Resources` folder in the project and ensure that the Build Action is set to `BundleResource`. Also ensure that the Copy to Output Directory setting is set to Always Copy. Figure 2-22 illustrates the result of these actions when performed in Visual Studio for Mac.

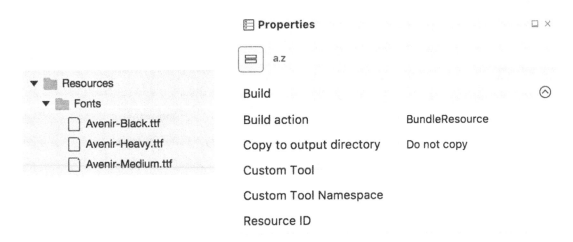

Figure 2-22. *Adding the custom font files to the iOS project*

After adding our fonts to the application, we will have to tell iOS where it can find these custom fonts. That is done by editing the Info.plist file. Open it up in the editor and add the Fonts Provided by Application key. We add all the fonts we want to use as separate keys within the array. Figure 2-23 illustrates how the end result would look for the font files we added in this example.

▼ Fonts provided by application	Array	(3 items)
	String	Fonts/Avenir-Black.ttf
	String	Fonts/Avenir-Heavy.ttf
	String	Fonts/Avenir-Medium.ttf

Figure 2-23. *Adding the custom font to the Info.plist file*

Adding a Custom Font in Android

When using Android, we add our custom font files to the Assets directory of the application. As a Build Action, we need to set the files to AndroidAsset. Contrary to iOS, we do not need to register these fonts anywhere else in our application. Figure 2-24 shows how to set up our custom fonts.

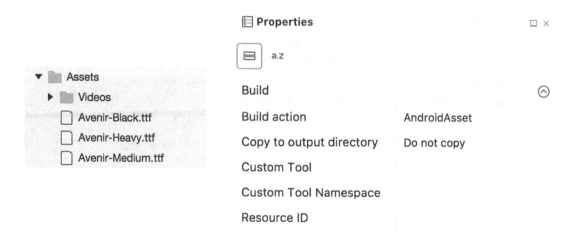

Figure 2-24. *Adding the custom font files to the Android project*

Finding the PostScript Name of the Font

Each font we add to the application has an internal font name (PostScript Name), which is not necessarily the same as the filename. This internal name is the name that we will need to use to reference the font when we use it in Xamarin.Forms. To figure out what name we need to use, we can use the following method on a Mac:

1. Install the font on the Mac.

2. Open the FontBook app.

3. Select the font and click on the Info button.

4. From the section that appears, we can use the PostScript name to reference the font.

A sample of how this dialog looks is shown in Figure 2-25 where the PostScript name of the selected font is *Avenir-Black*.

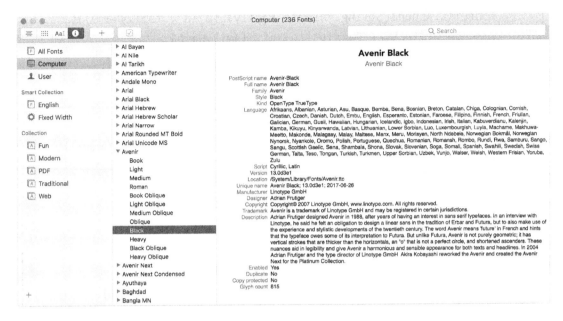

Figure 2-25. *A quick look at the Font Book on a Mac to find the PostScript name*

If you don't have a Mac but want to find out the PostScript name of a font, you need to do some additional work. On Windows it's not as easy to find the name we need. One way of figuring out the correct name is by incorporating a little code snippet in our iOS project's `AppDelegate.cs` class. The code in Listing 2-32 shows you which code we can use.

Listing 2-32. A Quick Code Snippet to Find Out What PostScript Font Name We Need to Use

```
public override bool FinishedLaunching(UIApplication app, NSDictionary options)
{
    // Nifty helper to get all fonts with the right names in your console
#if DEBUG
    var fontList = new StringBuilder();
    var familyNames = UIFont.FamilyNames;
    foreach (var familyName in familyNames)
    {
```

```
        fontList.Append(String.Format("Family: {0}\n", familyName));
        Console.WriteLine("Family: {0}\n", familyName);
        var fontNames = UIFont.FontNamesForFamilyName(familyName);
        foreach (var fontName in fontNames)
        {
            Console.WriteLine("\tFont: {0}\n", fontName);
            fontList.Append(String.Format("\tFont: {0}\n", fontName));
        }
    };
#endif

    // ... Rest of the initialization code here
}
```

When we add this code to the iOS startup class and run the app, we will see a list of all the fonts that are included in the app or available on the iOS platform listed in our Application Output window. The names of the fonts listed here are all PostScript names, so we simply find the font we want to use and copy its name from the output window. Do note that for this to work, we need to have performed the previous steps of adding the actual font into our app.

Tying It All Together in Shared Code

The last part we need to do is telling Xamarin.Forms which font we want to use. The important part of achieving this across both platforms is simply making sure that the FontFamily we set matches the font name to what each respective platform requires. To do this, we use the OnPlatform idiom to provide each platform with the correct value. The sample in Listing 2-33 shows how to do this in XAML.

Listing 2-33. Adding the Custom Font to Our XAML Page

```
<?xml version="1.0" encoding="UTF-8"?>
<ContentPage Title="Custom Fonts"
    xmlns="http://xamarin.com/schemas/2014/forms"
    xmlns:x="http://schemas.microsoft.com/winfx/2009/xaml"
    x:Class="CustomFonts.SamplePage">
```

```
<StackLayout VerticalOptions="Center" HorizontalOptions="Center">
    <Label Text="{Binding MyText}" FontSize="30" TextColor="#000000">
        <Label.FontFamily>
            <OnPlatform x:TypeArguments="x:String">
                <On Platform="iOS" Value="Avenir-Black" />
                <On Platform="Android" Value="Avenir-Black.ttf#Avenir-
                Black " />
            </OnPlatform>
        </Label.FontFamily>
    </Label>
</StackLayout>
</ContentPage>
```

In this sample, we define the FontFamily property for each platform. On iOS we can simply provide the PostScript name of the font and our custom font will get loaded. When it comes to using a custom font on Android there's a different approach necessary. We need to provide both the font filename and the PostScript name, separated by a hash/pound sign. After adding this we can run the app and admire our new font. Figure 2-26 shows how sample in Listing 2-33 looks on both iOS and Android.

Figure 2-26. *Using a custom font on iOS and Android*

Creating Reusable Controls

As a developer working with Xamarin.Forms, it is one of our main goals to optimize the amount of code sharing in our app while also decreasing code duplication. When creating a user interface, it is very easy to create duplicate code without even noticing it. Abstracting this duplicate code into reusable controls is a first step toward creating a more maintainable application.

Introducing a Simple Use Case

To explain the concept of creating reusable controls we will be creating a form that lets us enter data. Normally you could use something like a `TableView` for this task, but if you have to implement a custom UI design, creating your own form might be the easier solution. However, we want all our entry fields looking and feeling the same and ideally, we want to make changes to this control only once. This is where creating a custom control comes into play. Let's take a look at how we would create a simple form in XAML.

Listing 2-34. A Simple Form in XAML Without Using Custom Controls

```
<StackLayout>
    <StackLayout Orientation="Horizontal">
        <Label Text="Username" />
        <Label TextColor="Red" Text="*" />
    </StackLayout>
    <Entry Text="{Binding Username}" />
    <StackLayout Orientation="Horizontal">
        <Label Text="Email" />
        <Label TextColor="Red" Text="*" />
    </StackLayout>
    <Entry Text="{Binding EmailAddress}" />
    <StackLayout Orientation="Horizontal">
        <Label Text="Full name" />
    </StackLayout>
    <Entry Text="{Binding FullName}" />
</StackLayout>
```

As you can see in the sample in Listing 2-34, we are repeating ourselves a lot in this piece of code. For each entry control we repeat the same basic structure using a label above an entry field to indicate the field name and a required indicator asterisk that is omitted for some fields. This page works as expected, but it's far from optimal.

Creating a Custom Control

To abstract our sample into a custom control, we need to add a ContentView to our project, which is one of the options when creating a new file. This gives us both a XAML and a code file to work with. To add the UI for our custom control we can simply paste a part of our previous sample into the user control. This is illustrated in Listing 2-35, which shows the XAML file for our custom control.

Listing 2-35. The XAML File for the Custom Form Entry Control

```xml
<?xml version="1.0" encoding="UTF-8"?>
<ContentView xmlns="http://xamarin.com/schemas/2014/forms" xmlns:x="http://
schemas.microsoft.com/winfx/2009/xaml" x:Class="SampleApp.Views.
FormsEntry">
    <ContentView.Content>
        <StackLayout>
            <StackLayout Orientation="Horizontal">
                <Label x:Name="titleField" Text="Username" />
                <Label x:Name="required" TextColor="Red" Text="*" />
            </StackLayout>
            <Entry x:Name="entryField" Text="{Binding Username}" />
        </StackLayout>
    </ContentView.Content>
</ContentView>
```

As the sample shows, we've now abstracted away the look and feel of the repetitive part of our user interface. However, now our control can only work with the Username field, which doesn't make the control very reusable. We can get around this by creating a few bindable properties. To support this we already added an x:Name attribute to all of the parts of our custom control that will be dynamic once it's done.

Creating a Bindable Property

A bindable property is a property that is backed by a BindableProperty type instead of a field as would normally be the case. These types of properties allow us to data bind values to them, which allows us to populate our custom control with data. Properties like the `Text` property on existing Xamarin.Forms controls like the `Label` are also implemented using bindable properties. To create a bindable property, we need to do two things:

1. Create an instance of a `BindableProperty`.

2. Define accessors for the `BindableProperty` instance.

One thing to consider is that all `BindableProperty` instances must be created on the UI thread. Only code that runs on that thread can get or set the value of a bindable property. You can access them from different thread by marshaling to the UI thread using `Device.BeginInvokeOnMainThread`.

Let's start by creating a bindable property for the title of the entry field in the sample shown in Listing 2-35. Because all of our properties have the `x:Name` attribute set, we can access these controls in the code-behind of our custom control, which is what we'll be doing to set up the data bindings.

Listing 2-36. Adding a Bindable Property to Our Custom Control

```
public static readonly BindableProperty TitleProperty = BindableProperty.
Create(nameof(Title), typeof(string), typeof(FormsEntry), default(string),
Xamarin.Forms.BindingMode.OneWay);

public string Title
{
    get { return (string)GetValue(TitleProperty); }
    set { SetValue(TitleProperty, value); }
}
```

The sample in Listing 2-36 shows the bindable property we added to the code-behind of our custom control. Let's break down what we've added:

*   We use the static `Create` factory method to instantiate a `BindableProperty`.

*   The first parameter we provide is the name of the property that we want to make bindable, in our case this is the `Title` property. Using the `nameof` method, we prevent having to use magic strings to reference this property.

- The second parameter is the Type of the property we want to bind. Using the typeof method, we can retrieve the string type.

- The third parameter is the declaring type of our bindable property. In our case, this is FormsEntry.

- The fourth parameter is the default value we want our property to have. We want to use the default value for the string type.

- The fifth parameter is the binding mode our property should have. In our case, we want the binding to go one way, from the binding context to the control. More about the different binding modes is explained in Chapter 3.

- A Title property that gets and sets the value of the bindable property. This property can change the data-bound property on the binding context when we set it, depending on which binding mode we specified.

Now that we have a bindable property, we need to set the Text property of our Label when the Title property is changed. To do so we can override the OnPropertyChanged event and handle whenever the Title property is set.

Listing 2-37. Setting the Text Property of a Label When the Bindable Property Has Changed

```
protected override void OnPropertyChanged(string propertyName = null)
{
    base.OnPropertyChanged(propertyName);

    if (propertyName == TitleProperty.PropertyName)
    {
        titleField.Text = Title;
    }
}
```

The code in Listing 2-37 shows how to set properties on a control whenever a bindable property has changed. In this sample we set the titleField.Text property to the Title property if that is the property that has changed. Our sample also contained an

Entry field and a required field indicator that we can change into bindable properties in a similar fashion. The code in Listing 2-38 illustrates the resulting custom control after adding these additional properties.

Listing 2-38. The Completed Custom Control with Bindable Properties

```
public partial class FormsEntry : ContentView
{
    public static readonly BindableProperty TitleProperty =
    BindableProperty.Create(nameof(Title), typeof(string),
    typeof(FormsEntry), default(string), BindingMode.OneWay);

    public string Title
    {
        get { return (string)GetValue(TitleProperty); }
        set { SetValue(TitleProperty, value); }
    }

    public static readonly BindableProperty TextProperty =
    BindableProperty.Create(nameof(Text), typeof(string),
    typeof(FormsEntry), default(string), BindingMode.TwoWay);

    public string Text
    {
        get { return (string)GetValue(TextProperty); }
        set { SetValue(TextProperty, value); }
    }

    public static readonly BindableProperty IsRequiredProperty
    = BindableProperty.Create(nameof(IsRequired), typeof(bool),
    typeof(FormsEntry), default(bool), BindingMode.OneWay);

    public bool IsRequired
    {
        get { return (bool)GetValue(IsRequiredProperty); }
        set { SetValue(IsRequiredProperty, value); }
    }
```

```csharp
    public bool IsValid => !IsRequired || (IsRequired && !string.
    IsNullOrEmpty(Text));

    public FormEntry()
    {
        InitializeComponent();

        titleField.Text = Title;
        entryField.Text = Text;
        required.IsVisible = IsRequired;
        entryField.TextChanged += OnTextChanged;
    }

    private void OnTextChanged(object sender, TextChangedEventArgs e)
    {
        Text = e.NewTextValue;
        OnPropertyChanged(nameof(IsValid));
    }

    protected override void OnPropertyChanged(string propertyName = null)
    {
        base.OnPropertyChanged(propertyName);

        if (propertyName == TitleProperty.PropertyName)
        {
            titleField.Text = Title;
        }
        else if (propertyName == TextProperty.PropertyName)
        {
            entryField.Text = Text;
        }
        else if (propertyName == IsRequiredProperty.PropertyName)
        {
            required.IsVisible = IsRequired;
        }
    }
}
```

To complete our custom control, we've added a few things:

- A bindable property for both the Text and the IsRequired properties. The Text property has a binding mode of TwoWay, because we want to show the value in the Entry field and to be able to edit it.

- A TextChanged event, which handles changes to the Entry's values by setting the Text property.

- Both properties to the OnPropertyChanged method to set our controls values accordingly. By using the IsVisible property, we can hide and show the red asterisk required field indicator.

- An IsValid boolean, which we will cover in more detail in the next section.

Using a Custom Control

To use a custom control, we first need to add a namespace to the XAML page that we want to add the control to. This is done by referencing the namespace in which our control resides in the root XAML element. Next, we simply add our custom control to the page and set up all of the appropriate values, resulting in the code shown in Listing 2-39.

Listing 2-39. Our Custom Control Being Used to Create a Simple Data Entry Form

```
<ContentPage xmlns="http://xamarin.com/schemas/2014/forms"
             xmlns:x="http://schemas.microsoft.com/winfx/2009/xaml"
             xmlns:views="clr-namespace:SampleApp.Views ">
    <StackLayout>
        <views:FormsEntry Title="Username" Text="{Binding Username}"
        IsRequired="true" />
        <views:FormsEntry Title="Email" Text="{Binding EmailAddress}"
        IsRequired="true" />
        <views:FormsEntry Title="Full name" Text="{Binding FullName}" />
```

```
<Button Text="Save it now!" IsEnabled="false">
    <Button.Triggers>
        <MultiTrigger TargetType="Button">
            <MultiTrigger.Conditions>
                <BindingCondition Binding="{Binding
                Source={x:Reference Username}, Path=IsValid}"
                Value="true" />
                <BindingCondition Binding="{Binding
                Source={x:Reference Email}, Path=IsValid}"
                Value="true" />
                <BindingCondition Binding="{Binding
                Source={x:Reference Fullname}, Path=IsValid}"
                Value="true" />
            </MultiTrigger.Conditions>
            <Setter Property="IsEnabled" Value="true" />
            <Setter Property="BackgroundColor" Value="GreenYellow" />
        </MultiTrigger>
    </Button.Triggers>
</Button>
    </StackLayout>
</ContentPage>
```

Because the full name field is not required, we can omit the IsRequired property, which means it will default to its default value of false. By building this custom control we have significantly improved our code because the form now has less repetitive code. Future changes to the entry field only need to be made in one centralized location, which makes our app a lot more maintainable.

We also added a button to save our form, which uses a MultiTrigger option. Don't know what a MultiTrigger is? Shame on you, we covered that earlier on in this chapter! Go back and read up on that and come back here, we'll wait...

Read it? Good! The MultiTrigger checks each FormsEntry's IsValid property to see if a value is provided when the field is required. If every required field is filled, the trigger enables the Save button and gives it a satisfying green background color to indicate that the object can be saved.

Exploring Gestures

In this day and age of touch screen phones, a lot of navigation patterns rely on the use of gestures. Gestures, like pinching to zoom in and swiping left and right to go through a list of images, are commonplace in modern app user interfaces. Xamarin.Forms contains a few built-in gestures we can use to allow our app to respond and react to them. This is done through a concept called *gesture recognizers*. You can add these to any visual element and allow that element to respond to the following three gestures:

- Tap

- Pinch

- Pan

Adding a TapGestureRecognizer

By adding a TapGestureRecognizer, we can make any visual element clickable by tapping on it. This gesture recognizer supports both a Tapped method to hook up an event handler and a Command to bind to an action available in a view model. Adding both at the same time is not a common scenario. The sample in Listing 2-40 only shows both options for demo purposes.

Using the Command parameter is particularly useful when using the MVVM pattern. We can even provide a CommandParameter to provide our command with contextual information that we can use in our view model. Listing 2-40 shows an example of adding a TapGestureRecognizer and all of its possible properties.

Listing 2-40. Adding a TapGestureRecognizer to an Image to Make It Clickable

```
<Image Source="mypicture.jpg">
    <Image.GestureRecognizers>
        <TapGestureRecognizer
            Tapped="OnTapped"
            Command="{Binding TappedCommand}"
            CommandParameter="5218"
            NumberOfTapsRequired="2" />
    </Image.GestureRecognizers>
</Image>
```

The NumberOfTapsRequired property defines the amount of taps it takes before the event or command is executed. These taps need to happen in quick succession and when subsequent taps do not occur within that timeframe the tap counter is reset to zero. The maximum value for this property is 2 (only for Android), meaning anything more than a double tap would require you to write custom logic to handle the number of taps.

Adding a PinchGestureRecognizer

By adding a PinchGestureRecognizer, we can make any visual element respond to a pinch gesture. This gesture recognizer exposes the PinchUpdated event that's triggered whenever a pinch gesture is performed. Listing 2-41 shows how to add a pinch gesture recognizer to a visual element.

Listing 2-41. Adding a PinchGestureRecognizer to an Image to Be Able to Pinch It

```
<Image x:Name="myImage" Source="mypicture.jpg">
    <Image.GestureRecognizers>
        <PinchGestureRecognizer PinchUpdated="Handle_PinchUpdated" />
    </Image.GestureRecognizers>
</Image>
```

We will also need to handle the PinchUpdated event to perform an action based on the pinch gesture. In the sample shown in Listing 2-42, we are using a very basic approach to scaling the image based on the current pinch factor.

Listing 2-42. Handling the Pinch Gesture to Scale an Image on the Page

```
double currentScale = 1f;

public void Handle_PinchUpdated(object sender,
PinchGestureUpdatedEventArgs e)
{
    if (e.Status == GestureStatus.Running)
    {
```

```
        // Calculate the scale factor to be applied.
        currentScale += (e.Scale - 1);
        currentScale = Math.Max(1, currentScale);

        // Set the scale for the image.
        myImage.Scale = currentScale;
    }
}
```

In this sample, we define a global variable called currentScale that contains the current scaling factor for the image. When the pinch gesture is active, we take the current scale and adjust the currentScale variable accordingly before assigning it to the Scale property of the image. To do so, we use the argument's object that is being passed in to this event, which contains a Scale property. This holds the value that represents the scale factor of the pinch gesture that was performed by the user.

Adding a PanGestureRecognizer

By adding a PanGestureRecognizer, we can make any visual element respond to a pan gesture, which means we can drag that element around on the screen to position it. This gesture recognizer exposes the PanUpdated event, which is triggered whenever a pan gesture is performed. Listing 2-43 shows how to add a pan gesture recognizer to a visual element.

Listing 2-43. Adding a PanGestureRecognizer to an Image to Be Able to Pan It

```
<Image x:Name="myImage" Source="mypicture.jpg">
    <Image.GestureRecognizers>
        <PanGestureRecognizer PanUpdated="Handle_PanUpdated" />
    </Image.GestureRecognizers>
</Image>
```

We will also need to handle the PanUpdated event to perform an action based on the pan gesture. In the sample shown in Listing 2-44, we are using a very basic approach to move the image based on the current pan X and Y coordinates.

Listing 2-44. Handling the Pan Gesture to Move an Image on the Page

```
double x, y;

public void Handle_PanUpdated(object sender, PanUpdatedEventArgs e)
{
    if (e.StatusType == GestureStatus.Running)
    {
        myImage.TranslationX = Math.Max(Math.Min(0, x + e.TotalX), -Math.
        Abs(myImage.Width - DeviceDisplay.ScreenMetrics.Width));
        myImage.TranslationY = Math.Max(Math.Min(0, y + e.TotalY), -Math.
        Abs(myImage.Height - DeviceDisplay.ScreenMetrics.Height));
    }
    else if (e.StatusType == GestureStatus.Completed)
    {
        x = Content.TranslationX;
        y = Content.TranslationY;
    }
}
```

In this sample, we define two global variables called x and y that contain the current coordinates for the image. When the pan gesture is active, we take the current coordinates and adjust them according to the device's screen width and height. To do so, we use the argument's object that is being passed in to this event, which contains properties representing the X and Y coordinates of the pan gesture that was performed by the user.

The device width and height properties are retrieved using the APIs from the Xamarin.Essentials NuGet package, which contains a lot of useful helper methods. When the panning gesture is completed, we store the current X and Y coordinates.

Note   You can find out more about the Xamarin.Essentials package and all of the cross-platform APIs it contains on its GitHub page: https://github.com/xamarin/essentials.

Summary

This chapter covered most of the basics related to creating a good-looking user interface using Xamarin.Forms. We explained the basic layout controls that act as the building blocks for our user interface and how we can use them to create complex layouts by nesting them. A special mention was reserved for the `FlexLayout`, which adds a lot of flexibility to designing our apps by providing a lot of different layout options. We learned that we can use triggers to change our user interface based on actual data that is bound to it. Animations also impact the look and feel of our app considerably and we learned how to use the built-in animations or create our own animations. By using custom fonts, we can design our app to meet potential branding guidelines where the out-of-the-box fonts would not be enough. Lastly, we covered how we can use intuitive gestures to improve how our users interact with our app.

CHAPTER 3

Working with Data

When developing a mobile application, it's inevitable that you will need to work with data. Whether it's retrieving data or showing data on the screen, data is something every app will need to properly function. This chapter will cover some of the different options you have when presenting your data to the user.

We will take a look at some of the data binding features in Xamarin.Forms that allow us to be notified when data changes. We will also take a look at one of the essential controls within Xamarin.Forms: the ListView.

By using data templates, we can increase the reusability of our code, by consolidating cells that are used in various screens in our application into a single reusable template. We will also look into the default caching behavior of the ListView to improve the performance of our application.

Getting Data Onto the Screen

Most Xamarin.Forms applications will consist of one or more pages. These pages contain all sorts of views that represent data within the application. The application keeps track of all the values assigned to these views and handles changes within these values by displaying the appropriate new values to the user.

However, manually assigning values to properties of views can be a tedious and error-prone job, not to mention updating these values every time your data changes. Technologies that use XAML as its UI markup language, such as WPF, have always benefited greatly from the concept of data binding. Data binding is a technology that takes care of moving 7data between your UI layer and your data source while making sure it stays in sync. Luckily for us, when Xamarin.Forms was created, the UI markup language was based heavily on existing XAML specifications and integrated a full-fledged data binding engine.

© Gerald Versluis and Steven Thewissen 2019
G. Versluis and S. Thewissen, *Xamarin.Forms Solutions*, https://doi.org/10.1007/978-1-4842-4134-9_3

Data Binding Basics

The views that show the data in your application often get their data from an underlying *data source*. When this data changes we want to reflect those changes in our user interface. The same applies the other way around; when a user changes a value we also want this value to change in our data source. This is where data binding comes into play.

Essentially, data binding is a mechanism that triggers an event as soon as the value changes. This event can then be handled by the data source and the views to ensure that the data is successfully transferred from one side to the other, resulting in the correct current values showing in the user interface. Data bindings can be built in either the XAML file or in code, but putting them in the XAML file is the simpler, more common option.

Data Bindings in Xamarin.Forms

A data binding in Xamarin.Forms creates a link between a pair of properties of two objects. These two objects are called the *target* and the *source*.

- The target is the object and property on which the data binding is set, usually a View object in the user interface. However, it can be any type of object as long as it inherits from BindableObject and the property we're setting is a BindableProperty.

- The source is the object and property that usually contain the value we want to bind to the View object. This is the object that we reference in the data binding, which can be of any type. The property can be either a normal property or a BindableProperty.

Figure 3-1 illustrates this concept and aims to clarify the relationship between the target and source object and the role the binding plays between them.

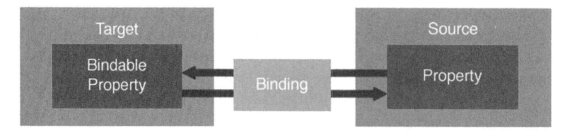

Figure 3-1. *The concept of data binding visualized*

The snippet shown in Listing 3-1 shows a data binding as you would normally set it up in XAML.

Listing 3-1. An Example of a Data Binding As It's Defined in XAML

```
<ContentPage xmlns="http://xamarin.com/schemas/2014/forms"
    xmlns:x="http://schemas.microsoft.com/winfx/2009/xaml"
    ... >
    <StackLayout>
        <Label x:Name="myLabel"
            BindingContext="{x:Reference Name=slider}"
            Text="{Binding Path=Value}"
            HorizontalOptions="Center"
            VerticalOptions="CenterAndExpand" />
        <Slider x:Name="slider"
                Maximum="100"
                VerticalOptions="CenterAndExpand" />
    </StackLayout>
</ContentPage>
```

So, what does this do? The first thing we did is tell our Label where to get its data from. This is done by setting the BindingContext. By using the built-in x:Reference markup extension, we can point to a view elsewhere on the page, in this case the Slider control. In order to do this, we need to set the x:Name property of our Slider, which will uniquely identify it on the page. Now we can use this name in our x:Reference markup extension to reference this control. We then use our Binding markup extension to specify which of the properties of the slider we want to bind to our label. In this case, we choose the Value property. Notice that we are specifying this using the Path= prefix. In this specific case this part can be omitted since the default property of a binding is its Path property. However, if we create a more complex binding by setting multiple properties on the binding, it is advised to add the prefix for the sake of clarity.

Because we've created a connection between these controls through data binding, changes are instantly propagating from one object to the other. This means that when we move the Slider it is instantly updating the value of our Label control.

In the example shown in Listing 3-1 we bind two controls to one another using data binding. This is what is known as a *view-to-view binding*. More often than not you may want to bind to a property of a business object of some sorts. To do so, simply set the BindingContext to an instance of your business object.

But wait, what is a binding context? Every bindable object has a binding context. Because the View object inherits from BindableObject, each view in Xamarin.Forms has a binding context. The binding context is the source of the object's bindings, so by setting it, we specify where the object should get its values from. When setting the binding context, each child object also receives the same binding context, which means we don't need to set it on each control individually.

Listing 3-2 shows an example of setting the BindingContext of the entire page in code.

Listing 3-2. An Example of Setting the BindingContext to a Business Object from Code-Behind

```
<ContentPage xmlns="http://xamarin.com/schemas/2014/forms"
    xmlns:x="http://schemas.microsoft.com/winfx/2009/xaml"
    ... >
    <StackLayout>
        <Entry x:Name="myEntry"
            Text="{Binding Path=Value1}"
            HorizontalOptions="Center"
            VerticalOptions="CenterAndExpand" />
    </StackLayout>
</ContentPage>

...


public partial class BindingContextSamplePage: ContentPage
{
    public MyObject Source { get; set; }

    public BindingContextSamplePage ()
    {
```

```
        InitializeComponent();
        Source = new MyObject(){ Value1 = "A" };
        this.BindingContext = Source;
    }
}
```

Because we set the BindingContext of the page, we can now use the Value1 in our data bindings on the page. When you run this sample, you will immediately see that the value we've set in code ("A") is shown in the textbox. Whenever we change this value it will also immediately reflect those changes in the property on our object. When using an MVVM framework a lot of this kind of plumbing code is done for you and the appropriate view model is set as the BindingContext of the page automatically.

Different Binding Modes

As described earlier in this chapter, data usually flows from the source to the target, but this is not always the case. It can also flow the other way or it can even flow both ways. This behavior is controlled by setting the Mode property on your data binding. The different possible binding modes are defined in the BindingMode enumeration.

- Default—One of the following values, as defined by the creator of the property.

- TwoWay—Data flows both ways between the source and the target.

- OneWay—Data flows from the source to the target.

- OneWayToSource—Data flows from the target to the source.

- OneTime—Data flows from source to target, but only when the BindingContext changes. The data binding is only executed once, when the BindingContext is initially set. This makes this ideal for labels bound to a value that will not be changed. The only way to update a OneTime binding is by setting the BindingContext again. This option was introduced in Xamarin.Forms 3.0.

Most bindable properties have a default binding mode of OneWay. Properties that support user input, such as the Text property on an Entry control, usually have a default binding mode of TwoWay. This is why the sample shown in Listing 3-2 works both ways, even though we never explicitly defined the binding as being a TwoWay binding.

113

Overriding the Default Binding Mode

Sometimes the default binding mode on a property doesn't suit your needs. In this case you can override the default binding mode by specifying your own. To do this, set the Mode property of the Binding markup extension to one of the binding modes in the BindingMode enumeration. An example of how to change the default binding mode is shown in Listing 3-3.

Listing 3-3. An Example of Overriding the Default Binding Mode of a Data Binding

```
<ContentPage xmlns="http://xamarin.com/schemas/2014/forms"
    xmlns:x="http://schemas.microsoft.com/winfx/2009/xaml"
    ... >
    <StackLayout>
        <Entry x:Name="myEntry"
            BindingContext="{x:Reference Name=slider}"
            Text="{Binding Path=Value, Mode=OneWay}"
            HorizontalOptions="Center"
            VerticalOptions="CenterAndExpand" />
        <Slider x:Name="slider"
                Maximum="100"
                VerticalOptions="CenterAndExpand" />
    </StackLayout>
</ContentPage>
```

In this sample we change the data binding of the Entry to become a OneWay binding. When we move the slider around, we will see the value shown in the entry field change. However, when manually editing the value in the entry field, the position of the slider is not updated. This is because the binding only flows one way.

Because the default binding mode of an Entry control is TwoWay we can omit the Mode property on the binding. If we do that we will see the entry value changing when we change the slider, but we can also enter a value in the entry field, which will make the value of the slider update.

Setting this binding to OneWayToSource will make sure that we will only see changes in the entry when we move the slider. Using the OneTime mode, we will see that our Entry control gets a default value, but both moving the slider and entering a value manually will not change anything. This is because the value is set only once, which sets it to the default value, after which it is never set again.

Notifying the App of Data Changes

So far, we've talked about data bindings and how our data flows through them but we haven't really touched on how our app knows that data has actually changed. There has to be a mechanism somewhere that tells our app that a property was changed, right? When using the MVVM architectural pattern, it is common practice to implement an interface called INotifyPropertyChanged on our view models. This is what lets the data binding engine know that a value has changed.

A view model that implements the INotifyPropertyChanged interface fires a PropertyChanged event whenever one of its properties has changed. To let the binding engine know which property has changed, the property name is passed into this event. The data binding mechanism in Xamarin.Forms attaches a handler to this PropertyChanged event so it can be notified when the property changes and keep the target updated with the new value. A basic implementation of the INotifyPropertyChanged event handler is shown in Listing 3-4.

Listing 3-4. The Basic Implementation of the INotifyPropertyChanged Interface

```
public class MyViewModel : INotifyPropertyChanged
{
    string _myProperty;
    public event PropertyChangedEventHandler PropertyChanged;

    public string MyProperty
    {
        get
        {
            return _myProperty;
        }
        set
        {
```

```
        if (_myProperty != value)
        {
            _myProperty = value;
            OnPropertyChanged();
        }
    }
}

protected virtual void OnPropertyChanged([CallerMemberName] string
propertyName = "")
{
    PropertyChanged?.Invoke(this, new PropertyChangedEventArgs
    (propertyName));
}
}
```

As the sample in Listing 3-4 shows, we added an event called PropertyChanged that is defined in the INotifyPropertyChanged interface. When our property changes we trigger the event and pass in the name of the property that changed. The binding engine then takes care of the rest for us and updates our targets accordingly.

Most people implement the INotifyPropertyChanged interface on a base view model class that all other view models inherit from. Alternatively, most MVVM frameworks offer their own implementation of the interface, which you can to use to raise the event. Another alternative is IL weaving, which is described in more detail in the next section.

Implementing INotifyPropertyChanged Using Fody

The sample given in Listing 3-4 shows how to implement the INotifyPropertyChanged interface, but it can get very repetitive if we have to implement this boilerplate code in every one of our view models. We could abstract parts of the boiler plate code away into a base view model class, but there is an even easier way—using *Fody*!

Fody is a framework that enables us to manipulate the intermediate language of an assembly when it's being built through a process known as *weaving*. In essence this means we can use it to improve our code automatically at the time of compilation.

The real magic usually happens in a Fody add-in that aims to solve a specific problem. In this case, we use the `PropertyChanged.Fody` add-in (available on NuGet), which allows us to inject code that raises the `PropertyChanged` event in all of the property setters of classes that implement `INotifyPropertyChanged`. This means we can significantly cut down on the amount of times we need to raise the `PropertyChanged` event in our properties. The view model shown in Listing 3-4 can be simplified using `PropertyChanged.Fody`, as shown in Listing 3-5.

Listing 3-5. The Simplified Version of Our View Model Using PropertyChanged.Fody

```
public class MyViewModel : INotifyPropertyChanged
{
    public event PropertyChangedEventHandler PropertyChanged;

    public string MyProperty { get; set; }
}
```

We could improve on the sample shown in Listing 3-5 even further by adding a base view model that implements the `INotifyPropertyChanged` interface. The resulting view model would only contain the `MyProperty` property, which is a significant improvement when looking at our lines of code.

There are a few additional attributes we can use on our properties to influence Fody's behavior:

- `AlsoNotifyFor`—By adding this attribute we can define other properties that should also have their `PropertyChanged` event called when the property that we added the attribute to has changed.

- `DoNotNotify`—This means that the property decorated with this attribute will not automatically raise its `PropertyChanged` event.

- `DependsOn`—By decorating a property with this attribute, we define that it depends on another property and injects this property to be notified when the dependent property is set. An example of a dependent property would be a full name property that depends on a first name and last name property.

Implementing PropertyChanged.Fody is not the solution to all of your problems. There are other solutions out there that work just as well and it all depends on personal preference. We've been using PropertyChanged.Fody in a few of our projects and decided to include it since it is a relatively unknown solution for implementing INotifyPropertyChanged.

Note   You can find out more about setting up Fody and the add-ins it currently supports on the GitHub page: `https://github.com/Fody/Fody/`

Working with Collections

So far, we've mostly looked into data binding a single object or value. When it comes to binding a collection of values there are some exceptions we need to consider. Looking at the sample in Listing 3-6, we have a List<string> type property that we initialize in the constructor of our view model. We also have an Add method that adds a new item each time it is called. Let's assume we have a data binding set up for this property that binds it to a view that can handle collections such as the ListView.

Listing 3-6.   A Sample of INotifyPropertyChanged with a List Type Property

```
public class MyViewModel : INotifyPropertyChanged
{
    public event PropertyChangedEventHandler PropertyChanged;

    public List<string> MyListProperty { get; set; }

    public MyViewModel()
    {
        MyListProperty = new List<string>() { "Item 1", "Item 2", "Item 3" };
    }

    public void Add()
    {
        MyListProperty.Add($"Item {MyListProperty.Count + 1}");
    }
}
```

When we call the Add method what do you think will happen in our user interface? Will we see items being added? As it turns out, nothing will happen. But why is that?

As was shown in Listing 3-4, the INotifyPropertyChanged mechanism works by sending out a PropertyChanged event when the setter of a property is called. However, making changes to a collection type by adding to or removing from it doesn't actually call the property setter. Since the setter is never called, there is no notification sent to the data binding, which is why we see no changes on the screen.

To ensure that our collections also trigger our data bindings accordingly we can use a specialized collection type called an ObservableCollection<T>. This is a generic implementation of a collection class that provides notifications when items get added or removed. To use this collection type, we can simply drop it into our code as a replacement of our List<T>, as shown in Listing 3-7.

Listing 3-7. Improving Our Collection Data Bindings Using an ObservableCollection

```
public class MyViewModel : INotifyPropertyChanged
{
    public event PropertyChangedEventHandler PropertyChanged;

    public ObservableCollection<string> MyListProperty { get; set; }

    public MyViewModel()
    {
        MyListProperty = new ObservableCollection<string>() { "Item 1",
        "Item 2", "Item 3" };
    }

    public void Add()
    {
        MyListProperty.Add($"Item {MyListProperty.Count + 1}");
    }
}
```

This works because `ObservableCollection` contains an event named `CollectionChanged` that is provided through the `INotifyCollectionChanged` interface. Because this behavior is defined through this interface, we can also create our own custom collection object and use it in data binding. The `CollectionChanged` event notifies any subscribers of changes to the collection in the same way that the `PropertyChanged` event handles changes to a property.

Converting Data Bound Values

When data binding values directly from and to an object, you may run into the scenario where you want to display a value in a slightly different way than its representation in the object. For example, you may want to format a date in a specific way, or perhaps you want to prefix a certain value with fixed text. To handle this scenario, you can use the `StringFormat` markup extension.

Normally you would use the static `String.Format` method to format a string. This same method powers the `StringFormat` markup extension, meaning you can use the same string formatting specifications you would normally use. An example of using `StringFormat` can be seen in Listing 3-8.

Listing 3-8. Formatting a String Value Using the Built-In StringFormat Markup Extension

```
<ContentPage xmlns="http://xamarin.com/schemas/2014/forms"
    xmlns:x="http://schemas.microsoft.com/winfx/2009/xaml"
    ... >
    <StackLayout>
        <Entry x:Name="myEntry"
            BindingContext="{x:Reference Name=slider}"
            Text="{Binding Path=Value, StringFormat='Slider value: {0:F2}'}"
            HorizontalOptions="Center"
            VerticalOptions="CenterAndExpand" />
        <Slider x:Name="slider"
                Maximum="360"
                VerticalOptions="CenterAndExpand" />
    </StackLayout>
</ContentPage>
```

The formatting string is delimited by single quote characters to ensure that the XAML parser doesn't treat the curly braces in the expression as another markup extension. In this example the value of the slider will be displayed with two decimal places due to the addition of the F2 specification in the formatting string.

Using ValueConverters to Tackle Complex Scenarios

A data binding transfers data from a source to a target property. But what if those two properties are not of the same type? Let's say for example that you want to bind a Boolean type property based on the value of an Enum type property. If you want to data-bind two properties that have incompatible types, you need a piece of code in between that converts the value from source to target type and back. This is what is called a ValueConverter. When looking at StringFormat we concluded that it can be used to convert anything into a string representation. Using a ValueConverter you can convert from and to any type of object.

A ValueConverter can be created by implementing the IValueConverter interface. Classes that implement IValueConverter are also often referred to as binding converters or binding value converters. A simple example of a value converter is shown in Listing 3-9. In this sample, we convert from a String value into a Boolean.

Listing 3-9. A Sample ValueConverter That Converts from String to Boolean and Back

```
public class YesNoToBoolConverter : IValueConverter
{
    public object Convert(object value, Type targetType, object parameter,
    CultureInfo culture)
    {
        switch (value?.ToString().ToLower())
        {
            case "yes":
                return true;
            case "no":
            default:
                return false;
        }
    }
}
```

```
public object ConvertBack(object value, Type targetType, object
parameter, CultureInfo culture)
{
    if (value is bool)
    {
        if ((bool)value)
            return "yes";
        else
            return "no";
    }

    return "no";
}
}
```

The `Convert()` method assumes that it receives a string as the input (as represented by the `value` parameter). It takes that value and converts it into a Boolean true or false value and falls back to false if the value is not "yes" or "no". This method is called when data moves from the source to the target in `OneWay`, `OneTime`, or `TwoWay` bindings.

The `ConvertBack()` method does the exact opposite: It assumes that the input value is a `Boolean` type and then returns the word "yes" or "no". This also falls back to "no" if the input is not a `Boolean` type. This method is called when data moves from the target to the source in `TwoWay` or `OneWayToSource` bindings.

With our converter defined we now need to instruct our data binding to use the converter. That is done by setting an instance of this class to the `Converter` property of the `Binding` markup extension, as shown in Listing 3-10.

Listing 3-10. Adding the Value Converter to the Data Binding

```
<ContentPage xmlns="http://xamarin.com/schemas/2014/forms"
    xmlns:x="http://schemas.microsoft.com/winfx/2009/xaml"
    xmlns:local="clr-namespace:ValueConverters"
    ... >
    <ContentPage.Resources>
        <ResourceDictionary>
            <local:YesNoToBoolConverter x:Key="yesNoToBool" />
```

```
        </ResourceDictionary>
    </ContentPage.Resources>
    <StackLayout>
        <Label Text="Hello!" IsVisible="{Binding MyBoolAsString,
        Converter={StaticResource yesNoToBool}}"
            HorizontalOptions="Center"
            VerticalOptions="CenterAndExpand" />
    </StackLayout>
</ContentPage>
```

First, we add an instance of our value converter to the page's resource dictionary. That means that our value converter is now known on the entire page by the name yesNoToBool. We can then add the value converter to our Binding using the Converter property. We do this by using the StaticResource markup extension, which points to the converter in our resource dictionary using the exact same key value that we've defined in the resource dictionary. Depending on the value of the MyBoolAsString property, the Label should become visible or invisible.

This is a rather simple scenario of what is possible with a value converter. Because you can use it on any type of data binding with any type of object, you can make them as simple or as complex as needed. Another added benefit of value converters is that you can reuse them. In the sample in Listing 3-10 we added the value converter to the page's resource dictionary. Alternatively, we could also add it to the resource dictionary of the app. That way, it becomes available for use throughout the entire app, which means that we don't need to define it on every single page where we want to use it.

Getting to Know the ListView

One of the most commonly used controls in any mobile app is the ListView. This view is the ideal solution for presenting lists of data, especially long lists that require scrolling. It comes in many shapes and sizes due to its versatility. The out-of-the-box ListView on each platform can be seen in Figure 3-2.

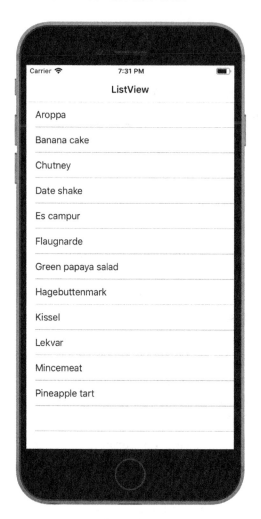

Figure 3-2. *The ListView in its default state on iOS and Android*

The ListView can be used in any situation where you are displaying scrollable lists of data. The ListView supports context actions and data binding and has a number of additional features available that you can use, like pull-to-refresh, headers and footers, grouping, and support for custom cells.

Understanding the Basics

The ListView is used for displaying lists of items and to do so we set the ItemsSource property. This property accepts any collection that implements IEnumerable. We can also run into the scenario where we want to use data binding to bind to a dynamic list of items from which we can add and remove items. To also allow data binding to show these changes to the list's content, we can use ObservableCollection<T>, as we mentioned earlier in this chapter.

Using the Built-In Cell Types

Each item in a ListView is represented by a ViewCell. These can be used for all sorts of things, such as displaying text and images, indicating a true/false state, and receiving user input. They define how each cell in your ListView looks and you can either customize them completely or you can use one of the built-in cell types in Xamarin.Forms:

- TextCell—Used for displaying text.

- ImageCell—Used for displaying an image with text.

- SwitchCell—Used for displaying a toggle control.

- EntryCell—Used for displaying a text entry control.

The TextCell is a cell for displaying text, optionally with a second line as detail text. The properties we can use to set these are Text and DetailText. Since these are rendered as native controls at runtime, their performance is optimized by the platform. They're limited in their customizability and only allow you to set a primary text, detail text, and the colors for both of these. An example of how the TextCell looks on each of the supported platforms can be found in Figure 3-3.

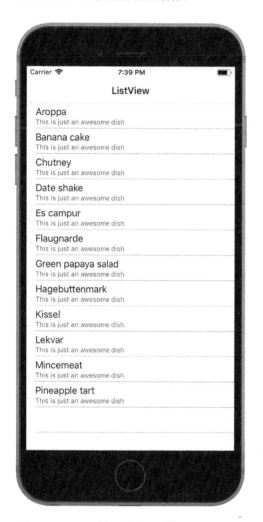
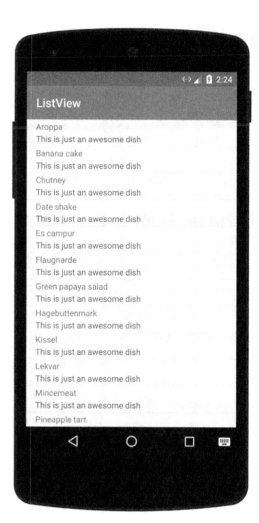

Figure 3-3. *The TextCell as it is rendered on iOS and Android*

The `ImageCell` is a cell that has the same text support as the `TextCell` but additionally allows you to show an image. This additional visual aspect is great to spice up an otherwise bland list of text. The properties we can use to set the text and image are `Text` and `ImageSource`, respectively. This cell is also natively rendered so the same performance optimizations apply. An example of the `ImageCell` is shown in Figure 3-4.

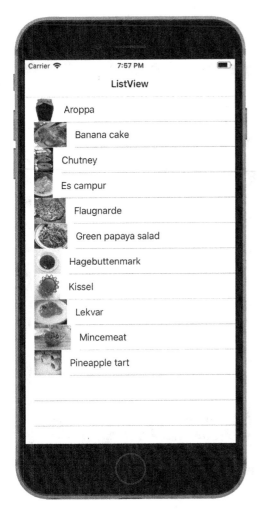

Figure 3-4. *The ImageCell as it is rendered on iOS and Android*

The SwitchCell is a cell that shows a toggle and a custom label text. The toggle control is rendered as a native toggle control as is defined by the platform we're running on. It has two interesting properties, namely Text and On, which can be used to set the label text and the toggle state. Since it's a control that requires user input, it has a TwoWay binding, meaning that any updates to the toggle are immediately reflected in our data source. An example of the SwitchCell is shown in Figure 3-5.

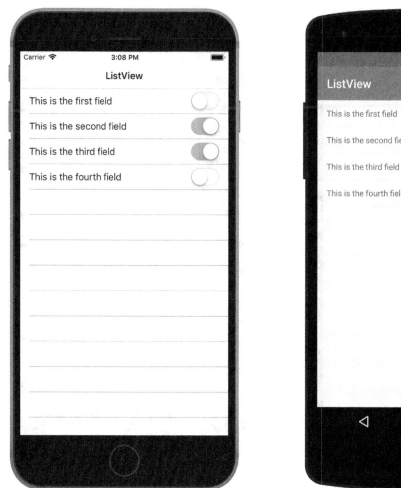
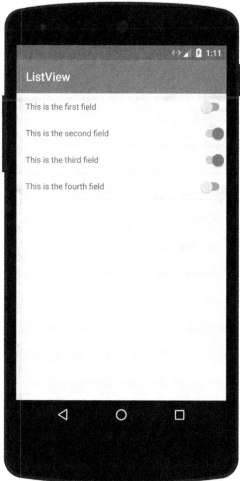

Figure 3-5. *The SwitchCell as it is rendered on iOS and Android*

The EntryCell is a cell that shows a text entry control. It's a common control to use when requiring data from the user. The text in the entry control is set through the Text property. This entry control is rendered using the native controls and, because it's a control that requires user input, it has a TwoWay binding by default. Any updates to the text value are therefore immediately reflected in our data source. An example of the EntryCell is shown in Figure 3-6.

Figure 3-6. *The EntryCell as it is rendered on iOS and Android*

Adding one of these existing cell types to your ListView is straightforward. The only thing you need to do is specify which cell type you want to use in the data template for the ListView (see Listing 3-11). More information about data templates and how you can create custom cells using them can be found later on in this chapter.

Listing 3-11. Using a TextCell and Binding a Value to it in the ListView

```
<ContentPage x:Name="MyPage" xmlns="http://xamarin.com/schemas/2014/forms"
    xmlns:x="http://schemas.microsoft.com/winfx/2009/xaml"
    ... >
    <ListView ItemsSource="{Binding MyItems}">
```

```
    <ListView.ItemTemplate>
        <DataTemplate>
            <TextCell Text="{Binding MyText}" />
        </DataTemplate>
    </ListView.ItemTemplate>
  </ListView>
</ContentPage>
```

In the sample shown in Listing 3-11, each item in the MyItems collection will be shown in its own TextCell instance, which is bound to the value of that item's MyText property.

Defining Separators and Row Height

In the samples shown in this chapter so far, you may have noticed the thin line between each of the items in the ListView. This line is a default feature of both iOS and Android and is known as the *separator line.* We can control whether these are displayed by setting the SeparatorVisibility property on the ListView to one of two values:

- *Default*—Shows the separator lines.

- *None*—Hides the separator lines.

Another thing we can influence when it comes to the separator lines is their color. To change the color, we can set the SeparatorColor property on the ListView to a valid predefined color object or a hexadecimal value. A XAML sample of this is shown in Listing 3-12.

Listing 3-12. Setting the SeparatorColor, HasUnevenRows, and RowHeight on the ListView

```
<ListView ItemsSource="{Binding MyItems}" SeparatorColor="Orange"
HasUnevenRows="false" RowHeight="60">
    <ListView.ItemTemplate>
        <DataTemplate>
            <TextCell Text="{Binding Text}" />
        </DataTemplate>
    </ListView.ItemTemplate>
</ListView>
```

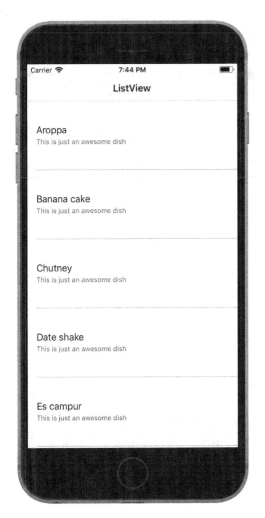

Figure 3-7. *Setting the RowHeight changes the height of all the rows in the ListView*

When using the out-of-the-box settings of the ListView, each item will have the
same row height. We can adjust this by setting the RowHeight property, which sets
the height for all rows, as shown in Figure 3-7. If you need individual rows to have
different heights, you can set the HasUnevenRows property to true. This will calculate
the row height for each row based on its contents, so you do not have to manually set
the RowHeight property anymore. An example of how this looks is shown in Figure 3-8.
Listing 3-12 illustrates how to set these properties.

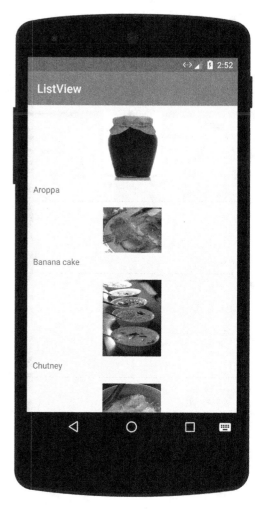

Figure 3-8. *Setting HasUnevenRows to true means each row calculates its own height*

Adding Headers and Footers

The ListView has the capability to place additional content above or below it that acts as a header or footer. This can be either a piece of text or a more complicated layout. To create a simple header/footer, just set the Header or Footer properties to the text you want to display. This can be done in either code-behind or XAML. The sample shown in Listing 3-13 shows how to set it in XAML.

Listing 3-13. Setting the Header and Footer on the ListView the Simple Way

```
<ListView Header="Look at our header!" Footer="Look at our footer!">
    ...
</ListView>
```

Figure 3-9 shows the results of this piece of sample code.

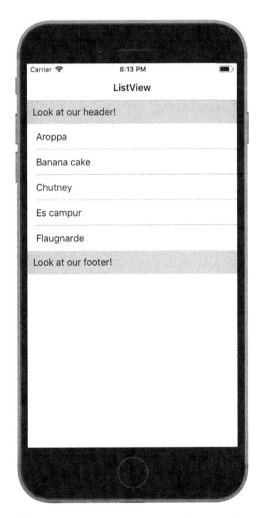

Figure 3-9. *A simple header and footer on iOS and Android*

If a more complicated header or footer is needed, the same properties can be used but they need to be set differently. Because we actually need to add multiple nested views to create a more complicated header or footer, we can use the templated version of these properties, as shown in Listing 3-14.

Listing 3-14. Setting the Header and Footer to a More Complicated Set of Views

```
<ListView ItemsSource="{Binding MyItems}">
    <ListView.Header>
        <StackLayout BackgroundColor="LightGray" Padding="20"
        Orientation="Horizontal">
            <Image WidthRequest="40" Source="xamarin.png" />
            <StackLayout>
                <Label Text="Look at my complicated header!" />
                <Label FontSize="14" Text=" Now with small titles and a
                logo " />
            </StackLayout>
        </StackLayout>
    </ListView.Header>
    <ListView.Footer>
        <StackLayout BackgroundColor="LightGray" Padding="20"
        Orientation="Horizontal">
            <Image WidthRequest="40" Source="xamarin.png" />
            <StackLayout>
                <Label Text="Look at my complicated footer!" />
                <Label FontSize="14" Text="Now with small titles and a
                logo" />
            </StackLayout>
        </StackLayout>
    </ListView.Footer>
</ListView>
```

Figure 3-10 shows the results of this piece of sample code.

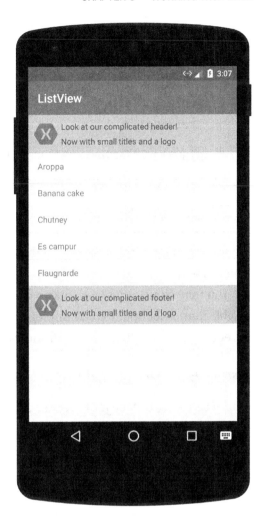

Figure 3-10. *A complicated header and footer on iOS and Android*

Selecting Items and Handling Tap Events

The ListView supports selecting items one at a time by default. Tapping on an item in the ListView triggers two different events:

- ItemTapped—Fires each time an item is tapped.

- ItemSelected—Fires only once for each item you tap. Also fires when an item is deselected.

The sample in Listing 3-15 shows how to implement the ItemSelected event.

135

Listing 3-15. Implementing the ItemSelected Event on the ListView

```
void ItemSelected(object sender, SelectedItemChangedEventArgs e)
{
    if (e.SelectedItem == null)
        return;

    DisplayAlert("Selected!", e.SelectedItem.ToString(), "OK");
}
```

Using the arguments that we get passed in from this event, we can retrieve the item that was selected and act on it. We also need to add a null check because this event also fires when an item is deselected. In this case, the SelectedItem property will be null, which is why we need to check for it.

You may come across a scenario where you don't want to be able to select items. To disable item selection, we can implement the ItemSelected event and manually set the SelectedItem to null. Listing 3-16 shows how this can be done.

Listing 3-16. Disabling the Item Selection by Setting the SelectedItem to Null

```
void ItemSelected(object sender, SelectedItemChangedEventArgs e)
{
    ((ListView)sender).SelectedItem = null;
}
```

Adding a Pull-to-Refresh

Refreshing a list by pulling it down is a gesture that has become increasingly popular in apps in the last few years. Users are expecting this behavior and luckily Xamarin.Forms has an easy implementation for it out-of-the-box, as shown in Listing 3-17.

Listing 3-17. Implementing the Pull-to-Refresh Mechanism in Xamarin.Forms

```
<ContentPage x:Name="MyPage" xmlns="http://xamarin.com/schemas/2014/forms"
    xmlns:x="http://schemas.microsoft.com/winfx/2009/xaml"
    ... >
    <ListView ItemsSource="{Binding MyItems}" IsPullToRefreshEnabled="true"
    RefreshCommand="{Binding RefreshCommand}" IsRefreshing="{Binding
    IsRefreshing}">
    </ListView>
</ContentPage>

...

public class MyViewModel
{
    public Command RefreshCommand { get; set; }
    public ObservableCollection<string> MyItems { get; set; } = new Observa
    bleCollection<string>();
    public bool IsRefreshing { get; set; }

    public MyViewModel()
    {
        RefreshCommand = new Command(AddItem);
    }

    public void AddItem()
    {
        IsRefreshing = true;
        MyItems.Add($"Item {MyItems.Count + 1}");
        IsRefreshing = false;
    }
}
```

The sample in Listing 3-17 shows how easy it is to implement pull-to-refresh. We start by setting the IsPullToRefreshEnabled variable to true on the ListView. To hook up some behavior to this event, we specify a Command that will be triggered as soon as the user pulls down the list. In this case we're simply adding a new item to the list on each refresh. The IsRefreshing property can also be bound to a value in your view model, which allows you to show or hide the loading indicator. By setting this value to true when we start loading and back to false when we're done, we can show and hide the loading indicator accordingly.

Using a Context Action to Act on a List Item

Sometimes you want your users to be able to perform an action on a list item. A common example of this is an email application, where you can swipe left or right to reveal additional actions you can take on an email, such as deleting it or marking it as read. On Android, this action can be reached by performing a long press on an item, whereas for UWP these are shown by right-clicking on an item. These actions are known as *context actions*.

In Xamarin.Forms you can create a context action by using `MenuItems`. Because the tap events are raised by the `MenuItem` itself, instead of the `ListView`, we do not have any context of which item was tapped at our disposal. This means that a `MenuItem` has no way of knowing which cell it belongs to. Luckily, we can use the `CommandParameter` property that the `MenuItem` provides to store objects, such as the object behind the `MenuItem`'s `ViewCell`. Listing 3-18 shows how to implement a context action in XAML.

Listing 3-18. A Context Action Implemented on a ListView in XAML

```
<ContentPage x:Name="MyPage" xmlns="http://xamarin.com/schemas/2014/forms"
    xmlns:x="http://schemas.microsoft.com/winfx/2009/xaml"
    ... >
    <ListView ItemsSource="{Binding MyItems}">
        <ListView.ItemTemplate>
            <DataTemplate>
                <ViewCell>
                    <ViewCell.ContextActions>
                        <MenuItem Command="{Binding Path=BindingContext.
                        DeleteCommand, Source={x:Reference MyPage}}"
                        CommandParameter="{Binding .}" Text="Delete"
                        IsDestructive="True" />
                    </ViewCell.ContextActions>
                    <Grid>
                        <Label Text="{Binding .}" VerticalOptions="Center" />
```

```
                </Grid>
            </ViewCell>
        </DataTemplate>
    </ListView.ItemTemplate>
  </ListView>
</ContentPage>
```

Because we are adding a context action to each cell, we need to add it in a custom data template. If you don't know what data templates are, you can read up on them later on in this chapter. In this example we are defining a ViewCell that has a ContextAction assigned to it. This context action has a Command and a CommandParameter, which we can use to trigger an action and pass data to that action. You can also define the text to display and determine whether or not the operation is a destructive one, which will alter the appearance of the context action on iOS.

One thing that may strike you as odd in this is that we're explicitly setting the source of our data binding. We covered using the binding context and source earlier in this chapter, but why do we need it here? This is due to the fact that we're inside a ListView where the data context for each ViewCell is the item that is bound to it. However, the Command we're referencing here does not exist on each ListView item, but exists on the page level in the view model. Therefore, we need to explicitly set the binding context of the Command we're trying to bind to the page.

We're also binding both the label's Text property and the menu item's CommandParameter to a period. What does that mean? The period references the root object that the current view is bound to, in this case the item in our list. This means we're sending the entire list item as a parameter to our command.

The view model associated with this XAML page is shown in Listing 3-19.

Listing 3-19. The View Model Associated with the XAML Shown in Listing 3-18

```
public class MyViewModel
{
    public Command DeleteCommand { get; set; }
    public ObservableCollection<string> MyItems { get; set; } = new Observable
    Collection<string>();
```

```
    public MyViewModel()
    {
        DeleteCommand = new Command<string>(DeleteItem);
    }

    public void DeleteItem(string item)
    {
        MyItems.Remove(item);
    }
}
```

As you can see, we have an ObservableCollection of strings that represent our items. Updates to this list, such as removing an item, are immediately visible in the UI. The Delete command is an instance of Command<string>, where the part in angle quotes represents the type of the parameter our command accepts. Our DeleteItem method accepts a string parameter, which is the value that it receives from the XAML binding and removes it from the list of items.

Adding a Jump List for Easy Navigation

When presenting a lot of items in the ListView, you will inevitably reach the point where finding an item in the list can become a hard task for the user. By grouping the items, you can improve the user experience because the content is organized in a way that the users can easily find what they're looking for. In Xamarin.Forms this is achieved by enabling grouping on the ListView. This adds a small header above each group and you also get a jump list to easily navigate to each group. Figure 3-11 shows an example of how this grouping looks across the different platforms.

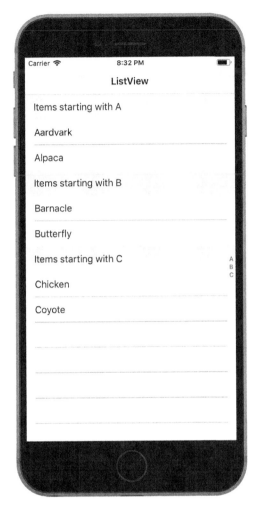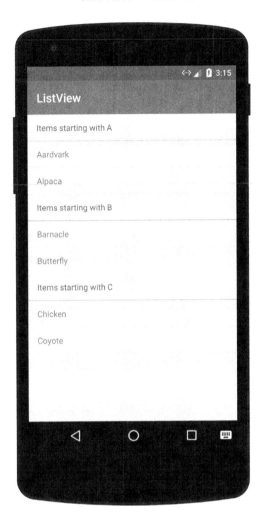

Figure 3-11. *Adding grouping to the ListView to improve the user experience*

To enable this grouping functionality, there are a few steps that need to be taken:

- Change your data source into a list of lists (each group has a list of items and is contained within a list itself).

- Set the ItemsSource property of the ListView to this list.

- Set IsGroupingEnabled to true on the ListView.

- Set the GroupDisplayBinding property to bind to the property of the groups that will be used as the header text for that group.

- Optionally, you can set the GroupShortNameBinding property to bind to the property of the groups that will be used as the jump list text.

First, we need to create a custom class that will represent one of our groups. See Listing 3-20.

Listing 3-20. A Simple Group Class That Can Serve As the Grouping for the ListView

```
public List<MyGroup> Items { get; set; }

public MyViewModel()
{
    Items = new List<MyGroup>() {
        new MyGroup("Items starting with A", "A") {
            new MyItem("Aardvark"),
            new MyItem("Alpaca")
        },
        new MyGroup("Items starting with B", "B") {
            new MyItem("Barnacle"),
            new MyItem("Butterfly")
        },
        new MyGroup("Items starting with C", "C") {
            new MyItem("Chicken"),
            new MyItem("Coyote")
        }
    };
}

...

public class MyItem
{
    public string ItemTitle { get; set; }

    public MyItem(string title)
    {
        ItemTitle = title;
    }
}
```

```
public class MyGroup : List<MyItem>
{
    public string Title { get; set; }
    public string ShortName { get; set; }

    public MyGroup (string title, string shortName)
    {
        Title = title;
        ShortName = shortName;
    }
}
```

In Listing 3-20 we create a new class representing the grouping we want to apply, called MyGroup. This class is basically a list of items with an added title and short name for the jump list added. We will be binding our ListView to an object of type List<MyGroup>. In the constructor for the view model, we populate the list with some values to complete the basic setup.

Listing 3-21. Setting Up the Grouping on the ListView in XAML

```
<ContentPage xmlns="http://xamarin.com/schemas/2014/forms"
    xmlns:x="http://schemas.microsoft.com/winfx/2009/xaml"
    ...>
    <ContentPage.Content>
        <ListView ItemsSource="{Binding Items}"
        GroupDisplayBinding="{Binding Title}"
        GroupShortNameBinding="{Binding ShortName}"
        IsGroupingEnabled="true">
            <ListView.ItemTemplate>
                <DataTemplate>
                    <TextCell Text="{Binding ItemTitle}" />
                </DataTemplate>
            </ListView.ItemTemplate>
```

```
        <ListView.GroupHeaderTemplate>
            <DataTemplate>
                <TextCell Text="{Binding Title}" />
            </DataTemplate>
        </ListView.GroupHeaderTemplate>
    </ListView>
  </ContentPage.Content>
</ContentPage>
```

The final step we need to take is setting up our grouping on the `ListView`. Listing 3-21 shows how to do so in XAML. We bind both the `GroupDisplayBinding` and the `GroupShortNameBinding` to their respective counterparts in our `MyGroup` object and simply enable grouping. The end result is that we get a grouped list of items and a jump list that lets you scroll toward related items quickly.

The sample in Listing 3-21 also shows that we have defined a custom group header template. Currently we only supply a simple text cell, but in the next section about data templates we will see that we can also create complicated data templates containing entire view hierarchies and use those as the group header.

Using Data Templates

A data template enables you to define the appearance of data and typically uses data binding to display the data. A common scenario can be found when using a `ListView` control. Each item in the list is shown using the defined data template, which enables you to define how an object is represented in the list. The fact that data templates are reusable means you only have to define the object's representation once and you can use it for as many lists as you want.

When the list you use to show your objects contains different types of objects or if data needs to be represented differently based on an object's properties, you can use a *data template selector*. The selector determines which template should be shown for each object in the list based on the criteria you define.

Creating a Data Template

A common use for a `DataTemplate` is displaying data from a collection of objects in a `ListView`. Because each item in a `ListView` is represented in a cell, each `DataTemplate` contains an object inheriting from the `Cell` data type. To define a custom look and feel, your best option is to use `ViewCell` because that gives you highest flexibility when defining your controls. Let's look at how a data template is created first. A data template can be created in different locations, which impacts where it can be used:

- Control-level (also known as inline)
- Page-level
- App-level

Each data template has an attribute named `x:Key` that enables you to specify a name for it. This name is used when referencing the data template and any other resource you put in a resource dictionary. You can create multiple data templates with the same `x:Key` value; however, the template that is defined at the lowest level will take precedent over the others. When the template is defined at the app level, it will be overridden by a template at the page level and when it's defined at the control level it will override a page-level template.

Create an Inline Data Template

An inline template, which is a template that's placed as the direct child of an appropriate control property, should be used if there's no need to reuse the data template elsewhere. The most well-known examples of this type of control property are `ItemTemplate`, `HeaderTemplate`, and `FooterTemplate`, which all exist on the Xamarin.Forms `ListView` control and can be seen in Listing 3-14. When a data template is defined in the control itself, you are only able to use it from within that control. A sample of this is shown in Listing 3-22.

Listing 3-22. A Basic Inline Data Template Containing a Label and an Image

```
<ListView ItemSource="{Binding MyItems}">
    <ListView.ItemTemplate>
        <DataTemplate>
            <ViewCell>
                <Grid>
```

```
                    <Label Text="{Binding Name}" FontAttributes="Bold" />
                    <Image Grid.Column="1" Source="{Binding
                    ProfilePicture}" />
                </Grid>
            </ViewCell>
        </DataTemplate>
    </ListView.ItemTemplate>
</ListView>
```

Create a Data Template in a Resource Dictionary

A data template can be defined in either the page's or the app's resource dictionary. The availability of your data template depends on which resource dictionary you choose to put it in, meaning that it can be reused on either the page or within the entire app. A sample of a data template in the page's resource dictionary is shown in Listing 3-23. Also note the ItemTemplate property of the ListView being set to the x:Key of our data template resource.

Listing 3-23. The Same Data Template Added as a Resource to the Page's Resource Dictionary

```
<ContentPage xmlns="http://xamarin.com/schemas/2014/forms"
    xmlns:x="http://schemas.microsoft.com/winfx/2009/xaml"
    ...>
    <ContentPage.Resources>
        <ResourceDictionary>
            <DataTemplate x:Key="MyCellTemplate">
                <ViewCell>
                    <Grid>
                        <Label Text="{Binding Name}" FontAttributes="Bold" />
                        <Image Grid.Column="1" Source="{Binding
                        ProfilePicture}" />
                    </Grid>
                </ViewCell>
            </DataTemplate>
        </ResourceDictionary>
    </ContentPage.Resources>
```

```
    <ListView ItemTemplate="{StaticResource MyCellTemplate}"
    ItemSource="{Binding MyItems}">
    </ListView>
</ContentPage>
```

Create a Custom Cell Type to Use in the Data Template

To create a custom cell type, we create a control that inherits from ViewCell. This custom control can then be placed directly inside of a data template. The advantage of this approach is that the appearance defined by the cell type can be reused by multiple data templates throughout the application. First, we need to create our own custom type, as shown in Listing 3-24, which should inherit from ViewCell.

Listing 3-24. The Data Template Created as a Custom Type

```
<ViewCell xmlns="http://xamarin.com/schemas/2014/forms"
xmlns:x="http://schemas.microsoft.com/winfx/2009/xaml"
x:Class="DataTemplates.MyCell">
    <Grid>
        <Label Text="{Binding Name}" FontAttributes="Bold" />
        <Image Grid.Column="1" Source="{Binding ProfilePicture}" />
    </Grid>
</ViewCell>

...


public partial class MyCell : ViewCell
{
    public MyCell()
    {
        InitializeComponent();
    }
}
```

With our custom ViewCell defined, we can add that to our data template. To do so, we need to add a namespace declaration to the XAML file that indicates where our custom cell type can be found, just like you do when using a custom control. Listing 3-25 shows how we can use our custom ViewCell in a data template.

Listing 3-25. The Same Data Template Added as a Custom Type to the ListView's ItemTemplate

```
<ContentPage xmlns="http://xamarin.com/schemas/2014/forms"
    xmlns:x="http://schemas.microsoft.com/winfx/2009/xaml"
    xmlns:local="clr-namespace:DataTemplates"
    ...>
    <ListView ItemSource="{Binding MyItems}">
        <ListView.ItemTemplate>
            <DataTemplate>
                <local:MyCell />
            </DataTemplate>
        </ListView.ItemTemplate>
    </ListView>
</ContentPage>
```

Dynamically Selecting a Data Template

So far, we've talked about data templates that were essentially hardcoded into our markup, resulting in each list item using the same template. But what if we would like to be able to dynamically switch our templates at runtime depending on the data? That's where the DataTemplateSelector comes into play. A DataTemplateSelector enables us to choose which DataTemplate we want to show, depending on the property values of the objects bound to the ListView.

So when would we use a data template selector? Because they have a performance impact, they should only be used if the data templates are significantly different from one another. If we can achieve the desired result by changing the visibility of controls, using value converters or using data triggers than using a data template selector is not necessary. If the content of the cell needs to be completely different, perhaps because the list has different types of objects, we can consider using a data template selector.

An example of a DataTemplateSelector is shown in Listing 3-26. So, what is happening here? By overriding the OnSelectTemplate method, we can return the appropriate DataTemplate for each item in the list. The item parameter, which contains the item that is bound to the ListView, can be used to create a condition that determines which template to return. This method is called for each item in the item source of our list, passing in the item as a parameter. This item can be used to check a property value or its type to determine which template we want to use to render the item. In this example there are two possible data templates that can be returned, but you're not limited to just two. Keep in mind though that the more data templates you add, the more of a performance hit your app will likely take.

Listing 3-26. The DataTemplateSelector Determines Which Template Needs to Be Used

```
public class MyCellDataTemplateSelector : DataTemplateSelector
{
    public DataTemplate TemplateA { get; set; }
    public DataTemplate TemplateB { get; set; }

    protected override DataTemplate OnSelectTemplate (object item,
    BindableObject container)
    {
        return ((MyItem)item).IsActive ? TemplateA : TemplateB;
    }
}
```

With our `DataTemplateSelector` defined, we need to hook it up to our `ListView`. We do this by adding an instance of our `DataTemplateSelector` object to either the page's or the app's `ResourceDictionary`. Where we add it depends on the scope of where we need to use the template selector, as you have learned earlier on in this chapter. After we've added the instance of our `DataTemplateSelector`, we need to set the two `DataTemplate` type properties that we defined in Listing 3-26 to point to the `DataTemplate` objects we want to use. These are also defined in the page's `ResourceDictionary` in the example shown in Listing 3-27. Our custom `DataTemplateSelector` is consumed by the `ListView` by assigning it to the `ItemTemplate` property. At runtime, the `ListView` will use our custom `DataTemplateSelector` to return the correct instance of a `DataTemplate` object returned by the `OnSelectTemplate` method.

Listing 3-27. Adding the DataTemplateSelector to the ListView

```
<ContentPage xmlns="http://xamarin.com/schemas/2014/forms"
    xmlns:x="http://schemas.microsoft.com/winfx/2009/xaml"
    xmlns:local="clr-namespace:DataTemplates"
    ...>
```

```
<ContentPage.Resources>
    <ResourceDictionary>
        <DataTemplate x:Key="MyCellTemplateA">
            <local:MyCellA />
        </DataTemplate>
        <DataTemplate x:Key="MyCellTemplateB">
            <local:MyCellB />
        </DataTemplate>
        <local:MyCellDataTemplateSelector x:Key="MyDataTemplateSelector"
        TemplateA="{StaticResource MyCellTemplateA}"
        TemplateB="{StaticResource MyCellTemplateB}" />
    </ResourceDictionary>
</ContentPage.Resources>
<ListView ItemTemplate="{StaticResource MyDataTemplateSelector}"
ItemSource="{Binding MyItems}">
</ListView>
</ContentPage>
```

Caching Data Using the ListView

The ListView is often used to display more data than can fit onscreen. If you have a lot of items that you want to show, it may be beneficial for the performance of the application if you use a caching mechanism because creating a new row for each item would result in poor performance.

To improve performance, the native ListView equivalents for each platform have built-in features that let you reuse existing rows. When you enable the cell reusing feature, only the cells visible onscreen are loaded in memory and the content is loaded into these existing cells. This prevents the application from instantiating a new cell for each item, saving time and memory.

Xamarin.Forms gives you the ability to influence the caching strategy it uses by setting the CachingStrategy property on the ListView. This is an enumeration that contains the following values:

- RetainElement—The default value. This will generate a new cell for each item.

- RecycleElement—This setting uses recycling to improve performance by minimizing the memory usage. When using a DataTemplateSelector to select a DataTemplate, this strategy will not cache the DataTemplate. This means that a DataTemplate is selected for each item in the list.

- RecycleElementAndDataTemplate—This setting builds on RecycleElement by also reusing any DataTemplate you may have set through a DataTemplateSelector. When using this strategy, a DataTemplate is selected once per *item type*, instead of once per item. This means that we can **only** use this strategy when we differentiate which template we want to use based on the type of item instead of a value within the item.

There are a few additional prerequisites to consider:

- In Xamarin.Forms 2.4 and onwards, a change has been made to the RecycleElement caching strategy. Each of the DataTemplate type properties in the DataTemplateSelector should return only one ViewCell type. If the same property returns different ViewCell types, Xamarin.Forms will throw an exception.

- When using the RecycleElementAndDataTemplate caching strategy, each DataTemplate returned by the DataTemplateSelector must use the DataTemplate constructor that takes a Type.

Summary

When it comes to displaying and working with data, Xamarin.Forms has a lot of options to help you get your data onscreen. Adhering to an MVVM framework will make your life a lot easier due to the easy binding support it gives you out-of-the-box. We learned about the ListView and some of the neat tricks it can do, such as showing a jump list with only a few lines of code. We also learned about data templates and that they're an easy way to standardize and reuse how we show our data. Lastly, we learned about dynamically showing a different template depending on our data by using a data template selector.

CHAPTER 4

Network and Security

In the previous chapter, we saw how to work with data. Most of this data will probably come from some kind of backend over a network. In this chapter, we see how we can transfer this data from a backend to our app in several ways. Associated with sending and receiving data is connectivity. How can we assure that we are actually connected to a network and act on changes in the network state? These are also things we will be looking at in this chapter.

Furthermore, especially on mobile, it is very important to consider that a network connection might not always be available or stable. To overcome this, we can take a look at how to cache data so the user isn't lost completely whenever no connection is available. All of this and even a little bit more like storing data secure, network resiliency, and saving bandwidth are all things we will learn in this chapter.

Connecting with REST APIs

A big part of most apps will be based on data that is sent to and received from a backend. This can be done in numerous ways, but the most popular one for a while now is *REST*. REST stands for REpresentational State Transfer and is based on the constraints and properties of HTTP. Explaining HTTP and REST could be done in a book of itself and thus beyond the scope of this book. I am going to assume that you grasp the concepts of REST. If you need help, here is a extensive introduction: `https://docs.microsoft.com/en-us/azure/architecture/best-practices/api-design`.

The Old-Fashioned Way

Since we can use good old C# in our Xamarin apps, you can simply use the `HttpClient` library to make HTTP requests. Imagine we are building an app that sends and retrieves data about people. A sample `GET` and `POST` method could then look like the code in Listing 4-1.

153

© Gerald Versluis and Steven Thewissen 2019
G. Versluis and S. Thewissen, *Xamarin.Forms Solutions*, https://doi.org/10.1007/978-1-4842-4134-9_4

Listing 4-1. Old-School HttpClient Communication with the Backend

```csharp
private HttpClient _httpClient = new HttpClient
{
    BaseAddress = new Uri("https://www.example.com/api")
};

public Person GetPersonById(int id)
{
    var personJson = _httpClient.GetStringAsync($"people/{id}");

    return JsonConvert.DeserializeObject<Person>(personJson);
}

public async Task AddPerson(Person person)
{
    var personJson = JsonConvert.SerializeObject (person);
    var content = new StringContent (personJson, Encoding.UTF8,
    "application/json");

    HttpResponseMessage response = await _httpClient.PostAsync
    ("people", content);

    if (!response.IsSuccessStatusCode)
    {
        throw new Exception("Something went wrong!");
    }
}
```

If you have worked with REST APIs in C# before, this code should look pretty familiar. We just create an instance of the HttpClient and use it to implement all of our needed requests. For basic apps, the is fine. You can probably come up with some optimizations to reduce your amount of duplicated code and handle errors in a graceful way.

However, there is a lot of boilerplate code in here. You can imagine, that if you have a dozen or more calls to implement, there are a lot of pretty similar lines of code to be found in your API client class. They will all serialize or deserialize an object and send some request. This can be done in a better way.

HTTP Requests with Refit

One way to overcome the redundant code from the "old-fashioned" way, is by using a library called *Refit*. With Refit, you can reduce your code needed to communicate to the backend to a simple interface. In that interface you decorate the method signatures with a couple of attributes, and the rest will be generated for you at compile-time. Let's see how this works.

To implement the calls that we saw back in Listing 4-1, we can now simply define their signatures in an interface. The result of this can be seen in Listing 4-2.

Listing 4-2. New Backend Client with Refit

```
public interface IBackendService
{
    [Get("/people/{id}")]
    Task<Person> GetPersonById(int id);

    [Post("/people")]
    Task AddPerson([Body]Person person);
}
```

From this interface, the full implementation will be generated at compile-time. It won't be exactly like the code in Listing 4-1, but it will look pretty similar. To be clear: this code lives in your client application, inside your app. Refit generates code from your interface definition to communicate with your backend. This saves you the trouble of writing (de)serialization or HTTP call code over and over again.

For each method signature, you can see I have adorned it with an attribute. The name of the attribute indicates what HTTP verb is to be used for that request. In the code of Listing 4-2 there are two methods: one uses the GET verb and one uses the POST verb. Of course, the other verbs are available as well.

As a parameter for the Get and Post attributes, you need to supply the relative endpoint at the backend. Later, we will provide a base URL for the client.

Tip   Don't forget to add a slash in front of the endpoint or your code will throw an exception at runtime!

Something cool is going on in the endpoint definition of the GetPersonById method. As you can see the "id" part of our endpoint is enclosed in curly brackets. The parameter of the method signature of the GetPersonById, is also named "id". By constructing the attribute this way, the value we supply to the id parameter will automatically be mapped onto the values between curly brackets in the endpoint with the same name.

When working with REST, it is a very common thing to retrieve an object by its ID. This ID is of course dynamic, which would cause a problem if we have to specify the endpoints on beforehand. By using this method with the curly brackets, we overcome this problem.

Another curious thing is going on with the AddPerson method. You can see a [Body] attribute inside of the parameter list. Depending on the HTTP verb, this means that the value will be read, or will be provided in the body of the request. Since we are doing a POST request in this example, the serialized object will be put in the body because of the [Body] attribute that is in front of it.

Another common thing that is used when sending HTTP requests is working with headers. Adding static headers is pretty easy to do, just add another attribute. You can add a header on either method or class level. When adding it on method level, the header is only sent for that specific method, on the interface level, it is sent for all methods in that interface. Defining a header is shown in Listing 4-3.

Listing 4-3. Adding Static Headers on Interface and Method Level

```
[Headers("User-Agent: My-Awesome-User-Agent")]
public interface IBackendService
{
    [Get("/people/{id}")]
    Task<Person> GetPersonById(int id);

    [Headers("Another: Header")]
    [Post("/people")]
    Task AddPerson([Body]Person person);
}
```

But a lot of times, you will want to add a variable value to your header. This method is much alike the [Body] attribute. Just add the [Header] attribute to a parameter and its value will be used as the value of the header. An example is shown in Listing 4-4.

Listing 4-4. Dynamic Header Value

```
public interface IBackendService
{
    [Post("/people")]
    Task AddPerson([Body]Person person, [Header("Authorization")]string
    authorization);
}
```

As a parameter for the [Header] attribute you supply the key of the header; the parameter that comes after it will be used as the value.

Of course, HTTP and REST have a lot more options that you can use. Think of query string parameters and file uploads for instance. This is all possible with Refit as well, and I encourage you to check it out yourself.

Note   All details about Refit and its capabilities can be found on the project's page on GitHub: `https://github.com/reactiveui/refit`.

An interface itself can't be called upon, so we still have to have some way of invoking the methods that are generated by Refit. Therefore, we still need a client class that acts as a wrapper for the interface we have defined. For clarity, we will end up with three components:

- The interface describing our endpoints on the backend.

- The generated class that implements the previously-mentioned interface. Based on the interface definition and the attributes, Refit will generate this for us.

- A wrapper class that will use the generated Refit class to retrieve data.

To retrieve a client for this, we can simply call: `RestService.For<IBackendService>("https://www.example.com");`. With the client we get out of this line of code, we can call the methods that we have defined in the interface for it. You probably want to wrap this into some kind of client of your own to handle errors, etc.

Probably a good thing to know is that when a call from Refit is not a HTTP success status code, so whenever a call is *not* a HTTP 200 OK, it will throw an exception. That in itself might be a reason to wrap it into a class and not repeat a lot of error handling code in your view models.

Other Libraries

There are, of course, other libraries out there that will help you with making HTTP requests. One of them is called *RestSharp*. This library, and others out there, of course have its own use but are not so extensive as Refit. Or at least extensive in its own way. RestSharp does not generate implementations for you; it just provides you with shorthand methods for HTTP calls. It will also take care of the serialization and deserialization for you. So, if you don't like to give out control on what your methods look like down to the letter, libraries like RestSharp might be better for you.

Note   For information on RestSharp, check out the project's website: `http://restsharp.org/`.

Connectivity

On a mobile device, it is not always a certainty that you have a network or Internet connection. It might be good to check if you are connected before starting some network intensive calls.

Nothing is built into this for Xamarin.Forms, but luckily this is solved by a library called `Xamarin.Essentials`. This NuGet package contains a whole number of very easy to use APIs that provide you with some much-needed functionality. The best thing is, it isn't just for Forms, you can also use this library in traditional Xamarin projects. You will probably see this library being referenced a couple of more times throughout this book.

Note   If you have been working with Xamarin for a longer time, the Essentials library might look familiar. The `Xamarin.Essentials` library is a bundle of a whole lot of separate libraries that were already out there and much used, most of them by James Montemagno.

The Essentials library supports the following platforms and operating systems:

- Android, version 4.4 (API 19) or higher

- iOS, version 10.0 or higher

- UWP, version 10.0.16299.0 or higher

The installation just goes through NuGet, so add the package as you normally would and find the `Xamarin.Essentials` package. At the time of writing, the package is still in preview, so you might need to enable the checkbox to include pre-release packages. See Figure 4-1.

Figure 4-1. *Adding the Xamarin.Essentials package to a project*

On Android, Essentials needs a little bit of initialization. In your Android project's `MainLauncher` or any `Activity` that is launched, you need to add this line in the `OnCreate` method: `Xamarin.Essentials.Platform.Init(this, bundle);`.

To handle runtime permissions on Android, you need to add this to all `Activity` classes in your project. For Forms, that should typically only be one. You can see the implementation in Listing 4-5.

Listing 4-5. Runtime Permissions Handling for Xamarin.Essentials

```
public override void OnRequestPermissionsResult(int requestCode, string[]
permissions, [GeneratedEnum] Android.Content.PM.Permission[] grantResults)
```

```
{
    Xamarin.Essentials.Platform.OnRequestPermissionsResult(requestCode,
    permissions, grantResults);

    base.OnRequestPermissionsResult(requestCode, permissions, grantResults);
}
```

Again, for Android we need something special to be able to use this. In this case the `AccessNetworkState` permission. To add this, open the `AssemblyInfo.cs` file in your `Properties` folder and add this line: `[assembly: UsesPermission(Android.Manifest.Permission.AccessNetworkState)]`. Or you can add it in the `AndroidManifest.xml` file, also under the `Properties` folder.

Under the `manifest` node, add this line: `<uses-permission android:name="android.permission.ACCESS_NETWORK_STATE" />`. There is a last way to do this, through the visual editor for permissions. Right-click the Android project and go to the properties. Find the Required Permissions section (long list of checkboxes) and find the `AccessNetworkState` there, then check it. The latter option is seen in Figure 4-2.

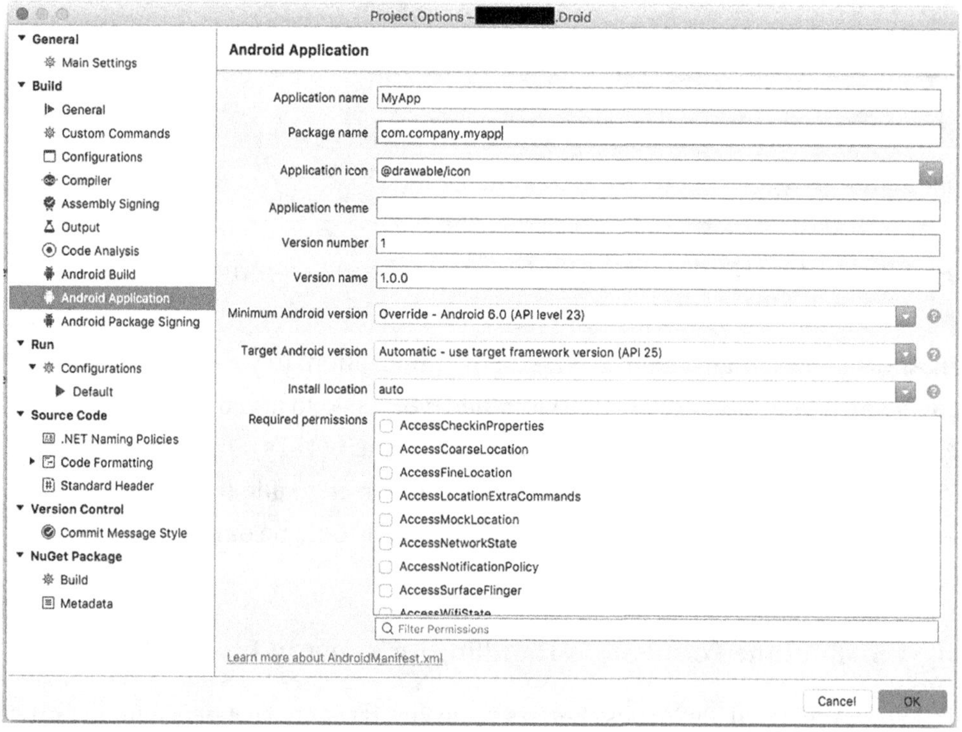

Figure 4-2. *Set the required permissions for the Android app*

Now we are all set to go!

The connectivity part of the Essentials library isn't very hard to use. It exposes a couple of methods and events that we can use to determine whether or not our app has any form of connection.

To check the current network access, we can simply execute the code in Listing 4-6.

Listing 4-6. Checking the Current Network Access

```
using Xamarin.Essentials;

// ... Rest of code. Namespace, class declaration, etc.

var current = Connectivity.NetworkAccess;

if (current == NetworkAccess.Internet)
{
    // Connection to internet is available
}
```

As you can see, we have a simple static class that we can interrogate on our connectivity questions. In the code in Listing 4-6, we are checking to see if the app has Internet access. The NetworkAccess enum has some other options as well, to get some more fine-grained information:

- *Internet*—The app has local and internet access. Note that Internet access can be reported "falsely". Due to the limitations of the implementation on each platform, it can only be guaranteed that a connection is available. For instance, the device can have a WiFi connection, but if the router is disconnected, no actual Internet access is available, although it will be reported as such by Essentials.

- *ConstrainedInternet*—This means limited Internet access. Usually means that you can connect to a portal where you have to accept the agreement and/or enter credentials to gain access to the internet.

- *Local*—The app has only local access to the network.

- *None*—No connection is available at all for the app.

- *Unknown*—The app is not able to determine whether there is a connection.

Besides knowing that you have a connection or not, it might also be useful to know what type of connection you have access to. For instance, if you want to sync large images, you might not want to do that over the cellular connection since it could incur costs for the user.

To check the type of connection, simply use the code of Listing 4-7.

Listing 4-7. Checking the Type of Connection

```
var profiles = Connectivity.Profiles;
if (profiles.Contains(ConnectionProfile.WiFi))
{
    // Active Wi-Fi connection.
}
```

Other options in the `ConnectionProfile` enum are:

- Bluetooth

- Cellular

- Ethernet

- Other

- WiFi

- WiMAX

Finally, you might be interested in the fact that the state of the network changes. You might want to show some icon or other visual indicator to the user that they are offline or start reaching for your cache when the connection drops.

There is an event available for you to detect this. In Listing 4-8, you can see some sample code that illustrates the use of this event.

Listing 4-8. ConnectivityChanged Event to Detect Changes in the Network State

```
public class SuperImportantConnections
{
    public SuperImportantConnections ()
    {
        // Hook into changes in connectivity, don't forget unsubscribe when
        you're done!
```

```
    Connectivity.ConnectivityChanged += Connectivity_ConnectivityChanged;
}

private void Connectivity_ConnectivityChanged(object sender,
ConnectivityChangedEventArgs  e)
{
    // Work with the new info
    var access = e.NetworkAccess;
    var profiles = e.Profiles;
}
}
```

And basically, that is all there is to it. The actual implementation of this can vary depending on your architecture and requirements. With the Connectivity plugin you can very easily gain access to information about the user's connection and use it to your advantage. We will see how to use it in conjunction with caching, for example, in the next section.

Caching

An important part of any application is caching. This is true especially on mobile where bandwidth can be limited and costly. But not only that, no one likes to look at an empty screen, right? When we cache some data we at least have *something* to show the user while we load actual new data in the background and present it to them when it's done.

Of course, you can do all of this yourself, which can be a lot of work. Luckily, there are already some smart people who have done the hard work for us. In this section, we will look at *Akavache* and *Monkey Cache*. Both do more or less the same thing but in a slightly different way. What they have in common that it is all about caching data and help us reduce network traffic and create a more responsive app.

Akavache

The Akavache library, originally by Paul Betts, is based on SQLite3 and provides us with an asynchronous and persistent key/value store. It is extremely suitable for expiring caching data but can also be used to save user settings or other data.

I have been using this plugin in a number of my projects because it just works and it is such an addition to the user experience. Before I knew Akavache, I just had users look at an empty list view that may or may not had a loading indicator. While it is functional, it might not be what users expect nowadays. If you look at other popular apps by big vendors, you will see that you are presented with data immediately and data is then loaded and replaced for you as you go. This makes for a much better experience for your users.

Before we start looking into implementing Akavache in code, let me tell you there are a couple of stores available where you can save data. These stores can be reached through a static object called `BlobCache`. This is also the object where you will invoke the methods on to save and retrieve items from the cache. I have summed them up here, together with their characteristics:

- `BlobCache.LocalMachine`—General cached data. Retrieved objects from a server, i.e. news items, list of users, etc.

- `BlobCache.UserAccount`—Settings that the user does within your app. Some platforms sync this to the cloud.

- `BlobCache.Secure`—If you are saving sensitive data, this is the place where you want to put it.

- `BlobCache.InMemory`—Like the name says; it holds the data in-memory, whenever your app is killed, so is the data in there.

Installing Akavache is easy and happens through a NuGet package. Go to the screen to add a NuGet package to your project and find the `akavache` and `akavache.sqlite3` packages. Add these to your shared project as well as all your platform projects. Failing to do so might result in using only the in-memory store, which is reset with every app start. Or your app might not work at all. Figure 4-3 shows the required packages being added in Visual Studio for Mac.

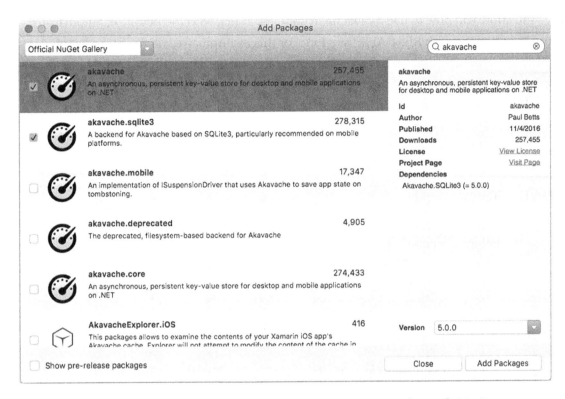

Figure 4-3. *Adding the Akavache packages to your project through NuGet*

Note   For your iOS project, make sure a class `AkavacheSqliteLinker Override.cs` is created. It might in some cases be needed by Android as well. This prevents the linker removing some much needed DLL files because they don't have a reference in your platform-specific platforms. The content for this class should be like in this link: `https://github.com/reactiveui/ Akavache#handling-xamarin-linker`

After installing the NuGets, you need to add a line of initialization code. With this line you set your application name and it will create a general caching store for you. In the case of a Xamarin.Forms app, a likely place to do this is in the `App.xaml.cs` file, App constructor. Just insert a line like this:

```
Akavache.BlobCache.ApplicationName = "YourAppName";
```

To show you how to use Akavache in code, let's stick with the people example from the "Connecting with REST APIs" section. For this example, we will retrieve a list of all people. Assume that we have implemented the REST client with Refit and hold an instance in the _restService variable.

Basically, what we will do is wrap the call to retrieve the data from a remote in another call that first checks the cache for us. The code can be seen in Listing 4-9.

Listing 4-9. Retrieve a List of People Through Our Akavache Cache

```
public IObservable<IEnumerable<Person>> GetPeople()
{
    return BlobCache.LocalMachine.GetAndFetchLatest("people",
        async () => await _restService.GetAllPeople(), (offset) =>
        {
            // return a boolean to indicate the cache is invalidated. When
            no network is available or cache is not expired, return false
            to just retrieve data from the cache
            if (Connectivity.NetworkAccess == NetworkAccess.None)
                return false;

            return (DateTimeOffset.Now - offset).Hours > 24;
        });
}
```

There is a couple of things that stand out in this piece of code. Let's go through it from top to bottom. First, notice that we now return an IObservable object. Objects that implement the IObservable interface can send push-based notifications to subscribers.

In our case with the caching, what will happen is:

1. The local cache will be checked. If something is in there it will be returned and subscribers are notified.

2. The cache expiry condition is evaluated.

3. Asynchronously, the data from the remote source is being fetched.

4. When remote data comes in, the subscribers are again notified, this time with the updated data.

Then we call the `GetAndFetchLatest` method on our `BlobCache.UserAccount` object. It takes three arguments:

- `"people"`—A string that identifies this specific cache. Since it uses SQLite under the hood, think of this as the table name where the cached records are stored. Each time data comes in from remote, this table is refreshed.

- `async () => await _restService.GetAllPeople()`—This holds the call to execute to fetch remote data. In our case this just calls the (Refit) REST client, which returns the list of people. You can supply your own method here with more extensive logic.

- `(offset) => { ... }`—This method will determine whether the cache is stale or not. As an input parameter you will receive the `DateTimeOffset` of the last time the cache was updated. This you can use to determine if the cache is expired or not. In this example we compare it to the current timestamp and if there is more than 24 hours in-between we expire the cache. But you can implement any logic here as you see fit. This should return a boolean: `true` means the cache is expired and remote data should follow. `False` means the cached data is enough for now.

There is another parameter that specifies an absolute point in time when the cache is expired as an addition to the expiration logic you might have in the third parameter.

In the expiration logic you can also see I incorporated the Connectivity plugin to first determine if we have a connection. If there is no connection available, we will just work with cached data.

To work with the retrieved data, we need to subscribe to this method. You can see this happening in Listing 4-10.

Listing 4-10. Subscribe to Our Cache Method

```
private void LoadPeople()
{
        _backendService.GetPeople().Subscribe((people) =>
        {
                People.Clear();
```

```
            foreach (var person in people)
            {
                    People.Add(person);
            }
    });
}
```

Imagine that this code lives in a view model and we have a variable _backendService that holds an instance to the class that retrieves our people. Because the GetPeople returns an IObservable, we can use the Subscribe on it.

The Subscribe method takes in a function with an input parameter of the type that we specified on GetPeople, in this case a collection of Person. When this method gets invoked, we clear People, which is a more global collection and start repopulating this collection. Probably because we are showing in in some kind of list in the UI.

If we only get cached data, we pass through here once and it will be lightning fast because we are loading data from this. When there is data in the cache, this will happen either way. So, the user is presented with the dataset that is already in there. When the cache is expired and we are able to retrieve new data from remote, we will pass through this method again, but now with new data. Because of the way the OS handles the UI updates, the user will barely notice that new data is coming in. And of course, you could make the updating of data a bit smarter than just replacing the whole thing.

The Subscribe method returns an IDisposable object. To avoid memory leaks, make sure that you dispose the observable whenever you do not need it anymore. You can do this by capturing the return value of the subscribe method in a variable like this: var subscription = _backendService.GetPeople().Subscribe(…); and then disposing it later, like this: subscription.Dispose();.

Tip   All in-depth details about Akavache can be found on the project's GitHub page: https://github.com/reactiveui/Akavache

---

Akavache has some more methods that are more or less shorthand for caching files, images, and secure data. They should be pretty self-explanatory.

One thing you need to know about the Akavache caching is: in order to not lose data, you need to shut down the cache store properly. While this sounds easy, on mobile it can be a bit hard, since you do not always have control over the lifecycle of your app. One way to get around this is wrapping the access to the cache in a repository pattern and each time you write to the cache, do a proper shutdown. A shutdown is easy and done in just one line:

```
BlobCache.Shutdown().Wait();
```

Monkey Cache

Another caching provider is *Monkey Cache*. This plugin is also very good but goes about things a little differently. First of all, it has different persistence providers. You can choose from SQLite, LiteDB, and FileStore or roll your own if you're feeling adventurous.

All of these providers end up doing the same thing—persisting data—but one has some small advantages over the other, mainly in terms of performance. When you are working with small amounts of data, under about 50 records, the differences are negligible. Above that, things start to matter. Figure 4-4 shows a screenshot of the test results as published by James Montemagno (the author of this plugin) himself.

Barrel	Add	Get	Get ETag	Empty	Number	Threads	Total	Total2
SQLite1	36	1	0	23	1	1	1	108
SQLite10	291	3	1	41	10	1	10	438
SQLite100	2319	8	8	25	100	1	100	2395
SQLite1000	22907	82	55	40	1000	1	1000	23110
SQLite4000	332504	1863	1709	480	1000	4	4000	84597
LiteDB1	96	46	0	16	1	1	1	181
LiteDB10	244	85	0	86	10	1	10	449
LiteDB100	1061	62	2	959	100	1	100	2181
LiteDB1000	9896	97	37	10132	1000	1	1000	20215
LiteDB4000	146951	44281	1583	100478	1000	4	4000	83940
FileStore1	59	0	0	1	1	1	1	89
FileStore10	77	2	0	3	10	1	10	154
FileStore100	223	13	0	24	100	1	100	489
FileStore1000	1833	134	0	230	1000	1	1000	2241
FileStore4000	42260	9013	0	1047	1000	4	4000	13663

Barrel	Add	Get	Get ETag	Empty	Number	Threads	Total	Total2
SQLite	81	4	1	23	1	1	1	354
SQLite	23184	124	90	30	1000	1	1000	23483
LiteDB	143	56	1	19	1	1	1	288
LiteDB	9901	80	32	9992	1000	1	1000	20053
FileStore	28	0	0	1	1	1	1	92
FileStore	2060	92	0	286	1000	1	1000	2521

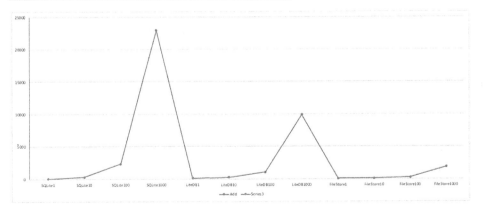

Figure 4-4. *Test results of the different persistence providers of Monkey Cache*

Unlike Akavache, in Monkey Cache, you do not get to choose where your data is persisted. Per platform it will get saved in a specific location. For all platforms this will be the local app's folder.

Installing Monkey Cache is just as easy as any other plugin; you can install it through NuGet. Just find the package named MonkeyCache and install it, together with MonkeyCache.SQLite, MonkeyCache.LiteDB, or MonkeyCache.FileStore. Make sure you also install this on your shared project as well as your platform projects.

You need to initialize with just one line, where you state your application name. This can be anything you make up and will be used as a name for your caching container. Just call Barrel.ApplicationId = " YourAppName"; before you call any other caching method.

Using the library is rather easy, but as I mentioned earlier, you will have to do some more manual work than with Akavache. In Listing 4-11, you can see a call that uses Monkey Cache to first check if there is cached data available and if it has not expired. If the cached data is valid, that data is returned, else it will be retrieved from remote.

Listing 4-11. Retrieving the Person Data with the Help of Monkey Cache

```
public async Task<IEnumerable<Person>> GetPeopleAsync()
{
    if(!Connectivity.NetworkAccess == NetworkAccess.None)
    {
        return Barrel.Current.Get<IEnumerable<Person>>(key: url);
    }

    if(!Barrel.Current.IsExpired(key: url))
    {
        return Barrel.Current.Get<IEnumerable<Person>>(key: url);
    }

    var people = _backendService.GetPeople();

    //Saves the cache and pass it a timespan for expiration
    Barrel.Current.Add(key: url, data: people, expireIn:
        TimeSpan.FromDays(1));

    return people;
}
```

The biggest difference here is that Monkey Cache will not present the user with cached data immediately while retrieving data remotely if needed. You as the developer are responsible for how data is cached and how it is presented to the user.

You should see some familiar things in the code from Listing 4-11 by now. First, we check if there is an Internet connection. If the device is offline, we always return the cached data. If we are online, see if our cached data is still valid. If so, return that cached data. If the data has expired, we get it from remote, put it in our cache, and return the just fetched data to the user.

To make your life easier, you can of course create some generic methods for this which you can reuse. Monkey Cache also has support for *ETags* to reduce network traffic. What this means exactly we will learn a little down the road in this chapter.

Tip   To get all details about Monkey Cache, check out the GitHub page: `https://github.com/jamesmontemagno/monkey-cache`.

Network Resilience

An app is usually more than just the piece of software running on the device. It almost always has some kind of backend where it gets its data from or sends its data to. This backend can be half a world away, though! With servers hosted anywhere and app stores distributing our apps globally, there can literally be a whole world between your app and the backend.

And don't forget the other way around: our users might be doing the craziest things. Travel at high speed through the air or over land, going through tunnels or even go into space in a cool electric car! These scenarios and much more can cause the network to be instable or not reachable at all. As the developer, we are expected to take all of these scenarios into account. If you don't, the user might decide your app doesn't work well

Of course, the easiest solution is to just check if a connection is available and decide what to do based on that. But even doing that might not be a 100% accurate. A next logical step would be to catch exceptions and let the user retry whenever something bad happens. This is of course a pretty viable and tried and tested method, but for most scenarios you, the developer, will probably know best how to handle certain situations.

To help you with that, there is a great NuGet package available named *Polly*. With this package, you can define certain policies (hence the name) for whenever something bad happens, instead of just asking the user to retry.

Table 4-1 shows the different policies that Polly has to offer, together with a short description.

Table 4-1. *Polly's Different Policies*

Policy	Premise	AKA	Mitigation
Retry	Many faults are transient and may self-correct after a short delay.	"Maybe it's just a blip"	Allows configuring automatic retries.
Circuit-Breaker	When a system is seriously struggling, failing fast is better than making users/callers wait. Protecting a faulting system from overload can help it recover.	"Stop doing it if it hurts" or "Give that system a break"	Breaks the circuit (blocks executions) for a period, when faults exceed some pre-configured threshold.
Timeout	Beyond a certain wait, a success result is unlikely.	"Don't wait forever"	Guarantees the caller won't have to wait beyond the timeout.
Bulkhead Isolation	When a process faults, multiple failing calls backing up can easily swamp resource (e.g., threads/CPU) in a host. A faulting downstream system can also cause "backed-up" failing calls upstream.Both risk a faulting process bringing down a wider system.	"One fault shouldn't sink the whole ship"	Constrains the governed actions to a fixed-size resource pool, isolating their potential to affect others.

(continued)

Table 4-1. (*continued*)

Policy	Premise	AKA	Mitigation
Cache	Some proportion of requests may be similar.	"You've asked that one before"	Provides a response from cache if known. Stores responses automatically in cache, when first retrieved.
Fallback	Things will still fail—plan what you will do when that happens.	"Degrade gracefully"	Defines an alternative value to be returned (or action to be executed) on failure.
PolicyWrap	Different faults require different strategies; resilience means using a combination.	"Defense in depth"	Allows any of these policies to be combined flexibly.

There is a lot of ground to cover with Polly and I don't get around to describing all of it. But let's look at some examples.

Retry Policy

The Retry policy is pretty self-explanatory: you are able to retry a request with conditions.

Observe the code in Listing 4-12 to see an example of a Retry policy implemented with Polly.

Listing 4-12. Getting People from the Remote Backend Wrapped in a Retry Policy

```
private async Task<IEnumerable<Person>> GetPeopleRemote()
{
    return await Policy
        .Handle<ApiException>(ex => ex.StatusCode != HttpStatusCode.NotFound)
        .WaitAndRetryAsync(retryCount: 3, sleepDurationProvider:
        retryAttempt => TimeSpan.FromSeconds(Math.Pow(2, retryAttempt)),
        onRetry: (ex, time) =>
```

```
        {
            Console.WriteLine($"Something went wrong: {ex.Message},
            retrying...");
        })
    .ExecuteAsync(async () =>
    {
        Console.WriteLine($"Trying to fetch remote data...");
        return await _restService.GetPeople();
    });
}
```

This code seems a lot to take in at first, but when you see all the different pieces, it's not so bad. Let's go through it step-by-step. The reason why the code seems so much is because it is actually a few methods chained together. If you look closely, you will see the Handle, WaitAndRetryAsync, and ExecuteAsync methods. To make it extra confusing, all methods have parameters that take a lambda expression.

All methods originate from the static Policy class. With the Handle method, we specify which kind of exceptions we want to handle with this policy. We can implement some logic here to make it even more flexible. In this example, the retry will happen only for the ApiException class and only when the ApiException.StatusCode not is NotFound. In other words, all ApiExceptions that return anything but a 404 will be retried.

This is a really powerful thing. Think about it: a 404 Not Found is very unlikely to recover when retried. The endpoint just is not there, so retrying a couple of times would make no sense. But for instance, a 500 Internal Server Error might be resolved within a small window of time and suddenly your code works again without bothering your user with any error that occurred in the background. Depending on your own requirements, you can implement a custom condition to suit your needs.

Then the WaitAndRetryAsync method tells the policy that it needs to retry for all the exceptions that come up. With the parameters you can specify how often a retry attempt should happen—three times in this case—and how long should be between retries. Again, here you can implement your own logic. On this line—retryAttempt => TimeSpan.FromSeconds(Math.Pow(2, retryAttempt)—you see the logic for the example code. From the policy, we get the current retry attempt as an input parameter.

With the value in there, we calculate a number of seconds to a power of two. So, each attempt will be the current attempt to the power of two: 1, 4, and 9 in our case. You could also choose to have a fixed time between retries. It is all up to you!

Optionally, you can execute your own logic whenever a retry attempt it done. In Listing 4-12, you see a line that writes something to the console, that will happen whenever an exception was cached and a retry was invoked.

In the ExecuteAsync, we write the logic that we wanted to execute in the first place. Here you will see the call through our REST client, trying to retrieve data from our backend. I have implemented another write line to the console here. If an exception happens but the code recovers, you will see something happening like that shown in Figure 4-5.

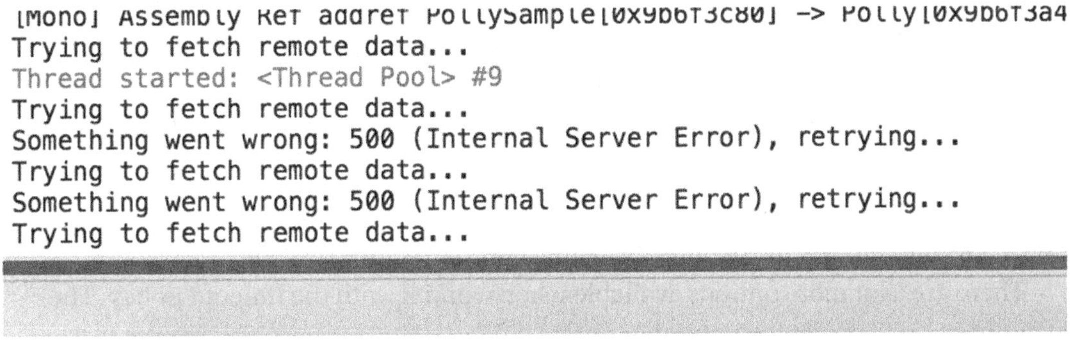

```
[Mono] Assembly Ref addref PollySample[0x9D6T3C80] -> Polly[0x9D6T3a4
Trying to fetch remote data...
Thread started: <Thread Pool> #9
Trying to fetch remote data...
Something went wrong: 500 (Internal Server Error), retrying...
Trying to fetch remote data...
Something went wrong: 500 (Internal Server Error), retrying...
Trying to fetch remote data...
```

Figure 4-5. *Retry output in the console window*

If, after the specified number of retries, the call still fails, the exception is still thrown. Take that into account. One way to do this is by using the PolicyWrap, which we will see a little bit later.

Timeout

The timeout policy does what it says. You can wrap your code in a timeout and when your code does not finish before the specified timeout, an exception is thrown. Look at the code in Listing 4-13.

Listing 4-13. The Polly Timeout Policy

```
return await Policy.TimeoutAsync(30, onTimeoutAsync: (context, timespan,
task) =>
{
    Console.WriteLine($"{context.PolicyKey} at {context.OperationKey}:
    execution timed out after {timespan.TotalSeconds} seconds.");
     return Task.CompletedTask;
})
.ExecuteAsync(async () => await _restService.GetPeople(id));
```

In this code, we see again the call to our REST service to obtain the people data. This time, it is wrapped in a `TimeoutAsync` method. The first parameter specifies that we want to wait for at most 30 seconds. The second parameter lets us specify a method that runs just before the exception is thrown when the method runs out of time. In this case we write a message to the console. The return of the `Task.CompletedTask` is needed to prevent warnings, because the lambda is an async method, but I don't await anything.

Basically, that is all there is to it. Just like with the Retry policy, you see a `ExecuteAsync` call, which contains the actual code we want to execute.

There are a lot more options available when working with the timeout policy. The biggest feature is the ability to implement it as a pessimistic or optimistic timeout. The default strategy is the optimistic strategy. When using the optimistic strategy, you have the ability to work with a `CancellationToken`. When implemented, you can allow your users to cancel the operation before the timeout hits. You can, of course, also have a programmatically implemented trigger that cancels the operation.

With the pessimistic strategy, you can implement a timeout for methods that normally don't support it. Also, cancellation before the timeout hits is not possible. To implement either the optimistic or pessimistic timeout strategy, simply pass in the corresponding value from the `TimeoutStrategy` enum into the `TimeoutAsync` method.

PolicyWrap

As you could imagine, it might be interesting to combine a couple of the policies we have already seen. With the `PolicyWrap` policy, you can do just that. `PolicyWrap` has a couple of different notations that all do the same. In Listing 4-14, you can see three lines that do the same thing.

Listing 4-14. Different Notations of the PolicyWrap

```
Policy.Wrap(fallback, waitAndRetry, breaker).Execute(action);

fallback.Wrap(waitAndRetry.Wrap(breaker)).Execute(action);

fallback.Wrap(waitAndRetry).Wrap(breaker).Execute(action);
```

In this code, variables like waitAndRetry, breaker, and fallback hold instances to the policies with the same name. Then in the Execute method, the code is inserted that you actually want to run. You need two or more policies to be able to use PolicyWrap.

When using multiple policies, the question arises how execution and errors are handled. When using the PolicyWrap, all policies act as layers. Each policy is wrapped in the next until the last one is reached which executes the actual logic from the Execute method. When reading the code, policies are wrapped from left to right. In the example from Listing 4-14, breaker executes the code and is wrapped in waitAndRetry and waitAndRetry is wrapped in fallback. When the code is executed and fails, it will execute whatever the policy prescribes and, if the policy is exhausted, it will bubble up to the policy wrapping.

For this example, this is what would happen:

- fallback is the outer policy and will pass execution along to waitAndRetry

  - waitAndRetry will pass it along to breaker

  - breaker is the most inner policy and executes the code, unless the circuit is open

  - The executed code succeeds, returns its result, or throws an error

  - breaker will update its status according to the policy configuration

  - waitAndRetry will wait and retry in case of a fault, fail completely when retry attempts are exhausted, or return in case of a success

- fallback will substitute the result for a fallback value or return the result in case of a success

As mentioned earlier, it would probably be too much to handle all the policies and their options here. I would like to invite you to try the rest of them for yourself and see what you can come up with.

177

Tip Like many of the packages out there today, Polly is also available on GitHub. See all the details about this project here: `https://github.com/App-vNext/Polly`

Conditional HTTP Requests

One more optimization that is worth noting can be accomplished with *conditional HTTP requests*. A conditional HTTP request is a request that is executed differently depending on the value of specific headers.

The conditional HTTP request falls basically into two categories:

- For *safe* methods, like GET, which usually retrieves data, the conditional request can be used to send back the data only if it is newer than the version retrieved earlier. This can spare bandwidth, something that is particularly interesting on mobile devices.

- For *unsafe* methods, like POST, which usually sends or updates data, conditional requests can be used to check the integrity of the data being sent.

To clarify a bit more on safe and unsafe methods—safe methods are the HTTP verbs that do not change the state on the server. They just retrieve data for consummation on the client. Unsafe methods are the opposite—they *do* mutate data on the server.

In this section, we just focus on the safe methods, since we are mostly interested in saving bandwidth.

The different headers involving conditional HTTP requests are:

- If-Match—The request yields a result whenever the *ETag* (a hash, which I will go into in a bit) matches in both the request as well as on the server.

- If-None-Match—The request yields a result whenever the ETag in the request and the server do not match.

- If-Modified-Since—The request yields a result whenever the date on the server is newer than the value in the request.

- `If-Unmodified-Since`—The request yields a result whenever the date on the server is older or equal to the date on the server.

- `If-Range`—Similar to `If-Match` and `If-Unmodified-Since` but can have just one ETag or one date (whereas the other headers could have multiple). If the condition matches, you will retrieve only a partial result that is relevant. If the condition fails, you will retrieve the full content.

If a result is sent back from the server, this will have a HTTP 200 OK result. If the condition from these headers is met and the server decides no data has to be transferred, you will receive a HTTP 304 Not Modified result with an empty body, saving you the bandwidth of retrieving a result you already had. The exception is `If-Range`, that will send back a 206 Partial Content when the condition is met and a 200 OK with the full content otherwise.

I have mentioned the term ETag a couple of times now, so let me explain to you what it is. The *ETag* stands for *Entity Tag*. Basically, it is a hash that uniquely identifies the data that you are requesting. The HTTP specification does not prescribe what type of hash it should be (MD5, SHA-1, etc.) or how it should be composed. This is totally up to you, as long as the hash that is produced is unique for that data.

To give you a concrete example, I show you how to work with the `If-None-Match` header, which is the most relevant in regard to mobile apps.

The flow for caching the data is like this:

- The app initiates a request to the server for the first time.

- The server returns the requested data together with an `ETag` header.

- The app saves the `ETag` together with the endpoint where the data came from.

- The next time the same endpoint is requested, the app adds an `If-None-Match` header to the request with the saved `ETag` hash from before.

- The server compares the incoming hash from the app to the hash computed from the requested data. If the hash is equal, the data is not sent back to the app. Instead a HTTP 304 Not Modified with an empty body is returned. If the hash is different, apparently something is changed and the full data is returned to the app.

The implementation for this solution needs to happen on the client application, our app, and the backend application. On the client, we have to create some kind of key/value store where the key is the endpoint that we request the data from and the value is the ETag hash that we retrieve from the server.

Look at the code in Listing 4-15, which shows you an implementation of a custom HttpClient to handle the incoming ETag and outgoing If-None-Match headers. It makes sense to do this in a central place like the HttpClient, so it will work automatically for all requests coming in and going out.

Listing 4-15. Handling the ETag and If-None-Match Headers from the HttpClient

```
public class EtagHttpClientHandler : HttpClientHandler
{
    protected override async Task<HttpResponseMessage>
    SendAsync(HttpRequestMessage request, CancellationToken
    cancellationToken)
    {
        // Everything before the base call is the request
        try
        {
            // See if we have a ETag for this endpoint and add it to the
            request
            var etag = await BlobCache.LocalMachine.
            GetObject<string>(request.RequestUri.ToString());

            if (!string.IsNullOrWhiteSpace(etag))
            {
                request.Headers.IfNoneMatch.Clear();
                request.Headers.IfNoneMatch.Add(new
                EntityTagHeaderValue(etag));
            }
        }
        catch
        {
            // Intentionally left blank, Akavache throws an exception if
            the key is not found
        }
```

```
// Do the actual network call
var responseMessage = await base.SendAsync(request,
cancellationToken).ConfigureAwait(false);

// Here we can handle the response
if (responseMessage.IsSuccessStatusCode)
{
    // If a ETag is provided with the response, cache it for future
    requests
    if (!string.IsNullOrWhiteSpace(responseMessage.Headers.ETag?.
    Tag))
        await BlobCache.LocalMachine.InsertObject<string>(re
        sponseMessage.RequestMessage.RequestUri.ToString(),
        responseMessage.Headers.ETag?.Tag);
}

    return responseMessage;
    }
}
```

All the heavy lifting is done in the SendAsync method. This method is invoked whenever a request is sent to the server. As denoted in the comments in the code, everything before the call to the base is before the actual request is sent. That is the place where you can enrich the outgoing request. In our case, we are checking our cache—implemented with Akavache—to see if we have a hash value available. If we do, it is attached in the If-None-Match header.

Then the actual network call happens, and when we get a (successful) result back, we check if there is an ETag header in there and save it in the cache.

Tip   The code from Listings 4-15 and 4-16 is part of a sample project available on: https://github.com/jfversluis/AirplaneModeProof/tree/master/AirplaneModeProof.Api/Middleware. The repository contains a working example of both the server and client application. To get a full understanding of how it all works together, it might be good to have a look at that. It also holds examples of other concepts we have seen in this chapter.

On the server side, the implementation varies depending on what technology you are using for your backend. The code shown in Listing 4-16 shows a so-called *middleware* for ASP.NET Core. Middleware is a piece of code that is registered in the request/response pipeline that can be used to enrich the request and/or response. To see how to register and work with this piece of middleware, look at the mentioned repository in the previous tip.

The concept is pretty similar to what we just saw with the HttpClient.

Listing 4-16. Calculate the ETag Value from ASP.NET Core Middleware

```
public class ETagMiddleware
{
    private readonly RequestDelegate _next;

    public ETagMiddleware(RequestDelegate next)
    {
        _next = next;
    }
    public async Task InvokeAsync(HttpContext context)
    {
        var response = context.Response;
        var originalStream = response.Body;

        using (var ms = new MemoryStream())
        {
            response.Body = ms;

            await _next(context);

            if (IsEtagSupported(response))
            {
                string checksum = CalculateChecksum(ms);

                response.Headers[HeaderNames.ETag] = checksum;

                if (context.Request.Headers.TryGetValue(HeaderNames.
                IfNoneMatch, out var etag) && checksum == etag)
                {
```

```
                response.StatusCode = StatusCodes.Status304NotModified;
                return;
            }
        }

        ms.Position = 0;
        await ms.CopyToAsync(originalStream);
    }
}

private static bool IsEtagSupported(HttpResponse response)
{
    if (response.StatusCode != StatusCodes.Status200OK)
        return false;

    // The 20kb length limit is not based in science. Feel free to change
    if (response.Body.Length > 20 * 1024)
        return false;

    if (response.Headers.ContainsKey(HeaderNames.ETag))
        return false;

    return true;
}

private static string CalculateChecksum(MemoryStream ms)
{
    string checksum = "";

    using (var algo = SHA1.Create())
    {
        ms.Position = 0;
        byte[] bytes = algo.ComputeHash(ms);
        checksum = $"\"{WebEncoders.Base64UrlEncode(bytes)}\"";
    }

    return checksum;
}
}
```

The magic in this case happens in the InvokeAsync method. There we check if the ETag header is supported. And if yes, we calculate a simple SHA1 hash from the response's body. There is a little helper method all the way down the bottom of the class to calculate the SHA1 hash.

That is all there is to it. In Figure 4-6, you can see two requests that implement this feature. In the screen at the top, a request is sent without an If-None-Match header and you only see the server responding with an ETag header.

In the screen at the bottom, the If-None-Match header from the client and the ETag from the server are identical, thus the server responded with an HTTP 304 (not visible in screenshot).

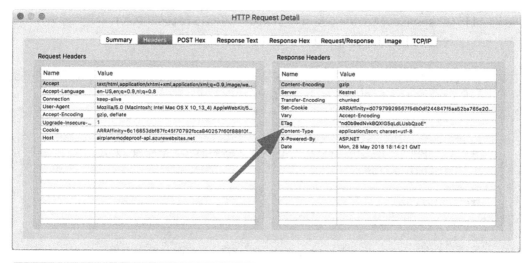

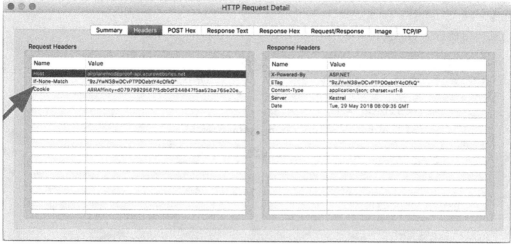

Figure 4-6. *Two requests with ETag and If-None-Match headers*

The Monkey Cache plugin we saw earlier has built-in support for using the `ETag` value.

Another thing that might be interesting to look at is implementing GZip/Deflate. This basically zips the contents of the request and unzips it at the other side. The implementation is not handled in this book.

Tip   If you want to read more extensively into the conditional HTTP requests, look at this documentation from Mozilla: `https://developer.mozilla.org/en-US/docs/Web/HTTP/Conditional_requests`

Sensitive Data

Besides just getting data across and optimizing that, there is also the matter of sensitive data. Not a day goes by without some kind of data breach that is in the news. As a developer, it is rapidly becoming more important to be aware of what sensitive data is and how to store and transfer it properly.

In this section, we learn how to save sensitive data properly and what we need to know about transferring data securely. Secure data can be anything. The most obvious is usernames, passwords, OAuth tokens, and other kinds of credentials. But anything that you deem sensitive should be saved securely. Especially with privacy laws like the GDPR, it might be worth double-checking the security of the data you're saving.

Storing Sensitive Data

There are a couple of solutions for storing data in a secure way. Each platform—at least iOS, Android, and UWP—has a dedicated store for secure data. On iOS it will be saved in the keychain, for Android in the keystore, and on UWP there is the *DataProtectionProvider*.

Multiple plugins have implemented functionality to save data in each respective secure store in Xamarin.Forms. Akavache that we have seen earlier, is actually one of them. But since we have seen that in action already, let's look at an alternative. The alternative plugin is one we have seen earlier as well, it's `Xamarin.Essentials`!

To set up the secure storage, there is a little platform-specific setup required for iOS. You need to enable the Keychain entitlement and add a keychain access group for the application's bundle identifier. To do this, open the `Entitlements.plist` file, find the keychain entitlement, and enable it. This will take care of the rest for you. Then go into your iOS project's properties and set the Custom Entitlements to the Entitlements.plist file under iOS Bundle Signing.

Now simply install the `Xamarin.Essentials` NuGet package on all your projects and we can start using it. In the code in Listing 4-17, you can see all methods of the secure part of the Essentials library. I added comments to explain what each method does.

Listing 4-17. Methods to Work with Secure Data in Xamarin.Essentials

```
// Add a value to the secure keystore. The first parameter is the key, the
second parameter is the value.
await SecureStorage.SetAsync("oauth_token", "secret-oauth-token-value");

// Retrieve a value from the store by its key
var oauthToken = await SecureStorage.GetAsync("oauth_token");
// Remove a value from the keystore by its key
SecureStorage.Remove("oauth_token");

// Purge the whole keystore associated to your app
SecureStorage.RemoveAll();
```

Tip   Read up on all the details of the secure storage part of `Xamarin.Essentials` on the Microsoft Docs website: `https://docs.microsoft.com/en-us/xamarin/essentials/secure-storage`

Transferring Data Securely

This part is actually pretty easy: make sure you only connect with HTTPS resources. On iOS, Apple already forces you to do this by default since iOS 9. Since the world isn't up to speed with that yet, there is a way around it, but I would discourage that. If you have control over the app as well as the backend, invest some time in installing a certificate to make the connection secure. Also, make sure to do it properly and do not bypass the validity or integrity of the certificate in any way. Android does not enforce anything of this kind (yet).

Since not too long ago, an SSL certificate was quite costly, but now with the Let's Encrypt service you can get certificates for free and in an automated way. That means there is no reason not to implement it and secure all the things!

When not using a secure connection, your app is vulnerable to all kinds of attacks. Malicious people might be able to change the content in your app or steal data from your users. If that happens and it gets out, people will not just stop using your app and prevent other users from ever installing it, but you might even face criminal charges depending on local laws. I would say that is reason enough to do everything in your power to prevent this from happening.

If you do need to get around the requirement for secure connections for iOS, because for instance you do not have the backend in your own management, you have a couple of keys to work with in the info.plist file.

The best thing to do is add an exception for a single domain. You can exclude one (or more) domains from the secure connection requirement. Excluding just a few domains is the best thing you can do, as it leaves your app as secure as possible.

In Listing 4-18, you can see a compact example of the example.com domain being allowed to load data without a secure connection.

Listing 4-18. Allowing the example.com Domain to Load Data Insecurely

```
<key>NSAppTransportSecurity</key>
<dict>
    <key>NSExceptionDomains</key>
    <dict>
        <key>example.com</key>
        <dict>
            <key>NSIncludesSubdomains</key>
            <true/>
        </dict>
    </dict>
</dict>
```

You can disable the requirement to load secure data altogether by adding the key from Listing 4-19.

Listing 4-19. Allow All Data to Be Loaded Insecurely

```
<key>NSAppTransportSecurity</key>
<dict>
    <key>NSAllowsArbitraryLoads</key>
    <true/>
</dict>
```

Note that when implementing the code in Listing 4-19, Apple might decline your app in the store if you do not have a good reason to disable this.

Note   To read up on all the details of the `info.plist` keys, refer to the Apple documentation: `https://developer.apple.com/library/ios/documentation/General/Reference/InfoPlistKeyReference/Articles/CocoaKeys.html#//apple_ref/doc/uid/TP40009251-SW33`

As mentioned, Android does not have any requirements for this just yet. It is unclear if Google will enforce anything like this. Nevertheless, just make sure to be as secure as possible.

Tying It All Together

You might have already noticed that I combined some of the concepts explained in this chapter here and there. Because it all has to do with networking and a bit of security, you can pull together some of the bits and pieces to make your app even more robust.

For instance, the check to see if there is an active Internet connection works great with the caching mechanism. And with Polly in the mix, you can anticipate certain errors and deal with them without the user ever having to know about them.

Each app is different, so it all depends on your requirements and time you have to spend on these kinds of solutions, but I would recommend you play with it a little. See what fits together and how it can work in your project structure. Start small and add a concept each iteration. Naturally over time, you will develop a pattern with these concepts that handles your network calls beautifully, making your more stable and robust and a delight to work with.

Summary

In this chapter we saw everything that has to do with networking and a bit of security. We learned how we can connect with REST APIs and how we can do it with the least amount of code possible by using libraries like Refit and RestSharp.

Also, saving bandwidth is an important factor on mobile. Not only that, while we're saving bandwidth, we can also attribute to the user experience. By implementing caching, we do not retrieve data unless we decide that it is needed and have the possibility to show data to our users while updating in the background.

A device goes anywhere the users go, which means walking through deserted places, sitting on high-speed trains that go through tunnels, or maybe even riding in an expensive sports car in space. This means a network connection might not always be available or at least not always stable. Because of this, we need libraries like `Xamarin.Essentials` and Polly to check if we have a connection and be able to recover from certain network errors gracefully. By doing so, our users might never even notice something went wrong and will be more pleased with the quality of our app.

Also, we saw how we can store certain data in a secure store, I have shown you a little trick to save even more bandwidth by using conditional HTTP requests and how all of this could work together in your own projects.

In the next chapter, we look at some common business concepts for apps, like scanning barcodes, showing PDFs, and much more.

CHAPTER 5

Business App Concepts

While a lot of the solutions in this chapter are applicable to any kind of app, these are common scenarios that you will find when developing apps in a business context. This means developing apps in an enterprise environment, where quality matters just a little bit more.

In this chapter we will see how to show PDF files, scan barcodes, and get a grip on our users' behavior when our app is released with App Center.

Also, we will see what the possibilities are for versioning your app and why that matters. And finally, we look at localization. Translating your app can really help improve the adoption of your app. While English makes your app available for a broad audience, there are still a lot of countries that aren't taught in English or people who simply prefer to use applications in their native tongue.

Showing a PDF File

Still one of the most used formats to transfer and show documents is PDF. Yet, this is not always widely supported, which is also true for Xamarin.Forms.

If you can or are willing to afford it, you can use third-party control libraries such as the one from Syncfusion. They offer an out-of-the-box PDF viewer that's very easy to implement and offers all the features that you might wish for.

When this is not an option, let me show you how you can implement a PDF viewer of your own. For this, we will need to implement code on the shared project as well as the platform projects. I will describe how to do it for Android and iOS as these are our primary platforms. You should be able to use the following technique to make it work for UWP and possibly other platforms as well.

© Gerald Versluis and Steven Thewissen 2019
G. Versluis and S. Thewissen, *Xamarin.Forms Solutions*, https://doi.org/10.1007/978-1-4842-4134-9_5

Shared Project

Implementation in the shared project is rather easy. To show a PDF file, we are going to use a custom control. Although this custom control will not be very custom. It is simply an inheritance of the default Xamarin.Forms `WebView`.

This is needed, so we can create a custom renderer for it, which we will need on the different platforms.

To create our "custom" control, simply use the code from Listing 5-1.

Listing 5-1. Custom PDF Control

```
public class PdfWebView : WebView
{
}
```

After defining the control, you can simply use this control in code, or in XAML as is shown in Listing 5-2.

Listing 5-2. Consuming the Custom PDF Control in XAML

```
<?xml version="1.0" encoding="utf-8"?>
<ContentPage xmlns="http://xamarin.com/schemas/2014/forms"
    xmlns:x="http://schemas.microsoft.com/winfx/2009/xaml"
    xmlns:controls="clr-namespace:pdfjs.Controls"
    x:Class="pdfjs.pdfjsPage">

    <Grid>
        <controls:PdfWebView x:Name="PdfView" />
    </Grid>
</ContentPage>
```

It is important to know that when we implement the code to retrieve the PDF on Android, we will first download it locally and then show it to the user. On iOS, this is not necessary. I will explain to you why in the following sections on iOS and Android.

To be able to download them locally, we need a dependency service. In shared code, we have to define an interface. In Listing 5-3 you can see how I have defined it.

Listing 5-3. Interface to Download PDF Files

```
public interface ILocalFileProvider
{
    Task<string> SaveFileToDisk(Stream stream, string fileName);
}
```

The implementation of this method will save a PDF file stream to disk and return the local path of where the file was saved.

For now, this is all that is needed in the shared code. We will have to come back here later to specify which PDF file to use.

iOS Project

On iOS showing the PDF is actually rather easy. The web control on iOS has support for PDF files, so you simply feed it with the right path or direct online URL to the PDF and it will show up nicely.

First, let's look at the custom renderer that is needed on iOS to render our custom PdfWebView control. The code is seen in Listing 5-4.

Listing 5-4. Custom Renderer for the PdfWebView on iOS

```
[assembly: ExportRenderer(typeof(PdfWebView), typeof(PdfWebViewRenderer))]
namespace pdfjs.iOS.CustomRenderers
{
    public class PdfWebViewRenderer : WebViewRenderer
    {
        protected override void OnElementChanged(VisualElementChanged
        EventArgs e)
        {
            base.OnElementChanged(e);

            if (NativeView != null && e.NewElement != null)
            {
                var pdfControl = NativeView as UIWebView;

                if (pdfControl == null)
                    return;
```

```
                pdfControl.ScalesPageToFit = true;
            }
        }
    }
}
```

Actually, the only reason this renderer exists is because we need to set the ScalesPageToFit property on the native web view. By doing this, we allow the user to zoom in and out on the PDF file.

If you first want to download the PDF locally, you will also need to implement a dependency service. We learned how to work with the dependency service back in Chapter 1.

As I have mentioned, on iOS this is not absolutely necessary, but you might have reasons to do so. In the service, you implement the ILocalFileProvider we saw earlier in the shared code.

In Listing 5-5, you can see how it is implemented in the iOS project.

Listing 5-5. Implementation of the Dependency Service to Download the PDF File on iOS

```
[assembly: Dependency(typeof(LocalFileProvider))]
namespace pdfjs.iOS.PlatformSpecifics
{
    public class LocalFileProvider : ILocalFileProvider
    {
        private readonly string _rootDir = Path.Combine(Environment.
        GetFolderPath(Environment.SpecialFolder.Personal), "pdfjs");

        public async Task<string> SaveFileToDisk(Stream stream, string
        fileName)
        {
            if (!Directory.Exists(_rootDir))
                Directory.CreateDirectory(_rootDir);

            var filePath = Path.Combine(_rootDir, fileName);
```

```
        using (var memoryStream = new MemoryStream())
        {
            await stream.CopyToAsync(memoryStream);
            File.WriteAllBytes(filePath, memoryStream.ToArray());
        }

        return filePath;
    }
}
}
```

And by implementing this, we are done with iOS. Let's see how we can implement this same concept on Android.

Android Project

For Android, and possibly other platforms, showing a PDF is a bit harder. They do not have built-in controls at the time of writing. Not wanting to write a whole PDF parser myself, I came up with a different solution.

There is a library called PDF.js, which is a JavaScript framework created by Mozilla for showing PDF files. By loading this into a web view and pointing it to a (local) PDF file, we can easily show PDF files to our users.

Tip   You can also use PDF.js for your web application or any other solution where you might want to show PDF files and have a web browser available. Find all information on their website: https://mozilla.github.io/pdf.js/.

First, go to the website of PDF.js (https://mozilla.github.io/pdf.js/) and download the latest version. Add this to your Android project under the Assets folder. Your final folder structure should look like Figure 5-1.

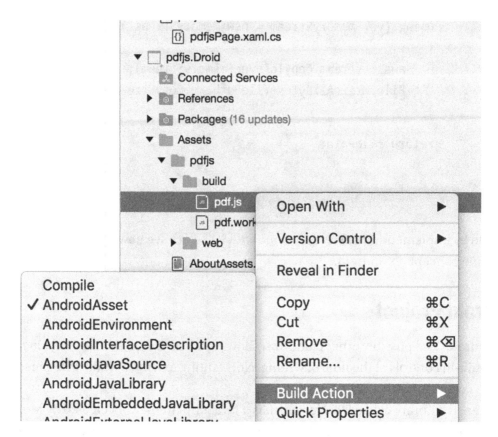

Figure 5-1. *Folder structure and build action for the PDF.js library*

Put a `pdfjs` folder under your `Assets` folder and in there the `build` and `web` folder from the version of PDF.js that you have downloaded. Also seen in Figure 5-1 is setting the Build Action for each file under the `pdfjs` folder to `AndroidAsset`.

After doing this, it is time to implement the dependency service for Android. You can see it in Listing 5-6.

Listing 5-6. Implementation of the Dependency Service to Download a PDF on Android

```
[assembly: Dependency(typeof(LocalFileProvider))]
namespace pdfjs.Droid.PlatformSpecifics
{
    public class LocalFileProvider : ILocalFileProvider
```

```
{
    private readonly string _rootDir = Path.Combine(Android.
    OS.Environment.ExternalStorageDirectory.Path, "pdfjs");

    public async Task<string> SaveFileToDisk(Stream pdfStream, string
    fileName)
    {
        if (!Directory.Exists(_rootDir))
            Directory.CreateDirectory(_rootDir);

        var filePath = Path.Combine(_rootDir, fileName);

        using (var memoryStream = new MemoryStream())
        {
            await pdfStream.CopyToAsync(memoryStream);
            File.WriteAllBytes(filePath, memoryStream.ToArray());
        }

        return filePath;
    }
}
}
```

You might notice that the implementation looks pretty similar to iOS. The reason we need to implement it on both iOS and Android is that the calls to determine the right location on disk will differ per platform.

To be able to download and read the file from a local path, make sure you have set the READ_EXTERNAL_STORAGE and WRITE_EXTERNAL_STORAGE permissions on your Android app.

To finish off, let's go back to the shared project one more.

Showing the PDF File

Back in our shared project, we now need to set the Source property of the custom control to show our PDF.

For the purpose of this demo, I will simply hook up the PDF to our custom control from the code-behind of our page. In a real-life and especially enterprise scenario, you are probably using MVVM or a similar architectural pattern. The concept remains the same, setting the property will only happen a bit different.

Let me show you the code in the code-behind and walk you through it. It is seen in Listing 5-7.

Listing 5-7. Loading the PDF in the Custom Control

```
public partial class pdfjsPage : ContentPage
{
    public pdfjsPage(string url)
    {
        InitializeComponent();

        var localPath = string.Empty;

        if (Device.RuntimePlatform == Device.Android)
        {
            var dependency = DependencyService.Get<ILocalFileProvider>();

            if (dependency == null)
            {
                DisplayAlert("Error loading PDF", "Computer says no", "OK");

                return;
            }

            var fileName = Guid.NewGuid().ToString();

            // Download PDF locally for viewing
            using (var httpClient = new HttpClient())
            {
                var pdfStream = Task.Run(() => httpClient.
                GetStreamAsync(url)).Result;

                localPath =
                    Task.Run(() => dependency.SaveFileToDisk
                    (pdfStream, $"{fileName}.pdf")).Result;
            }
```

```
        if (string.IsNullOrWhiteSpace(localPath))
        {
            DisplayAlert("Error loading PDF", "Computer says no", "OK");

            return;
        }
    }

    if (Device.RuntimePlatform == Device.Android)
        PdfView.Source = $"file:///android_asset/pdfjs/web/viewer.
        html?file={WebUtility.UrlEncode(localPath)}";
    else
        PdfView.Source = url;
    }
}
```

A lot seems to be going on here. From top to bottom this is happening: we check to see if the app is running on Android. If it is, then we download the file locally with the dependency service we implemented. There is some error handling in there, but for the happy path the PDF file is downloaded and saved for us to view.

Then near the end, we again check on what platform we are currently running the app. For Android, you will see that I set a special kind of URL. With that URL, I point to the PDF.js library and open the local viewer.html file. To that HTML page, I can supply the local path to my downloaded PDF file with the file query parameter.

In the case that we are running on iOS, we simply set the source of our control to the URL of the PDF file. On iOS you can show a remote PDF file just like that. If you have chosen to also download the PDF file locally on iOS, simply remove the if statement and let both Android and iOS point to the local PDF.js URL.

Note   If you need a working example of how to show a PDF, look at this sample project I have created. This sample repository uses the exact same code as described in this chapter. The repository can be found here: `https://github.com/jfversluis/pdfjs`.

Scanning Barcodes

Barcodes are still very much present in our daily lives. It is a quick and easy way to store and read information or show a unique identifier on an object. It is not a big surprise that scanning barcodes is something that is often requested in apps.

While mobile devices often aren't specialized in scanning barcodes, they are very suited because of the great cameras that are available. In this section, we look at how to implement a barcode scanner into our own app.

To pull this off, I will use the ZXing library, which also has bindings for Xamarin and Xamarin.Forms. ZXing (which gets the name from Zebra Crossing) is a library that allows you to scan barcodes as well as generate barcodes. To provide you with an alternative, there is also the Scandit library, although that one will not be described in this book. The basic functionality comes down to the same thing: scanning barcodes.

For this example, we will be using a Xamarin.Forms app, but the ZXing library is also available for traditional Xamarin apps.

Barcode formats that are supported by ZXing are:

- AZTEC

- CODABAR

- CODE_39

- CODE_93

- CODE_128

- DATA_MATRIX

- EAN_8

- EAN_13

- ITF

- MAXICODE

- PDF_417

- QR_CODE

- RSS_14

- RSS_EXPANDED

- UPC_A

- UPC_E

- UPC_EAN_EXTENSION

- MSI

- PLESSEY

- IMB

Installing ZXing

Adding ZXing to your app is as easy as installing a NuGet package on your projects. Remember to install the package on all of your projects: the shared code project as well as your platform projects. The package that you are looking for is the ZXing.Net. Mobile package. When developing for Xamarin.Forms, you want to use the ZXing.Net. Mobile.Forms package. At the time of writing, installing the Forms specific package does not install the necessary required regular package on Android. In your Android project, manually also install the ZXing.Net.Mobile package together with the ZXing.Net. Mobile.Forms package.

You will also need to add the right permissions for using the camera and the flashlight as well as a small line of initialization code. Let me show you how on the different platforms.

iOS

In the AppDelegate.cs file of your iOS project, add the following line in the FinishedLaunching method:

```
ZXing.Net.Mobile.Forms.iOS.Platform.Init();
```

In addition, you will need to add the right key(s) to your info.plist file to request the right permissions for the camera. At the time of writing, you will need to add the entry of Listing 5-8 in your info.plist file.

Listing 5-8. The Info.plist key to Acquire Permissions to the Camera in iOS

```
<key>NSCameraUsageDescription</key>
<string>We would like to use your camera to be able to scan barcodes</
string>
```

You should now be all set on iOS.

Android

For Android the exercise is mostly the same but a bit more extensive. In the
MainActivity.cs file, inside the OnCreate method, add this line:

```
 ZXing.Net.Mobile.Forms.Android.Platform.Init();
```

To accommodate for the new permissions model in newer Android versions, you
also need to add the code of Listing 5-9. This also needs to go into the MainActivity.
cs file.

Listing 5-9. New Permissions Model for Android

```
public override void OnRequestPermissionsResult(int requestCode, string[]
permissions, Permission[] grantResults)
{
        global::ZXing.Net.Mobile.Android.PermissionsHandler.
        OnRequestPermissionsResult (requestCode, permissions,
        grantResults);
}
```

With this code the permissions for the camera are requested as needed. To also
support older Android versions, you need to add the permissions to the Android
Manifest file. The camera permission should be included already for you when installing
the ZXing library. If you also want to be able to use the flashlight, you will need to add
this attribute on top of a namespace declaration somewhere in your Android project.
It makes sense to do this on top of the MainActivity.cs file. A sample can be seen in
Listing 5-10.

Listing 5-10. Adding the Flashlight Permission to Your Android App

```
[assembly: UsesPermission (Android.Manifest.Permission.Flashlight)]
namespace MyApp.Droid
{
    public class MainActivity : FormsAppCompatActivity
    {
        // Your code...
    }
}
```

If the camera permission was not added automatically, you can do it the same way as shown here, just replace flashlight with camera.

You can also add the permissions directly to the AndroidManifest.xml file under the Properties folder. You can see a sample AndroidManifest.xml file in Listing 5-11, which holds the camera and flashlight permissions.

Listing 5-11. Adding Android Permissions to the AndroidManifest.xml File

```
<?xml version="1.0" encoding="utf-8"?>
<manifest xmlns:android="http://schemas.android.com/apk/res/
android" package="com.app.your" android:installLocation="auto"
android:versionName="1.0.0" android:versionCode="1">
    <uses-sdk android:minSdkVersion="23" />
    <uses-permission android:name="android.permission.INTERNET" />
    <uses-permission android:name="android.permission.CAMERA" />
    <uses-permission android:name="android.permission.FLASHLIGHT" />
    <application android:label="YourApp" android:icon="@drawable/icon">
    </application>
</manifest>
```

The only thing the assembly attribute does is generate these lines at compile time. It does not matter which of these options you chose to add the permissions, the result will be the same. Although, do not add them both, as this will result in errors that permissions are declared multiple times.

There is also a visual editor for the AndroidManifest.xml file that allows you to simply check the camera and flashlight checkbox.

For Android, that should be all there is to it.

UWP

In the main page's constructor, simply add this line:

```
ZXing.Net.Mobile.Forms.WindowsUniversal.ZXingScannerViewRenderer.Init();
```

This should be located in the `MainPage.xaml.cs` file. Make sure that, in the UWP manifest file, you enable the `webcam` permission to be able to use the camera.

Tip   The project website for the ZXing library for Xamarin can be found here: `https://github.com/Redth/ZXing.Net.Mobile`.

Now that we know how to install and set up the ZXing library in our app, it is time to see how we can start using it.

Implementing Barcode Scanning

Scanning barcodes can be done in two ways: a single barcode or continuously. With the first option you show a page with the camera open, and you scan a barcode and do something with the result. In continuous mode, you can keep scanning barcodes one after another and do something with the incoming results, for instance add them to a list in the background.

All the features work both in code as well as in XAML with data binding supported. I will be showing sample code with XAML, since I am just such a fan. The easiest way to implement a view that can scan barcodes is by using the ZXingScannerPage object. By creating a page of that type and navigating to it, you will have a full screen barcode scanning screen. The page shows an overlay to give it a barcode scanner look. You can see it in the screenshot in Figure 5-2.

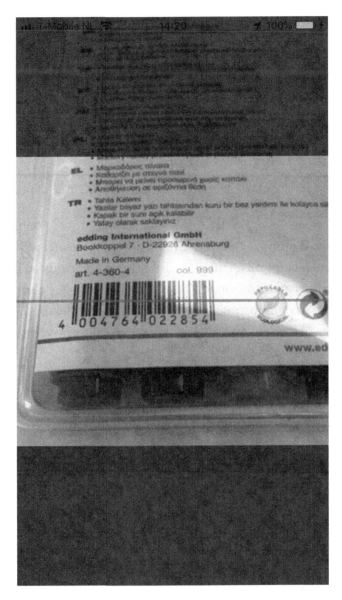

Figure 5-2. *Sample of the ZXingScannerPage on iOS*

In the code of Listing 5-12, you can see all the code that is needed to set up the page
and start scanning barcodes. Note that your code-behind also needs to inherit from the
ZXingScannerPage. The implementation of the Handle_OnScanResult we will see a bit
later on.

Listing 5-12. Code for the ZXingScannerPage

```
<?xml version="1.0" encoding="utf-8"?>
<zxing:ZXingScannerPage xmlns="http://xamarin.com/schemas/2014/forms"
    xmlns:x="http://schemas.microsoft.com/winfx/2009/xaml"
    x:Class="ZXingSample.MainPage"
    xmlns:zxing="clr-namespace:ZXing.Net.Mobile.Forms;assembly=ZXing.Net.
    Mobile.Forms"
    OnScanResult="Handle_OnScanResult" IsScanning="true">

</zxing:ZXingScannerPage>
```

You can however, customize the view if you want to. You can use the
ZXingScannerView object for this. This class can be used to be nested in any other layout
element. That way, you can incorporate a barcode scanner in any custom view you
might want to create. To demonstrate this, look at the code in Listing 5-13, which shows
a layout that consists of three blocks, where only the middle one will show the camera
image and scan barcodes.

Listing 5-13. Custom Layout with a ZXingScannerView

```
<?xml version="1.0" encoding="utf-8"?>
<ContentPage xmlns="http://xamarin.com/schemas/2014/forms"
    xmlns:x="http://schemas.microsoft.com/winfx/2009/xaml"
    x:Class="ZXingSample.PartialScreenScanning"
    xmlns:zxing="clr-namespace:ZXing.Net.Mobile.Forms;assembly=ZXing.Net.
    Mobile.Forms"
    Title="Partial screen">
    <Grid>
        <Grid.RowDefinitions>
            <RowDefinition Height="*" />
            <RowDefinition Height="Auto" />
            <RowDefinition Height="*" />
        </Grid.RowDefinitions>

        <BoxView Grid.Row="0" BackgroundColor="Chocolate"/>
        <zxing:ZXingScannerView Grid.Row="1" x:Name="_
        scanView" OnScanResult="Handle_OnScanResult"
```

```
        IsScanning="true"                              WidthRequest="200"
        HeightRequest="200" />
        <BoxView Grid.Row="2" BackgroundColor="Blue" />
    </Grid>
</ContentPage>
```

While this layout isn't very visually appealing, it does show you how you can incorporate the barcode scanner anywhere in your design. It will behave just like any other visual element you are used to work with.

To catch the result of the barcode scanning I have used an event in the code of Listing 5-12 and Listing 5-13. Whenever you point the camera at a barcode, the event will be raised and you will receive data about the barcode that was detected.

If you want to use a design pattern like MVVM, you would want to stay clear of events. No worries, that is also possible with the ZXing library. There are bindable properties and commands available to use from your view model.

To complete the section on barcode scanning, let me show you the code in the code-behind of the sample code, to handle the results of the barcode scanning. You can see it in Listing 5-14.

Listing 5-14. Handling Scan Results

```
public void Handle_OnScanResult(Result result)
{
    Device.BeginInvokeOnMainThread(async () =>
    {
        await DisplayAlert("Scanned result", result.Text, "OK");
    });
}
```

You can see how a Result object comes in that holds all the details of our barcode scanning action. From the Text property, you can get the scanned value. There are other properties available that tell you something about the orientation and barcode format, etc.

Of course, if you are working with an architectural pattern like MVVM, you shouldn't use events. To accommodate for that, there are bindable properties and commands in place. For instance, if you want to catch the scan result with the ZXingScannerPage, you can bind to the Result property and for the ZXingScannerView, you can use the ScanResultCommand.

> **Tip**   A working sample repository that shows scanning and generating barcodes
> can be found here: `https://github.com/jfversluis/ZXingSample`.

Implementing Generating Barcodes

You can also find yourself in the situation that you might need to generate a barcode.
This is also something that can be achieved through the ZXing library. For this, the
`ZXingBarcodeImageView` element is available. Using it is very easy; you can see a sample
in Listing 5-15.

Listing 5-15. Sample Usage of the ZXingBarcodeImageView

```xml
<?xml version="1.0" encoding="UTF-8"?>
<ContentPage xmlns="http://xamarin.com/schemas/2014/forms"
             xmlns:x="http://schemas.microsoft.com/winfx/2009/xaml"
             x:Class="ZXingSample.GenerateBarcodePage"
             xmlns:zxing="clr-namespace:ZXing.Net.Mobile.
             Forms;assembly=ZXing.Net.Mobile.Forms"
             xmlns:zxcm="clr-namespace:ZXing.Common;assembly=zxing.
             portable">

             <zxing:ZXingBarcodeImageView WidthRequest="300"
             HeightRequest="300" BarcodeValue="1337" BarcodeFormat="QR_CODE"
             HorizontalOptions="Center" VerticalOptions="Center">
                 <zxing:ZXingBarcodeImageView.BarcodeOptions>
                     <zxcm:EncodingOptions Width="300" Height="300" />
                 </zxing:ZXingBarcodeImageView.BarcodeOptions>
             </zxing:ZXingBarcodeImageView>
</ContentPage>
```

This sample code shows a QR code with the value of `"1337"` on a very simple page.
But you can use the image component anywhere in your layout.

You might wonder why the separate `EncodingOptions` are declared within the
image view. If you do not provide these, then the generated barcode image will show
up blurry.

Now you know all there is to know about scanning and generating barcodes. As mentioned, there are some alternatives out there that might have some different features that better suit your needs. But the ZXing library seems to do the trick rather well.

App Center Integrations

When releasing apps into the wild, you want to keep grip on what is going on. Is your app crashing? And how are people using it? That are two very important questions you might want answers to.

If you have created and released apps before, you might know that users aren't the most reliable source for crash reports and analytics. There are some great services out there that provide you with exactly that: detailed and insightful reports. One of these services is Microsoft's App Center.

What Is App Center?

App Center is a service by Microsoft that combines all kinds of features that have to do with mobile. It's even not just for Xamarin apps; you can also use it with your native Java, Objective-C/Swift, or Cordova apps.

You can use App Center for *continuous integration* and *continuous deployment* (CI/CD) as well as automated UI testing, sending push notifications, and much more. While this is all great stuff, we will focus on the crash reporting and analytics functionality.

Most of the services are free, at least to start off with. You can find App Center at `https://appcenter.ms/`. You can set up an account by using your Microsoft account and start using the features.

When you have created your account, you can create an unlimited number of apps in your account. Within each app you can then mix and match the services that you want to use. Do you want to use crash reporting but not the build pipeline? You can do that. Do you want to build your app in Azure DevOps but distribute via App Center? That is possible as well!

These mix and match functionalities are not something we will go into detail about in this book. Instead, we will describe what features are available to integrate in your app and how to use them to your advantage. This also means we will not handle building, testing, and distributing in detail.

Creating Your App in App Center

When you have set up your account and logged in to the portal, you will land on a rather empty screen. On the left side of the screen you can see your user account. You can also create organizations within your App Center account. These will show up on this left side as well. By switching between these, it filters between what apps are held in that account.

At the center of the screen is where most of the action will happen. This is where you get an overview of your app and where all configuration options, etc. will appear while you navigate through the App Center portal.

The top bar will have some context actions and/or filters for you to use on the screen you are currently reviewing. When you're on the landings page, you can add a new app, right from that top bar. Find the blue bottom in the top-right and click Add New App.

In the next screen, seen in Figure 5-3, you need to provide some details about the app to create. You will have to give it a name, specify the targeted operating system (OS), and choose the platform that the app is built in, i.e. Xamarin or React Native. Optionally, you can enter a description and specify a different owner for this app. Don't worry, you can change the owner later as well.

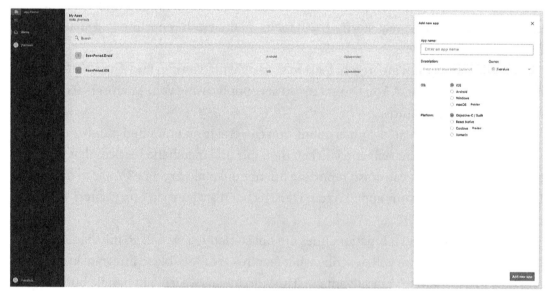

Figure 5-3. *Adding a new app to your App Center account*

Click the Submit button, and your new app definition within App Center is created for you! You will now be brought to the landings page for that specific app. You will notice how the left bar on the screen has changed as well. This will now show you the different features of App Center. By clicking on each of them, you can configure that specific part for your app.

Building, Testing, and Distributing

While a big part of the power of App Center is in automated building, testing, and distributing, it is a bit beyond the scope of this book. I do want to emphasize how great these features are. Within a matter of minutes, you can set up a full continuous integration and continuous deployment pipeline, all for free!

You don't need to do any extensive configuration, just the bare basics and you can get started. Since you have already specified for which OS the app is meant to be and in what language it is built, App Center already has a lot preconfigured for you. From the automated builds, you can then, with a simple checkbox, specify you want to distribute the outcome of this build to a group of people.

Also, a very powerful feature is the automated UI testing. You might know this from earlier as Xamarin Test Cloud. With this solution you can write coded test scenarios and upload them together with your app to the cloud. There, your app will go through the scenarios you drafted on actual *physical* devices. This makes the service very unique and as close as real life as possible. You have control over the devices that the tests run on. That way you can find out how that nasty bug happens on just that one device or OS version. This saves you the trouble of finding that device yourself, which is impossible to do for all scenarios in the world.

Of course, there is a price to all this. The service starts at $99 per month at the time of writing. This gives you one concurrent build and four build hours per month. This means that you can run one test at most at a time and, when one test takes 10 minutes, you can run it 240 times within that month. At the end of the month it resets. Higher tiers are available that give you more concurrent devices mostly. That means you can run tests on more devices simultaneously. Also, there are enterprise plans available that will give you unlimited test minutes.

All in all, very great stuff and I would like to encourage you to check it out yourself!

Crash Reporting

Let's see how to use crash reporting in our app. Actually, the most basic implementation is rather easy. You just need to add the NuGet package to your projects and add a line of initialization code. That is enough to get reports of unhandled exceptions into your App Center portal.

In your Visual Studio instance, add the `Microsoft.AppCenter.Crashes` NuGet package. Make sure that you install the package in both your shared code project as well as all targeted platform projects like iOS and Android.

To enable the crash reporting, you need to add a line of initialization code to your shared code library. At least, for Xamarin.Forms. On other platforms you might need to initialize it elsewhere. See the code in Listing 5-16 for Xamarin.Forms.

Listing 5-16. Initializing Crash Reporting in Xamarin.Forms

```
// Add this line in the App.xaml.cs file inside the OnStart method
AppCenter.Start("android={Your Android App secret here};" +
                "uwp={Your UWP App secret here};" +
                "ios={Your iOS App secret here}",
                typeof(Crashes));
```

The app secrets can be found in the App Center portal. If you want this to work on all three platforms, you will need to create three separate app definitions within App Center. If you don't need a platform, simply remove it from the initialization line. You can find the app secret in the form of a GUID on the "Getting Started" page of your app. At the time of writing, you can only view your crash reports or analytics per app definition, i.e. per app per platform. There is no way of combining the same app but on different platforms into a single view, but this is something that is being worked on by Microsoft.

Now, when your app crashes you've configured App Center in your code with the correct app secret, you will get detailed reports back in your App Center portal. It will contain a full stack trace, and if debug symbols are available, you can see the precise line numbers of where the error occurs. A sample crash report can be seen in the screenshot in Figure 5-4. The crash reporting is categorized under Diagnostics in App Center. "Crashes" are the unhandled exceptions and "errors" are handled exceptions, which we will see in a minute.

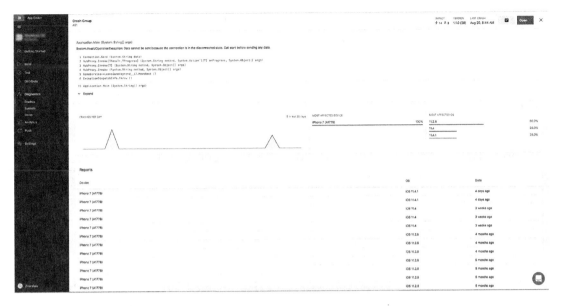

Figure 5-4. *Crash report in App Center*

This is very valuable information that you typically don't get back from your users. Also, the information comes in near real time so you know a crash happened even before a user has the chance to report it to you. Or, if the error caused the app to terminate, the report will be sent the next time the user starts the app again.

Note   Inform yourself with local laws and rules on what data you can and cannot collect. It is always a good idea to at least inform your users or even provide them with the option to disable the collection of data. This applies to both the crash reporting and even more so for the analytics.

You can also track handled exceptions. Within a `try/catch` block, you can report the exception to the App Center portal by simply calling it, as shown in Listing 5-17.

Listing 5-17. Reporting a Handled Exception

```
try
{
    // Your code here
} catch (Exception ex){
    Crashes.TrackError(ex);
}
```

Whenever an exception happens here, it will show up under Issues in the App Center portal. The level of information is the same, it's just a different categorization.

Note   The handled crash reporting is only available for Xamarin apps at the time of this writing. This includes Xamarin.Forms apps.

You can also collect some additional details when reporting a crash. The `TrackError` method also has an optional parameter that takes a `Dictionary<string, string>` object. That way you can send data along with the crash report in a key/value store. Note that some limitations apply. You can send at most 20 extra properties and the key and value can be a maximum of 125 characters long. If one of these requirements is not met, you might now be able to see your crash report in the portal.

Within the crash reports you can see all kinds of statistics about how much users are affected, what devices they are using with which version of the OS, etc. With that information you can prioritize the crashes and even mark them as open or closed. Chances are that you already have a bug tracking system in place, in the settings you have the ability to open an issue whenever a crash happens. You can integrate with Jira, GitHub, and Azure DevOps at the time of writing.

Analytics

The App Center analytics can be used to track your user's behavior inside your app. You can define events inside your code, which are weaved into a traceable path in the App Center portal. That way, you can determine whether a certain functionality is used and how.

The process of enabling analytics is pretty much the same as for crash reporting. Install the analytics package `Microsoft.AppCenter.Analytics` and add an initialization line. Actually, when you are already using crash reporting, you can simply add analytics to the existing initialization line. You can see this in Listing 5-18.

Listing 5-18. Initializing Analytics in Xamarin.Forms

```
// This line is in the App.xaml.cs file inside the OnStart method
AppCenter.Start("android={Your Android App secret here};" +
                "uwp={Your UWP App secret here};" +
                "ios={Your iOS App secret here}",
                typeof(Crashes), typeof(Analytics));
```

Note how the typeof(Analytics) was added. If you only want to use one of them, remove one of the options. The app secrets are the same in both cases.

When integrating the analytics NuGet package, you will get a lot of information for free, just like with the crashes. You can see how much active users there have been over time, daily sessions, which devices your users are using with your app, and much more. But it doesn't stop there.

You can now add lines anywhere in your app to track certain events. Simply add Analytics.TrackEvent("My custom event"); and define your own event names to have it show up in your App Center portal. By defining these events, you can see how the user moves through your application.

Just like when reporting a crash, you can also add custom information to the event you are tracking. Look at Listing 5-19 for an example.

Listing 5-19. Tracking a Custom Event with Additional Properties

```
Analytics.TrackEvent("Person details opened", new Dictionary<string, string> {
        { "Category", "Employees" },
        { "IsAdmin", "yes"}
});
```

I can't stress enough that you have to be careful with which data you collect and that you need to inform your users about this. Privacy is a very important topic and very current; you don't want to end up in the news that your app is misusing any sensitive information.

You can enable or disable the analytics functionality at runtime by calling this line:

```
Analytics.SetEnabledAsync(false);
```

The parameter value enables or disables the functionality. This allows you to provide the option to your end-user to opt-in or out. You can then determine at runtime if the functionality is enabled with:

```
await Analytics.IsEnabledAsync();.
```

In conjunction with crashes, these events are also shown leading up to the crash. There the events are referred to as *breadcrumbs*. This combined information makes it easier to pinpoint the cause of any errors.

The last feature that is available when using analytics is *Log Flow*. With Log Flow you are able to follow analytics messages coming in, in near real time. This can be very useful when testing your implemented events or walking through a reproduction and following along in the logs.

Figure 5-5 shows a sample Log Flow output.

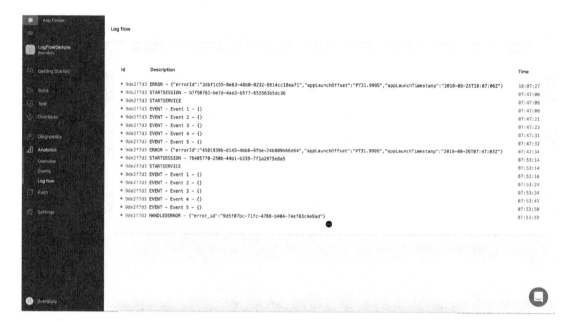

Figure 5-5. *Sample output in App Center Log Flow*

In the screenshot in Figure 5-5, you can see two sessions being started and which events are hit within that session. You can also see what crashes happen during the session. Or which crashes happened during last session, but got sent after starting the app again. This is all in near real time. This makes it easier to sit down with a user (or remotely of course) and let them reproduce a certain case while you can inspect the logs while reproduction is happening.

Tip   The documentation about App Center can be found on the Microsoft Docs website. It has a more extensive explanation of all features for you to try out. You can find it here: `https://docs.microsoft.com/en-us/appcenter/`.

This concludes the section about App Center. As mentioned, there is a lot more powerful stuff in here, and there is a lot more to come in the future.

App Versioning

When rolling out apps in a more corporate or enterprise environment, or simply when you have released a version to your end users, versioning becomes important. A version identifies a certain point in time and represents a certain state of your codebase.

Chances are that you want to continue improving your app, while a version is being used in the wild. The potential problem that arises is that users will start pointing out bugs to you, while you are long gone and working with a radically changed codebase. This problem only grows when a bigger variety of versions have been released. Because of this, it is good to have some good versioning in place that helps you identify a certain state of your repository. Or maybe when push comes to shove, you find yourself needing to create a hotfix on your old codebase, but not wanting to release all kinds of new, unfinished, features. That is why versioning matters.

That being said, let's just put this out there: there is no one way of doing this. There is no wrong or right, basically. It all comes down to your requirements and how you organize your repositories, code, builds, and releases. The important thing is traceability. The user can identify that your app is a certain version, and you are able to trace that back to a certain point in the codebase.

A typical version number will look like three integers, separated by dots. For example, 1.2.3 or 3.4.2, also known as *semantic versioning*. This stands for: major. minor.patch, so three levels of how much your code or functionality has changed. The patch level is also often just a counter of the build. So, each build that is created, the patch level will just go plus one. Another asset that is being used by more and more projects is the Git commit hash that was used to create this build.

When you are using Git, you have probably seen this kind of (SHA-1) hashes: c26cf8af130955c5c67cfea96f9532680b963628. Because of how Git works, this is more often than not abbreviated to c26cf8a. With the first seven characters, Git is able to identify a commit uniquely. Since a commit is a certain state of the code in time, this can also be very useful and act as a version number for your app. It is often used together with the "traditional" version number. This would produce something like: 1.2.3 (c26cf8a).

As a developer, you now know exactly where to look.

For the user to be able to report this number to you, make sure it is visible somewhere within the app. When using solutions like App Center, the version number associated with your app is automatically included and used for categorization.

Since there are numerous tools and ways to use when producing a binary for your app, it would be impossible to describe it all in here. Underneath, I will tell you about how and where the version numbers are composed in iOS and Android and what to look for when using Azure Pipelines as your build server to set these version numbers.

Note   Even though we are talking about Xamarin.Forms apps here, setting version numbers is still something that we need to do per platform. This is because each platform has a specific way of setting the version number.

---

iOS

On iOS, most of the metadata is saved in a file called the info.plist. This is where you will also find the version number. Or actually, version numbers, plural. For iOS, Apple has a pretty strict version number format. There are two fields that are of importance: the version and the build. These are represented by CFBundleVersion and CFBundleShortVersionString in the info.plist file.

As per the Apple documentation CFBundleVersion has to be a string comprised of three non-negative integers, separated by periods. Just like the example we saw earlier. In reality, this field can contain other values as well. Even a date-time stamp is possible. However, I recommend against it.

The CFBundleShortVersionString is the version that is shown to the end user in the App Store. Whenever you provide a new version to the App Store, you will have to increment the version numbers or it will be rejected by Apple.

I recommend that you keep both fields in sync with the same value; this is easiest and most common in the .NET ecosystem.

In Figure 5-6, you can see the info.plist editor in Visual Studio for Mac where you can set these fields. The Version field equals the CFBundleShortVersionString field and Build equals the CFBundleVersion field.

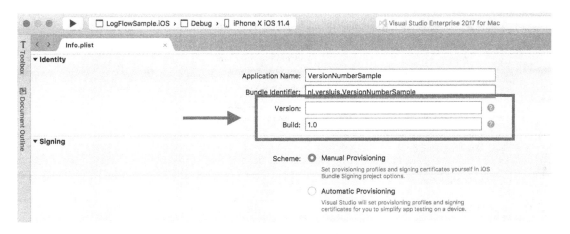

Figure 5-6. *Setting the version number from the info.plist editor in Visual Studio for Mac*

Tip   For more information on how to use the version numbers on iOS, check out the documentation by Apple here: `https://developer.apple.com/library/archive/technotes/tn2420/_index.html`.

Android

Setting the version number for an Android app happens in the `AndroidManifest.xml` file. You can find this in your Android project, in the `Properties` folder.

On Android, there are also two fields that matter: *version code* and *version name*.

The *version code* is the one that actually matters. This is just a positive integer that increases with each release. It does not need to correlate with the version name in any way. The version code is an internal version number, used to determine if a version is newer than last. You can compare it to the API levels that Android uses themselves.

The *version name* is a string value that is shown to your users. It has no other purpose than that. Still, I recommend using it as a unique version number system, but there is no restriction from Android that prevents you from doing otherwise. In Visual Studio there is also an editor available for the `AndroidManifest.xml` file; you can see it in the screenshot depicted in Figure 5-7.

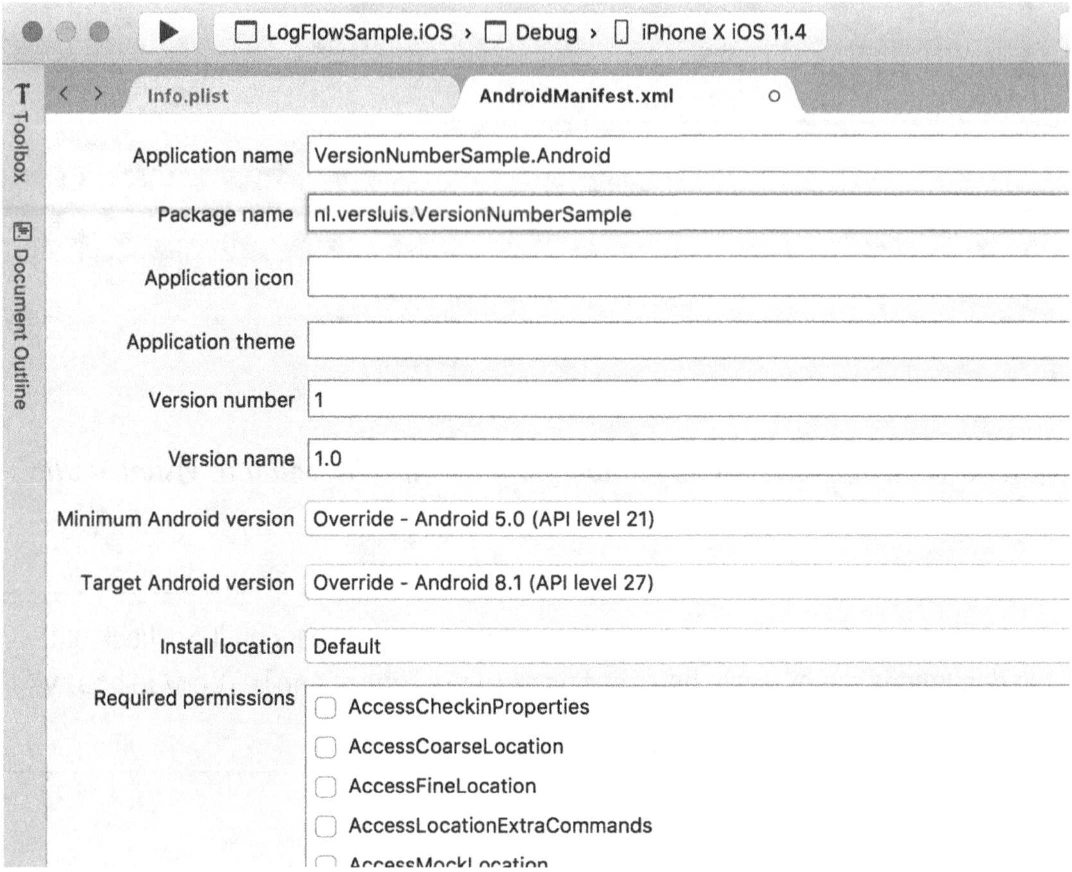

Figure 5-7. *Editing the AndroidManifest.xml in Visual Studio for Mac*

Tip   All information on the Android versioning can be found in the Android documentation: `https://developer.android.com/studio/publish/versioning`.

Setting the Version Number with Azure Pipelines

Depending on what build system you use, there are different ways to set the version number. As we have seen in the previous sections, they are simply set through some XML files. This text transformation should be fairly easy to implement with any CI/CD pipeline.

When using Azure DevOps Pipelines, there are probably some built-in tasks to achieve this, but you can also use a custom build task by Colin Dembovsky. With his custom *version assemblies* task, you can easily replace a version number (or anything else for that matter) with the use of a *regular expression* (regex) pattern. In this build task, you can specify a file—or files with wildcards—and replace the regex matches with a variable value or the build number from the current build definition in Azure Pipelines. In the screenshot of Figure 5-8, you can see how this particular build task can be configured.

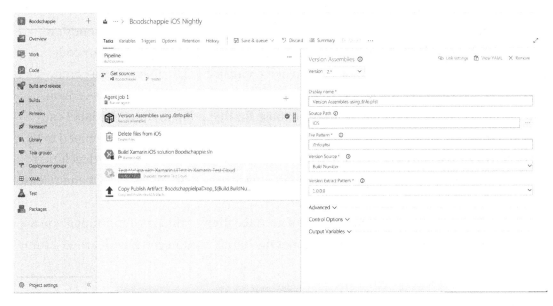

Figure 5-8. *Configuration of the version assemblies task*

In the repository from Figure 5-8, we look for the `info.plist` file in the iOS folder. In that specific file, we look for a pattern that looks like 1.0.0.0 and replace it with the value from our build configuration. Note that you will have to make sure that you provide a valid version number. The version number in this pipeline can be found on the Options tab in the bar. It defaults to a version number, which includes the date and time of the current build. This will not produce a valid version number for iOS or Android. Make sure that you enter something correct.

In the `info.plist` and `AndroidManifest.xml` files, you can simply leave the version number to something like 1.0.0. This makes it easy to find the build task we have seen and the version number will only become important whenever it is released to other people, not while developing. Also, by making the incrementation of your version number part of your build pipeline, you remove the pain from having to remember doing it by hand whenever you commit a new version of your code.

Tip   The version assemblies task is part of a bigger suite called Colin's ALM Corner Build & Release Tools. You can find all the info and install it into your Azure DevOps account here: `https://marketplace.visualstudio.com/ items?itemName=colinsalmcorner.colinsalmcorner-buildtasks`.

Remember, there is no wrong or right way of doing this. It all mostly depends on your procedures and requirements. It might also be a good thing to label your code whenever you release a version. In Git, you can create a label that points to a certain state in your code. By also adding a label to your code whenever you create a new version, you can easily identify the state of your codebase for that point in time. The label can have the name of the version number of your app build. Now, whenever you need to fix something in your released app, but do not want to release all kinds of half-developed features along with it you can go back to your label, create a branch with a fix and release just that.

Versioning can be a really powerful tool for traceability, which is important if you are developing apps in a business context. Hopefully in this section you have learned a thing or two that can help you achieve this.

Localization

Another thing that is often requested in enterprise environments is localization. Even in non-enterprise settings, it can be very useful to localize your applications. While you might be accustomed to English while developing, speaking English might not be that natural for everyone.

This is also true the other way around. If you want your app to target people outside of your native language, you might want to add support for other languages as well. By doing that, you can all of a sudden double or triple your target audience and make your app a big hit.

In this section, we see how we can easily localize our Xamarin.Forms apps and discuss some things that need some extra attention.

Localize Using Resource Files

For as long as I can remember, the .NET Framework has support for localization out-of-the-box. This works based on so-called *resource files* (or *resx* files, after their extension). You do not have to implement anything special here to make it work. Although it needs some special treatment, while loading the translations from resource files is supported, we do need some extra code to actually show the translations for each platform.

It all starts by adding a resource file to your shared project. Typically, you will have one that does not have a locale indicator. This file will act as the fallback whenever a localized file is not found. This means if the device is set to, for instance, Spanish, but your app does not contain a Spanish translation, it will default to the resource file with no language specified. Depending on your use case, this fallback resource file will probably contain English or the language that you were targeting in the first place. For this example, let's name our file Language.resx.

For each language that you want to add, you can add a separate file with the ISO, two-letter language code right before the extension. The OS will choose the right language based on the filename convention.

If we were to add Spanish to our app, this would be Language.es.resx or Dutch would be Language.nl.resx. You can also add the full indicator, for instance to distinguish British English and U.S. English. In these cases, you could create files like Language.en-US.resx and Language.en-UK.resx. If you just want to support English and not treat British or U.S. English separately, you can simply create a file called Language.en.resx.

A sample setup can be seen in the Solution Explorer that is shown in Figure 5-9. In the Localizations folder, you can see three files: the fallback without any language code and two files with English (en) and Dutch (nl) values.

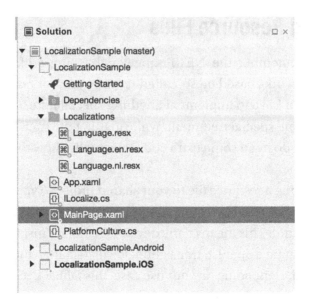

Figure 5-9. *Resource files in a sample project*

The resource files are XML files and, when they're saved, an equivalent C# class is generated. By default, this class is declared with the `internal` modifier. While this is usually enough for usage inside your app, it does not work if you want to access them from XAML. On Windows, Visual Studio has a built-in editor for resource files. When you go in there, you have the ability to set the access level. Visual Studio on Mac does not have an editor at the time of writing. To mark the generated class as public, you need to go to the properties of the resource file and set the value for Custom Tool to `PublicResXFileCodeGenerator`. You can see the Properties editor in the screenshot in Figure 5-10.

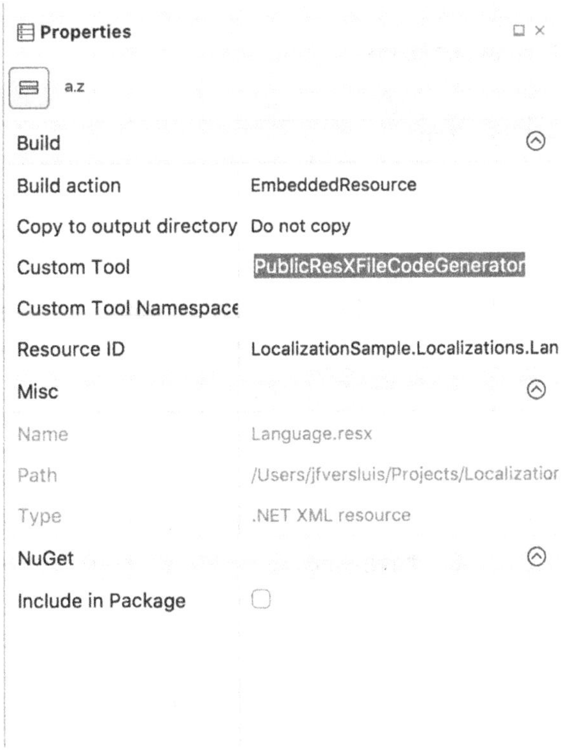

Figure 5-10. *Setting the Custom tool to generate a public class*

To be sure a new class is generated, open the resource file (in this case Language. resx), make a trivial change like adding a space, and save the file.

Note   The generated class is only important for the generic resource file. While classes are generated for the language-specific files, those could be omitted if you want.

Now we can start creating content in our resource files and start consuming them in our app. Again, on Windows there is a nice editor for resource files that you can use. In Visual Studio for Mac this is not yet available. Let's look at a sample XML resource file. You can see it in Listing 5-20.

Listing 5-20. Sample Resource File in English

```
<?xml version="1.0" encoding="utf-8"?>
<root>
```

```
<resheader name="resmimetype">
    <value>text/microsoft-resx</value>
</resheader>
<resheader name="version">
    <value>2.0</value>
</resheader>
<resheader name="reader">
    <value>System.Resources.ResXResourceReader, System.Windows.Forms,
    Version=4.0.0.0, Culture=neutral, PublicKeyToken=b77a5c561934e089</
    value>
</resheader>
<resheader name="writer">
    <value>System.Resources.ResXResourceWriter, System.Windows.Forms,
    Version=4.0.0.0, Culture=neutral, PublicKeyToken=b77a5c561934e089</
    value>
</resheader>
<data name="WelcomeToXamarin" xml:space="preserve">
    <value>Welcome to Xamarin.Forms!</value>
    <comment>Text for welcome label</comment>
</data>
</root>
```

The most important node here is the data node. The rest should be there by default and should be kept in there, but the data nodes will contain your translations. In the name attribute, you define the key that will be used to retrieve the translation. This needs to be the same in all your translated resource files. The xml:space attribute is needed to preserve the spaces in your values. Then in the enclosed value node, you specify the actual human-readable version of your string. With the comment node, you can add a comment for the translator to give some context on how this value is used. This will become a comment that is shown in the IntelliSense in the generated C# class for that resource file. The comment node is optional.

Note   If you want to use characters that are also part of the XML format, like < or > or &, remember to escape them in their encoded format like <, >, and &, respectively.

You can now start consuming your resources in your XAML or code. Observe the code in Listing 5-21 to see a simple sample page that shows the text from the resource file.

Listing 5-21. Consuming the Resource File to Translate Our UI

```
<?xml version="1.0" encoding="utf-8"?>
<ContentPage xmlns="http://xamarin.com/schemas/2014/forms"
xmlns:x="http://schemas.microsoft.com/winfx/2009/xaml" xmlns:i18n="clr-
namespace:LocalizationSample.Localizations" x:Class="LocalizationSample.
MainPage">
    <StackLayout>
        <Label Text="{x:Static i18n:Language.WelcomeToXamarin}"
        HorizontalOptions="Center" VerticalOptions="CenterAndExpand" />
    </StackLayout>
</ContentPage>
```

With the static markup extension, you can easily access keys in your resource files. The Label in these code references the key in our resource file in the Text property. To make this possible, you need to import the right namespace to the resource file. In this case, it is declared with the i18n: prefix.

We now have everything in place to work with our translations. However, they will not be shown just yet. We have to do some extra work to make them visible. This involves creating a per-platform service with the use of the dependency service.

In the shared code of the project, define an interface like the one shown in Listing 5-22.

Listing 5-22. Interface in Our Shared Code for Use with the Dependency Service

```
public interface ILocalize
{
    CultureInfo GetCurrentCultureInfo ();
    void SetLocale (CultureInfo ci);
}
```

As you can see, the classes that will implement this interface need to implement a method to return the current culture and set a culture. This is mostly needed because the way an OS handles localization differs. There is even some difference is a few localization codes between platforms.

Also, in your shared code, go into your `App.xaml.cs` file and add the piece of code from Listing 5-23 in your app loading sequence. You can add it in the constructor of the App object.

Listing 5-23. Setting the Right Culture on App Startup

```
if (Device.RuntimePlatform == Device.iOS || Device.RuntimePlatform ==
Device.Android)
{
    var ci = DependencyService.Get<ILocalize>().GetCurrentCultureInfo();
    Resx.AppResources.Culture = ci;
    DependencyService.Get<ILocalize>().SetLocale(ci);
}
```

You will notice that we are only running this code on iOS and Android. For Windows platforms, the language is automatically set and picked up, so we do not need to do anything special there. You might need to repeat calling this code whenever the user can choose a language at runtime. Note that you will also have to implement some mechanism to reload your bindings on your labels at runtime.

Before we go and look at the code that is needed for the specific platforms, we need to implement a small helper class that is used in the platform implementations of the `ILocalize` interface. You can see it in Listing 5-24.

Listing 5-24. Helper Class for Setting and Retrieving the Culture

```
public class PlatformCulture
{
    public PlatformCulture (string platformCultureString)
    {
        if (String.IsNullOrEmpty(platformCultureString))
        {
            throw new ArgumentException("Expected culture identifier", name
            of(platformCultureString));
        }
        PlatformString = platformCultureString.Replace("_", "-"); // .NET
        expects dash, not underscore
        var dashIndex = PlatformString.IndexOf("-", StringComparison.Ordinal);
```

```
        if (dashIndex > 0)
        {
            var parts = PlatformString.Split('-');
            LanguageCode = parts[0];
            LocaleCode = parts[1];
        }
        else
        {
            LanguageCode = PlatformString;
            LocaleCode = "";
        }
    }
    public string PlatformString { get; private set; }
    public string LanguageCode { get; private set; }
    public string LocaleCode { get; private set; }
    public override string ToString()
    {
        return PlatformString;
    }
}
```

First, let's look at how we can implement this on iOS. You can see it in Listing 5-25. iOS uses underscores instead of dashes, which is used in .NET, for the culture identifiers. That is why we need the helper class.

Listing 5-25. Implementation of ILocalize on iOS to Set and Retrieve the Culture

```
[assembly:Dependency(typeof(LocalizationSample.iOS.Localize))]
namespace LocalizationSample.iOS
{
    public class Localize : ILocalize
    {
        public void SetLocale (CultureInfo ci)
        {
            Thread.CurrentThread.CurrentCulture = ci;
            Thread.CurrentThread.CurrentUICulture = ci;
        }
```

```
public CultureInfo GetCurrentCultureInfo ()
{
    var netLanguage = "en";

    if (NSLocale.PreferredLanguages.Length > 0)
    {
        var pref = NSLocale.PreferredLanguages [0];
        netLanguage = iOSToDotnetLanguage(pref);
    }

    // this gets called a lot - try/catch can be expensive so
    consider caching or something
    System.Globalization.CultureInfo ci = null;
    try
    {
        ci = new System.Globalization.CultureInfo(netLanguage);
    }
    catch (CultureNotFoundException e1)
    {
        // iOS locale not valid .NET culture (eg. "en-ES" : English
        in Spain)
        // fallback to first characters, in this case "en"
        try
        {
            var fallback = ToDotnetFallbackLanguage(new
            PlatformCulture(netLanguage));
            ci = new System.Globalization.CultureInfo(fallback);
        }
        catch (CultureNotFoundException e2)
        {
            // iOS language not valid .NET culture, falling back to
            English
            ci = new System.Globalization.CultureInfo("en");
        }
    }
    return ci;
}
```

```csharp
private string iOSToDotnetLanguage(string iOSLanguage)
{
    var netLanguage = iOSLanguage;

    //certain languages need to be converted to CultureInfo equivalent
    switch (iOSLanguage)
    {
        case "ms-MY":    // "Malaysian (Malaysia)" not supported
        .NET culture
        case "ms-SG":    // "Malaysian (Singapore)" not supported
        .NET culture
            netLanguage = "ms"; // closest supported
            break;
        case "gsw-CH":  // "Schwiizertüütsch (Swiss German)" not
        supported .NET culture
            netLanguage = "de-CH"; // closest supported
            break;
        // add more application-specific cases here (if required)
        // ONLY use cultures that have been tested and known to work
    }
    return netLanguage;
}

private string ToDotnetFallbackLanguage (PlatformCulture
platCulture)
{
    var netLanguage = platCulture.LanguageCode; // use the first
    part of the identifier (two chars, usually);

    switch (platCulture.LanguageCode)
    {
        case "pt":
            netLanguage = "pt-PT"; // fallback to Portuguese
            (Portugal)
            break;
        case "gsw":
```

```
                netLanguage = "de-CH"; // equivalent to German
                (Switzerland) for this app
                break;
            // add more application-specific cases here (if required)
            // ONLY use cultures that have been tested and known to work
        }
        return netLanguage;
    }
  }
}
```

The SetLocale method is very simple; we just set the current thread culture references to a new instance with the new culture and it is set. The GetCurrentCultureInfo is a bit more extensive. You can see some translating to .NET culture names going on. Also, here are some private helper methods to make this all possible.

To also translate the OS controls for your iOS app, you need to add the supported languages to your info.plist file. OS-specific controls are, for instance, the Done button on a datepicker. In Listing 5-26, you can see a sample key that you need to add to the info.plist file.

Listing 5-26. The Info.plist keys to Translate the OS Controls

```
<key>CFBundleLocalizations</key>
<array>
    <string>de</string>
    <string>es</string>
    <string>nl</string>
</array>
```

This key will enable your app to show localized controls for German, Spanish, and Dutch. English is always included by default.

On Android, we have a similar class that implements the ILocalize interface. You can see it in Listing 5-27. Android also uses underscores instead of the dashes that .NET needs to recognize the culture.

Listing 5-27. Implementation of ILocalize on Android to Set and Retrieve the Culture

```
[assembly:Dependency(typeof(LocalizationSample.Android.Localize))]
namespace LocalizationSample.Android
{
    public class Localize : ILocalize
    {
        public void SetLocale(CultureInfo ci)
        {
            Thread.CurrentThread.CurrentCulture = ci;
            Thread.CurrentThread.CurrentUICulture = ci;
        }

        public CultureInfo GetCurrentCultureInfo()
        {
            var netLanguage = "en";
            var androidLocale = Java.Util.Locale.Default;
            netLanguage = AndroidToDotnetLanguage(androidLocale.ToString().
            Replace("_", "-"));
            // this gets called a lot - try/catch can be expensive so
            consider caching or something
            System.Globalization.CultureInfo ci = null;
            try
            {
                ci = new System.Globalization.CultureInfo(netLanguage);
            }
            catch (CultureNotFoundException e1)
            {
                // iOS locale not valid .NET culture (eg. "en-ES" : English
                in Spain)
                // fallback to first characters, in this case "en"
                try
                {
                    var fallback = ToDotnetFallbackLanguage(new
                    PlatformCulture(netLanguage));
```

```
            ci = new System.Globalization.CultureInfo(fallback);
        }
        catch (CultureNotFoundException e2)
        {
            // iOS language not valid .NET culture, falling back to
            English
            ci = new System.Globalization.CultureInfo("en");
        }
    }
    return ci;
}

private string AndroidToDotnetLanguage(string androidLanguage)
{
    var netLanguage = androidLanguage;
    //certain languages need to be converted to CultureInfo
    equivalent
    switch (androidLanguage)
    {
        case "ms-BN":   // "Malaysian (Brunei)" not supported .NET
                        culture
        case "ms-MY":   // "Malaysian (Malaysia)" not supported
                        .NET culture
        case "ms-SG":   // "Malaysian (Singapore)" not supported
                        .NET culture
            netLanguage = "ms"; // closest supported
            break;
        case "in-ID":   // "Indonesian (Indonesia)" has different
                        code in  .NET
            netLanguage = "id-ID"; // correct code for .NET
            break;
        case "gsw-CH":  // "Schwiizertüütsch (Swiss German)" not
                        supported .NET culture
            netLanguage = "de-CH"; // closest supported
            break;
            // add more application-specific cases here (if required)
```

```
            // ONLY use cultures that have been tested and known to work
        }
        return netLanguage;
    }
    string ToDotnetFallbackLanguage(PlatformCulture platCulture)
    {
        var netLanguage = platCulture.LanguageCode; // use the first
        part of the identifier (two chars, usually);
        switch (platCulture.LanguageCode)
        {
            case "gsw":
                netLanguage = "de-CH"; // equivalent to German
                (Switzerland) for this app
                break;
                // add more application-specific cases here (if required)
                // ONLY use cultures that have been tested and known to
                work
        }
        return netLanguage;
    }
}
}
```

This class is basically the same exercise as with iOS. The SetLocale is even identical to the one on iOS. In the GetCurrentCultureInfo method, there is also some translation to the .NET ecosystem going on.

Like I have mentioned, on Windows this just works, so this does not need any specific implementation.

This is everything that is needed to add translations to your app. As I have said— when you do not implement anything specifically to reload the language at runtime, you will only see the newly set language on new pages or for the whole app when you restart it. In a moment we will see how we can account for this a bit easier.

If you want to test a specific culture without having to switch the emulator or device's culture, you can use this line of code:

```
AppResources.Culture = new CultureInfo("fr-FR");
```

This sets the locale to French. Set this as early as possible when loading your app. This can also be used to set the locale independent of the device if you choose to provide your users with such a feature.

Tip   For everything on localization, you can also see the Microsoft Docs page for more information: `https://docs.microsoft.com/en-us/xamarin/ xamarin-forms/app-fundamentals/localization/text`.

Besides the built-in resource loading mechanism, you could also choose to implement an extension. This extension will work for XAML and will load the right extension through code. You can see the implementation of this extension in Listing 5-28.

Listing 5-28.   Implementation of a Markup Extension to Translate Text

```
[ContentProperty("Text")]
public class TranslateExtension : IMarkupExtension
{
    private readonly CultureInfo ci = null;
    private const string ResourceId = "LocalizationSample.Localizations.
    Language";

    static readonly Lazy<ResourceManager> ResMgr = new
    Lazy<ResourceManager>(
        () => new ResourceManager(ResourceId, typeof(TranslateExtension).
        GetTypeInfo().Assembly));

    public string Text { get; set; }

    public TranslateExtension()
    {
        if (Device.RuntimePlatform == Device.iOS || Device.RuntimePlatform
        == Device.Android)
        {
            ci = DependencyService.Get<ILocalize>().GetCurrentCultureInfo();
        }
    }
```

```
    public object ProvideValue(IServiceProvider serviceProvider)
    {
        if (Text == null)
            return string.Empty;

        var translation = ResMgr.Value.GetString(Text, ci);
        if (translation == null)
        {
#if DEBUG
            throw new ArgumentException(
                string.Format("Key '{0}' was not found in resources '{1}'
                for culture '{2}'.", Text, ResourceId, ci.Name));
#else
            translation = Text; // HACK: returns the key, which GETS
            DISPLAYED TO THE USER
#endif
        }
        return translation;
    }
}
```

What this extension does is take in the key that is specified in XAML and go through the resource files to get the corresponding value. This is basically what the .NET Framework normally does for you. This extension gives you a number of advantages.

For one, you can extend it. At some point in a project, the designers wanted to show text in uppercase for some headings. This can easily be done by adding a property to this extension and returning the text as uppercase depending on that property value.

Another thing you might notice is that it returns a key as a value whenever no translation is found. While this is not ideal, it helps you identify untranslated texts in a certain language.

Lastly, you can incorporate logic in here to reload the extension on the fly, eliminating the need to restart the app to show a new language after the user has changed it in-app.

Tip   For a sample repository showing the different ways of localization, look at `https://github.com/jfversluis/LocalizationSample`.

Localize Using i18n Portable

There is also a pretty good extension out there that can help you translating your UI. This plugin is called *I18N-Portable*. It is very easy to implement and takes a couple of things out of your hands. The most notable one is the option to really easily reload languages at runtime.

Installation happens through NuGet. Just add the I18NPortable package. You will only need to add it to your shared code. After the installation is complete, we need a couple of lines to initialize the plugin. You can do the initialization in a fluent way, which allows you to configure some settings while you're at it. Look at Listing 5-29 for a sample initialization.

Listing 5-29. Initializing the I18NPortable Plugin

```
I18N.Current
    // Optional: when a key is not found, it will appear as $key$
    .SetNotFoundSymbol("$")
    // Optional but recommended: locale to load when system locale isn't
    supported
    .SetFallbackLocale("en")
    // Optional: Throws exception when keys aren't found (recommended only
    for debugging)
    .SetThrowWhenKeyNotFound(true)
    // action to output traces
    .SetLogger(text => Debug.WriteLine(text))
    // Optional: Directory containing resource files (defaults to "Locales")
    .SetResourcesFolder("I18NPortable")
    // assembly where locales live
    .Init(GetType().GetTypeInfo().Assembly);
```

You should place this code somewhere early on in your app to load the correct language. A good place would be when instantiating the App object in your App.xaml. cs file. The most important line is the last one, starting with Init. With this line you specify in which assembly the localization files are situated. The other options from top to bottom are explained in the comments.

With the code in Listing 5-29, there should be a folder called `I18NPortable` that holds the files with the different languages. The file structure is different than the resource files we have seen before. By default, it is a flat TXT file in the following format: `TranslationKey = Translated Text`. The filename indicates the locale, for instance, for English the filename would be `en.txt` and for Dutch `nl.txt`. There is support for multiline—both with \n and line breaks—string formats and normal string of course. There is also a JSON reader available if you'd like your locale files to be in JSON format. If you want another format you have the ability to roll your own. Don't forget to set the build action of your files to Embedded Resource.

There are several ways to translate your text. From code you could do: `"TranslationKey".Translate();`. This will translate it to the right value depending on the current locale. You even have the possibility to translate enum values. Imagine you have an enum called `Animals`, which list a couple of types of animals. In your locale text file, define the translations, as shown in Listing 5-30.

Listing 5-30. Defining enum Translations for I18NPortable

```
# Enums are supported
Animals.Dog = Perro
Animals.Cat = Gato
Animals.Rat = Rata
Animals.Tiger = Tigre
Animals.Monkey = Mono
```

As you can see, you will define each value of the enum together with the translated value. In code, you can get the translated value like this:

```
string dog = Animals.Dog.Translate();
```

Of course, all of this goodness can also be used from XAML. Because the I18N class implements the `INotifyPropertyChanged` interface, it makes it ideal for reloading translations.

The easiest would be is to create a public property to expose the current I18N instance in a base class. A sample can be seen in Listing 5-31.

Listing 5-31. Sample Implementation to Expose the Translations in a View Model

```
public abstract class BaseViewModel
{
    public II18N Strings => I18N.Current;
}
```

Now, each class that inherits from the `BaseViewModel` will have a property `Strings`. With that property you can retrieve translations by its key. To reload them at runtime, you might need to implement some code to let the UI know a "change" has happened when the language is switched. More on this in a little bit. First, let's look at how to define a translation in XAML. To show a translated value in a label control you could define it like this: `<Label Text="{Binding Strings[TranslationKey]}" />`. When running the app, it will show the associated, translated, text.

Back to the reloading. When I have implemented this in a project, what I did was add a handler through the Xamarin.Forms MessagingCenter. By subscribing to an event, I did a reload of the `Strings` property. When setting a new locale from within the app I fire a message that triggers the event. You can see the relevant pieces of code in Listing 5-32.

Listing 5-32. Reloading the Language Runtime

```
// Put a message on the bus indicating the language changed
MessagingCenter.Send(this, "lang_changed");

// Act on the message and let the current view model know to reload the
locale
MessagingCenter.Subscribe<SettingsViewModel>(this, "lang_changed", (vm) =>
{
    OnPropertyChanged(nameof(Strings));
});
```

By implementing it like this, all translated text will be reloaded.

Note   All details about the I18N-Portable plugin can be found on the project website: `https://github.com/xleon/I18N-Portable`. It is also in the example repository that was mentioned earlier.

With this, I leave you to discover the rest by yourself. There are some more details to discover, but this is the most important part when using I18NPortable.

Summary

In this chapter we saw a couple of business use cases that can be realized with Xamarin. Forms apps. Of course, there are infinitely more scenarios that we can come up with, but I hope this will give you a good overview.

PDF files are still a very common file format for sending documents and it is no surprise that a lot of companies want to show invoices or signed documents from within their app. We have seen how we can show a PDF file across platforms.

Another technology that has been around for a long time are barcodes. In a warehouse or other product-handling scenarios, barcodes are still heavily used. We have learned how we can incorporate a barcode scanner in our app and extract data from it. With that data you can do the rest of the processing. Also, when you want to show data in barcode form, that is something we can do now as well.

Gathering analytics or crash reports can be invaluable when your app is released into the wild. Information that you get from the user is not always that reliable. Remember, they might not have the technical background that you have. In their world it just doesn't work. They cannot provide you with the detailed information that you need. By incorporating App Center into your apps, it is very easy to extract the information you need and gain valuable insights on what happens with your app.

When you do release multiple app versions, versioning is a big topic. You want to be able to identify what happens in a specific version and how that ties into your code. This makes for better traceability and maintainability.

Lastly, we saw how to translate the UI of our app. If we want more users to get engaged with our app, we must speak their language! Make sure translations are a part of your app and the user will feel more at home.

CHAPTER 6

Advanced Topics

While working with Xamarin over the years, we've noticed that there are certain topics that we come across regularly in forums or websites like our beloved StackOverflow. These topics are apparently causing problems for a lot of people out there. This chapter bundles a few of these topics with the goal of clarifying a bit of background and offer a solution.

That is basically what we have been doing throughout the course of this book, but this chapter will cover some more extensive topics. We will start you off with converting your *Portable Class Libraries* (PCL) projects to .NET Standard. You might have some "legacy" projects lying around which use an older PCL library. With the introduction of .NET Standard, PCLs have become obsolete and will be replaced by .NET Standard from now on.

The size of a Xamarin app will always be slightly more than a truly native app. This is caused by the fact that we have to incorporate .NET assemblies. When building an app with the Android or iOS runtime, their libraries will already be available on the device. In this chapter, we will show you how to reduce the size of your app as much as possible by using the linker and some other techniques.

Another common issue is the signing and distribution of apps. This can be a bit of a painful process. Especially the timing isn't optimal: you just worked hard and overcame all kinds of challenges while building a beautiful app, thinking you're done, only to find one last bump in the road. No more! In this chapter we will tell you all there is to know for iOS and Android. Publishing your app will be a breeze after this.

For several years now, Xamarin.Forms has been opensource. This not only means that you can have a look under the hood, it also means that you can start tinkering under that same hood. We have been doing contributions to Forms, simply because we were missing some feature or we wanted to give something back to the product that we love to use. Therefore, the last part of this chapter—and this book—will tell you a little bit

© Gerald Versluis and Steven Thewissen 2019
G. Versluis and S. Thewissen, *Xamarin.Forms Solutions*, https://doi.org/10.1007/978-1-4842-4134-9_6

about the process of contributing to Xamarin.Forms. Not necessarily an issue that you would want a solution for, but hopefully still interesting to read and it might inspire you to contribute as well!

Converting a PCL to .NET Standard

For years the Portable Class Library (PCL) was the go-to solution to host our shared code (let's ignore Shared Projects). It's the type of project Xamarin provided us with out-of-the-box so you may have some of these projects lying around. However, with the rise of .NET Standard libraries it is quickly becoming the less popular option. At the time of writing there is no reason to not use a .NET Standard library instead, so let's take a look at how we can upgrade our existing project.

Why Should We Upgrade?

.NET Standard is a specification of the .NET APIs that can be used on all of the Xamarin platform projects like iOS, Android, and UWP. It is similar to a PCL, but it's easier to use and contains a universal set of classes from the base class library (BCL). That means we can be sure that our library can be used anywhere where .NET Standard can run. This has a few advantages compared to using a PCL:

- *Interchangeable*—.NET Standard contains a set of APIs that are carefully selected and known to be interchangeable.

- *Platform independent*—The predefined PCL profiles are simply representations of the different platforms while .NET Standard is independent of any of them.

- *Versioned*—.NET Standard is versioned and is completely backward compatible.

Besides these advantages it is also considered to be the waytogo moving forward. It replaces PCLs and Shared Projects.A lot of existing NuGet packages have already migrated to .NET Standard and so should we!

Upgrading to .NET Standard

The process of upgrading our PCL project to .NET is relatively simple. We need to perform a few simple steps:

1. Create a backup of our solution, just to be sure.

2. Open the .csproj file for our shared project in a text editor and delete everything in it. Alternatively, you could unload the project in Visual Studio and edit the .csproj file from there.

3. Copy the code shown in Listing 6-1 into the .csproj file.

4. Add back all the NuGet packages that the PCL project had. The simplest way to do this is to open the packages.config file and add all of the packages references.

5. Delete the AssemblyInfo.cs and packages.config files.

6. Add back any references to other projects.

And that's it! We've now successfully upgraded our PCL project to .NET Standard. Whenever we want to create a new Xamarin.Forms application .NET Standard is the way to go because it's the next evolution of Portable Class Libraries.

As of this writing the only problem we might run into is when we are using a NuGet package that does not support .NET Standard yet. The other way around can be the case as well. There are libraries that only support .NET Standard, so you should either install an older version (and be aware of all of the risks that come with it) or find an alternative package.

Listing 6-1. An Empty .NET Standard Project Template

```
<Project Sdk="Microsoft.NET.Sdk">
<PropertyGroup>
<TargetFramework>netstandard2.0</TargetFramework>
</PropertyGroup>
<ItemGroup>
<!-- This is an example of how NuGet packages are listed in .csproj
<PackageReference Include="Xamarin.Forms" Version="3.0.0.482510" />
    -->
</ItemGroup>
</Project>
```

Reducing the Size of Our App

When creating our app, we also need to take the size of the final binary into consideration. Adding images or other media to our application can quickly increase the file size of our app, making it less appealing for users to download over a non-WiFi connection due to the additional costs incurred. If the users have to wait an extended period of time before they can start the app, because it takes a long time to download, they may uninstall it before it was even opened. Disk space on a user's device is also limited, so we need to ensure that we don't take up the majority of it. This section will cover some tips and tricks that can help reduce the size of our app.

What Does Xamarin Already Do for Us?

Xamarin already uses a variety of mechanisms to minimize package size for us while maintaining an efficient debug and release deploy process. One of these mechanisms is the *linker*. The linker runs static code analysis over our application and will remove assemblies, types, members and other code that is not used or referenced by our code. This process is often referred to as *linking*. The linker settings can be found by going to the Options of our iOS or Android project and looking at the platform-specific Build settings. See Figure 6-1.

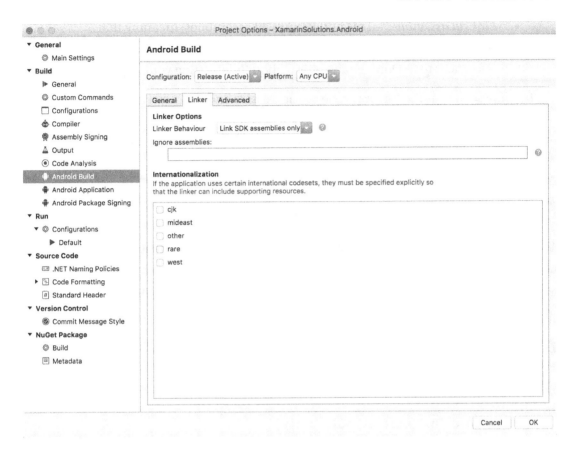

Figure 6-1. *The Linker Behavior setting in the Android Build options*

Figure 6-1 illustrates the location of the Linker Behavior setting for a Xamarin. Android project. It is in a similar location for Xamarin.iOS. This setting has one of three possible values:

- *Don't link*—This option completely turns off the linker, which is useful for troubleshooting problems we may encounter at runtime, to see if the linker is responsible. All .NET assemblies, types, and members will be included in our app package, even though we don't use them in our code. It is not advised to use this setting for production builds.

- *Link SDK assemblies only*—The safest option of the three, which should be your default choice. This option only links assemblies that come with the platform (Xamarin.iOS or Xamarin.Android). In other words, only code in these SDK assemblies is stripped by the linker. All of the other assemblies such as our own code are not stripped.

- *Link all assemblies*—This option links all assemblies, meaning that some of our own code may also be removed if there are no static references to it. Don't enable this without fully testing your app.

In some scenarios the linker can be too aggressive and proceeds to strip away code that it should not have removed. A common occurrence of this is when an object is only referenced through reflection. When this happens, you will run into errors like a `MissingMethodException`.

Fixing Errors Caused by the Linker

To fix any errors created by the linker stripping out code, we can create a simple class containing method calls to the methods the linker is removing. This is the easiest way to solve the issue because it creates a reference to our code causing the linker to ignore it. See Listing 6-2.

Listing 6-2. Creating a Fake Class to Fool the Linker Into Thinking We're Using It

```
public class DontLinkThese
{
    public void Init(OurCustomClass arg)
    {
        arg.DontRemoveThisMethod();
    }
}
```

The method shown in Listing 6-2 will never actually be called by our code. Its only function is to reference the `DontRemoveThisMethod` method so the linker cannot remove it. Another trick we can use is to add the `Preserve` attribute to a class or method, which will instruct the linker to ignore it. The code in Listing 6-3 shows how to apply this attribute.

Listing 6-3. Using the Preserve Attribute to Instruct the Linker to Not Remove a Specific Class

```
// We can use it on the assembly level
[assembly: Preserve (typeof (MyClass), AllMembers = true)]
```

```
// Or add it above a class or method
[Preserve (AllMembers = true)]
public class MyClass
{
    ...
}
```

If this doesn't cover your needs we can also define our linker configuration through XML. We can provide extra definitions to the linker to ensure that certain types, methods and/or fields are not stripped from our application. We do this by creating a new XML file and adding it to our iOS and Android projects and setting the Build Action for these files to LinkDescription. Listing 6-4 shows an example of such a configuration file.

Listing 6-4. Configuring Our Linker Through XML

```
<linker>
<assembly fullname="mscorlib">
<type fullname="System.Environment">
<field name="mono_corlib_version" />
<method name="get_StackTrace" />
</type>
</assembly>
<assembly fullname="Just.Another.Assembly">
<type fullname="MyType" preserve="fields">
<method name=".ctor" />
</type>
<type fullname="MySecondType">
<method signature="System.Void .ctor(System.String)" />
<field signature="System.String _myParameter" />
</type>
<namespace fullname="Just.Another.Namespace" />
<type fullname="Just.Another*" />
</assembly>
</linker>
```

We defined an XML file where the top-level `linker` element contains two `assembly` nodes, which in turn contain `type` nodes, which in turn contain `method` and `field` nodes. In this sample, the linker will only apply linking to the `mscorlib` and `Just.Another. Assembly` assemblies.

In the first sample, we tell the linker that it shouldn't touch both the `mono_ corlib_version` field and the `get_StackTrace` method in the `System.Environment` assembly. This means they will not be stripped from the assembly, even if the linker can't find any references to them. Note that the `StackTrace` property getter method is used here instead of the property name. This is due to the linker working with Intermediate Language (IL), which means it doesn't understand the actual properties.

The second sample ensures that all of the fields in the `MyType` type are preserved together with all of its constructors. It also uses the `MySecondType` declaration to ensure that a specific constructor and field are preserved. The third entry in this definition ensures that the entire `Just.Another.Namespace` and all of its containing types are preserved. Lastly, the fourth entry defines that any type containing the `Just.Another` prefix is preserved.

Using an Icon Font Instead of Images

There are a lot of different devices and form factors out there in the mobile world. All of these devices have different screen densities and resolutions to consider. When we're adding an image to our application the platform would like us to provide this image in different resolutions to be able to support all of these different devices.

Let's imagine we're creating an application which contains a lot of image resources such as icons. Some of these icons may even be present in different colors throughout the design of the application. If each of these icons has to be created in a variety of resolutions and different colors, the number of image files grows exponentially, which in turn bloats the file size of our app. As can be seen in Figure 6-2, we need at least nine images to support the entire range of screen densities on Android and iOS.

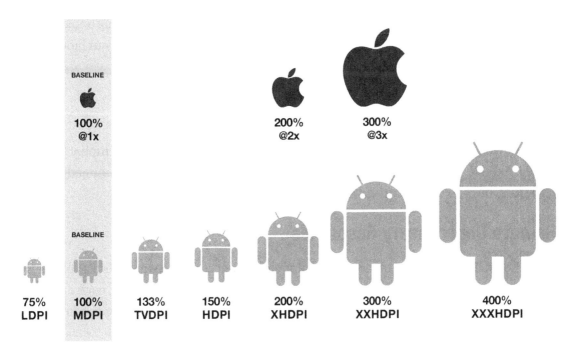

Figure 6-2. *The different image densities as required on Android and iOS*

Replacing Images with an Icon Font

A very simple solution that can eliminate the need for a lot of these icon-like images is to
create a font out of them. There are existing icon fonts out there, such as FontAwesome,
which may suit our needs. However, if the customer requires us to add custom
iconography to the app turning these icons into a font has a few added benefits:

- Significantly smaller file size—A font file containing around 40 icons
  comes in around 10 KB in file size. That's less than just one of our old
  PNG files!

- Unlimited scaling—Because the icons are added into the icon font as
  vectors, they can be scaled infinitely. If the customer decides that an icon
  needs to be bigger ,it's simply a matter of increasing the font size instead
  of going into an image editing tool and creating nine different new icons.

- Extensive color possibilities—Since we're using a font we can use all
  of the available text colors of the platform to color our icons. That's
  like 16 million colors we can use without having to ever touch an
  image editing tool!

Adding a custom font has been extensively discussed in Chapter 2 of this book. After adding the custom font, we can use all of the available glyphs as the text of our labels, buttons, and other elements within the app!

Additional File Size Improvements

The following sections describe some additional techniques that you can employ to reduce file size. Some of the techniques may seem obvious, like removing unneeded resources, but you'd be surprised at how often that work goes undone.

Remove Unnecessary Resources

It may seem like stating the obvious, but removing unnecessary resources is one of the easiest things we can do to decrease the size of our app. During its lifetime, each app goes through a lot of changes, some of which can make certain resources redundant. If we don't actually remove these resources they still add to our file size.

Splitting Your App Binary

When supporting multiple architectures, it may be beneficial to split the Android APK file. This is done through the Multiple APK support feature on Google Play,by enabling Generate One Package (.apk) Per Selected ABI in the options of our Android project. This results in separate APK files for each architecture we support, meaning we limit the amount of overhead to support other architectures in our binary.

Similar functionality is available for iOS where it's called app thinning. This is a feature that's available on the AppStore and enables Apple to only send you the necessary code for the architecture you're running on when downloading an app.

Compress Images

Besides icons that we can extract into a font, our app might also contain other high-quality images such as full color pictures. If these images are bundled within the app they will add to the file size of the binary. Compressing these images can result in an impressive reduction in file size.

Signing and Deploying Our Code

For the majority of this book we have been talking about developing our application. However, at some point we will have to deploy it to the AppStore and/or Play Store. To get our app binaries submitted to the store successfully, we will first need to sign them. This process ensures that the code has not been altered or corrupted since it was signed and confirms that the signing party is who they say they are.

Automatic Provisioning on iOS

Debugging on a physical device is always beneficial for the development of our app. We get to see how our app will behave when it's out there "in the wild" instead of in a mocked local environment such as the iOS simulator. However, the process around iOS device provisioning is one of the biggest gripes most Xamarin developers have with iOS. The provisioning process contains a lot of moving parts, such as:

- Enrolling in Apple's Developer Program

- Creating a certificate to sign the app

- Creating an app ID

- Registering our device with Apple

When all of these steps have taken care of, we need to sign our app build with the certificate that our device has been granted access to through a provisioning profile. This provisioning profile controls which devices are allowed to have a certain build of the app installed. Setting all of this up manually is a tedious and fault-intolerant process. Luckily, to take a lot of this hassle out of our hands, the Xamarin team has created an Automatic Provisioning feature.

Note   Due to the fact that manual provisioning for iOS is an extensive process, it will not be covered in depth in this book. At this point in time automatic provisioning is the preferred approach. If you want to learn more about manual provisioning, check out the Microsoft Docs page about this topic at:

```
https://docs.microsoft.com/en-us/xamarin/ios/get-started/
installation/device-provisioning/manual-provisioning
```

Introducing Fastlane

Automatic Provisioning is done through Fastlane, which is an open source platform aimed at simplifying Android and iOS deployment. It can be used in a variety of ways, from manually entering terminal commands to using environment variables in automated builds. Xamarin uses this tool from within Visual Studio to automatically handle the provisioning and signing process for us. This means we can actually focus on creating an awesome app instead of worrying about all of the complicated specifics around iOS provisioning and signing.

Connecting the Apple Account to Visual Studio

To get started with Automatic Provisioning, we first need to connect our Apple account to Visual Studio. By signing in, we enable Visual Studio to perform all the steps described previously automatically. To sign in to our Apple account, we navigate to our Visual Studio for Mac preferences and look at Apple Developer Accounts in the Publishing section (see Figure 6-3).

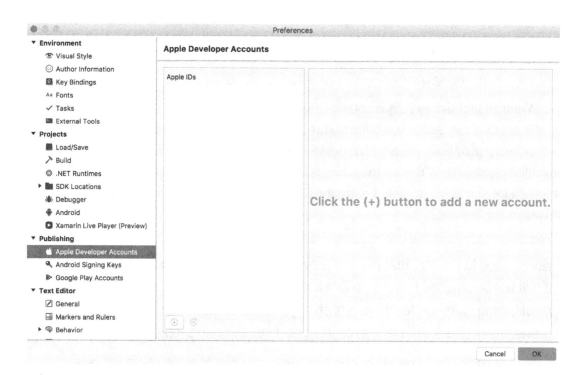

Figure 6-3. *The Apple Developer Accounts section in the Visual Studio for Mac preferences*

From here we can click the Add button and are asked to login to our Apple account with our Apple ID and password. These credentials are saved in a secure location and are securely sent through Fastlane.

Enabling Automatic Provisioning

Once our Apple account is successfully linked to Visual Studio, we can proceed with enabling Automatic Provisioning. This is done in the `Info.plist` file in our Xamarin.iOS project where it's located in the Signing section. See Figure 6-4.

Figure 6-4. *Enabling Automatic Provisioning in Visual Studio for Mac*

After enabling the Automatic Provisioning feature, we will be asked to select a team that will be used to create all the necessary certificates and profiles. If our Apple account contains multiple teams this is where we can distinguish between them. Selecting a team starts the automatic provisioning process, creating an app ID, generating provisioning profiles, and creating a signing identity so we can sign our build.

There are a few scenarios where the Automatic Provisioning feature will update our provisioning artifacts when necessary:

- When a new iOS device is plugged in to the Mac build host —Visual Studio will check to see if the device is already registered on the Apple Developer Portal for the selected team. If this is not the case the device will be added and a new provisioning profile is generated and downloaded which includes this device.

- When the bundle ID of our app is changed—Visual Studio will change the app ID to match the new bundle ID. A new provisioning profile containing this app ID is then generated and downloaded.

- When a supported capability is enabled in the `Entitlements.plist` file—The new capability is added to the current app ID and a new provisioning profile is generated and downloaded. However, at the time of writing not all of the existing iOS capabilities are supported.

Signing and Publishing on iOS

The previous section already described some of the things we will run into when creating a build for a physical iOS device. This chapter will assume that all of the necessary certificates and provisioning profiles are in place. We will describe the process from creating a build to publishing it to the AppStore.

Archive for Publishing

To create a valid app binary that we can deploy to the AppStore, we first need to build our application in Release mode. This strips out all the debug code and performs additional optimizations.

To get an IPA file that we can use for publishing, we need to *archive* our release build. This can be done by choosing Build ➤ Archive for Publishing. It is important to note that the device you've selected cannot be an iOS Simulator. If you do not have a physical device to connect to, you can choose Generic Device from the list of devices. See Figure 6-5.

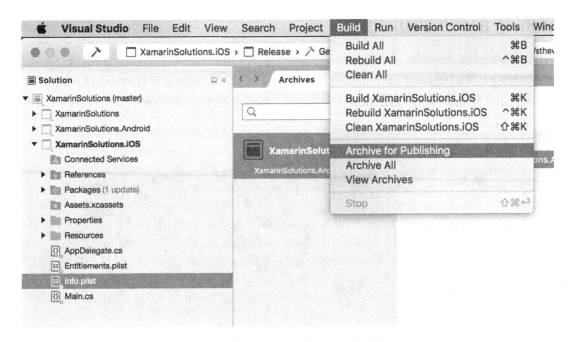

Figure 6-5. *Archiving our iOS release build for publishing*

The resulting archive is the app binary that we can deploy to the AppStore. When the archiving process is done, the Archive Manager is shown. It lists all of our previously created archives, which we can delete or comment on. We can also open the Archive Manager without actually archiving a build by choosing Build ➤ View Archives. See Figure 6-6.

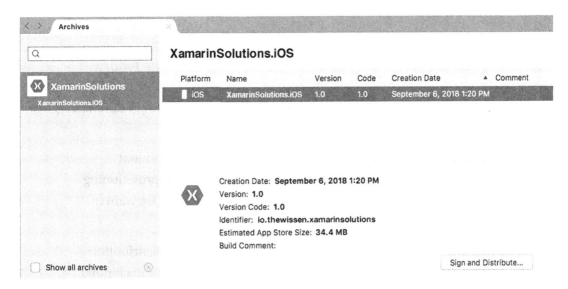

Figure 6-6. *The Archive Manager holding our archived build for iOS*

Signing and Publishing

When we've successfully created an iOS archive, it's time to start signing and publishing it. To sign our application, we simply click the Sign and Distribute button in the Archive Manager. We are then presented a dialog giving us three options, as shown in Figure 6-7.

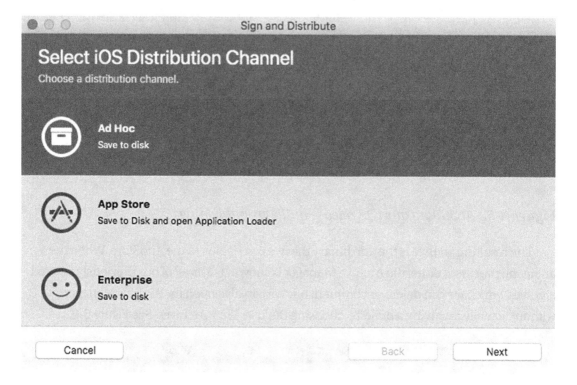

Figure 6-7. *Choosing the right distribution channel for our app binary*

These three different types of distribution channels all create a very different type of app binary.

- *Ad Hoc*—This creates an app build that can only be distributed among people whose devices are present in the Ad Hoc provisioning profile that is used to sign the app. We choose this when we want to create a build for our testers.

- *App Store*—This creates an app build that is suitable for distribution through the AppStore. The AppStore is the main distribution channel when we want to push a new version into production.

- *Enterprise*—This channel enables us to push a new production build outside of the AppStore. To be able to create an Enterprise build, we need to have a valid Apple Developer Enterprise Program, which enables us to create builds for enterprise apps.

All of these options create an IPA file that's stored on disk. However, where these binaries can be deployed to depends on the next step in the process. After choosing our distribution channel and clicking Next, we need to pick a provisioning profile. See Figure 6-8.

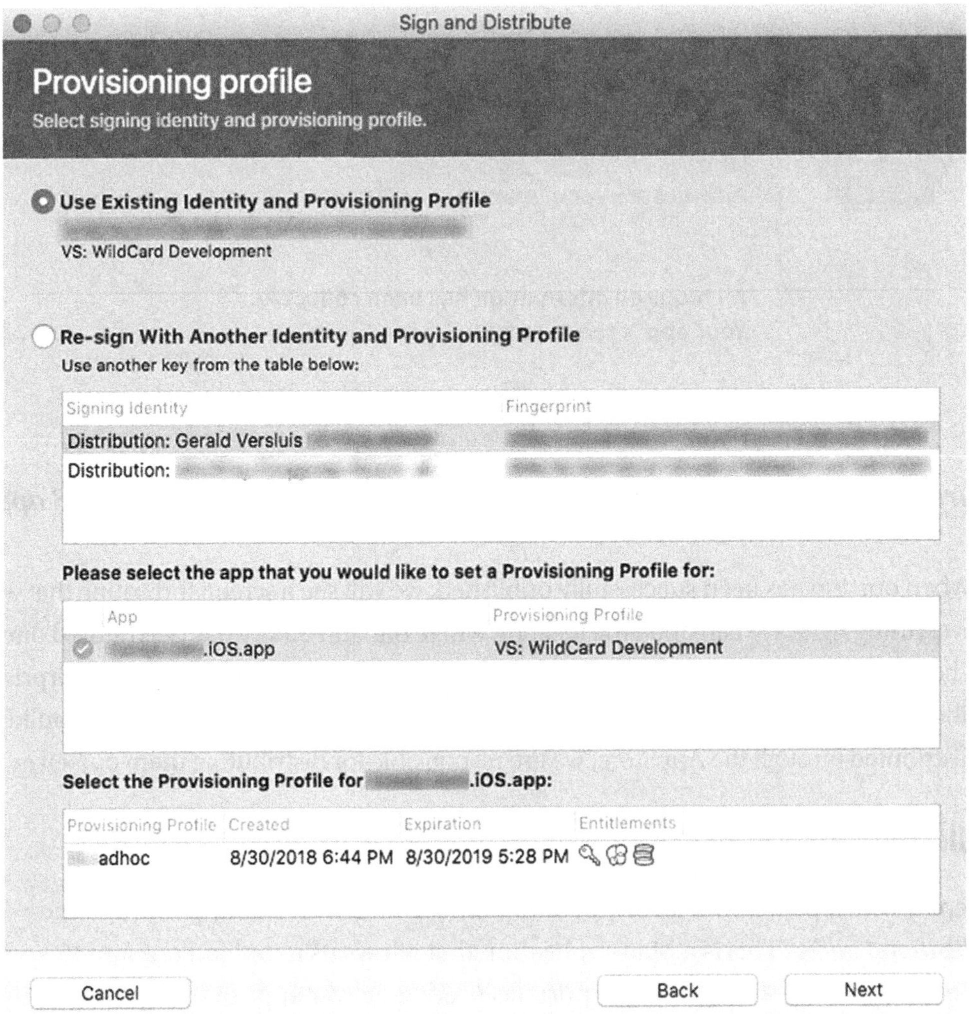

Figure 6-8. *Choosing the provisioning profile to use when publishing an iOS build*

We can use the existing identity and provisioning profile, which is the one that is currently selected in the active project. Another option is to pick a different identity and provisioning profile thatexists in our Apple Developer account. After choosing the profile we want to use, we clickNext and get a quick summary of what app we're publishing. ClickPublish and the publishing process will start. See Figure 6-9.

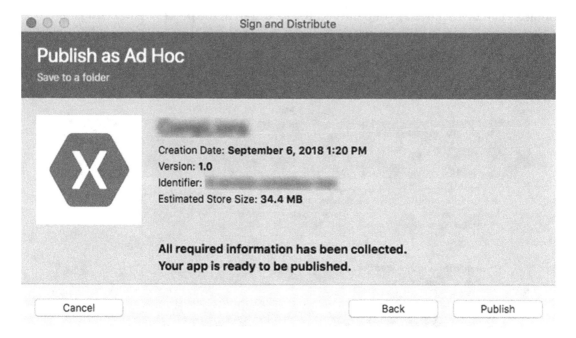

Figure 6-9. *The screen shown when we're ready to start publishing our iOS app*

When our app has been successfully published, we will see a screen indicating that we did everything right. We can open the location where our app binary has been stored directly from here, so we can easily move on to the next step. When choosing Ad Hoc or Enterprise distribution we can immediately start distributing the resulting IPA file. Since these builds are not distributed through the AppStore, we are responsible for distributing them ourselves.

Publishing to the AppStore

To deploy our application to the AppStore, we need to deliver our app through the *Application Loader*. This is a Mac application that allows us to upload our app to *iTunesConnect*. The iTunesConnect portal is used to deliver apps to the AppStore. After starting the Application Loader, we can click on the Deliver Your App button, which will prompt us to select our IPA file. See Figure 6-10.

Figure 6-10. *The Application Loader, which enables us to upload our app to iTunesConnect*

After a few confirmation dialogs, the Application Loader will start the upload process. It also performs a lot of checks to see whether or not your binary conforms to Apple's guidelines (see Figure 6-11). If any problems arise at this point, the Application Loader will notify you of it.

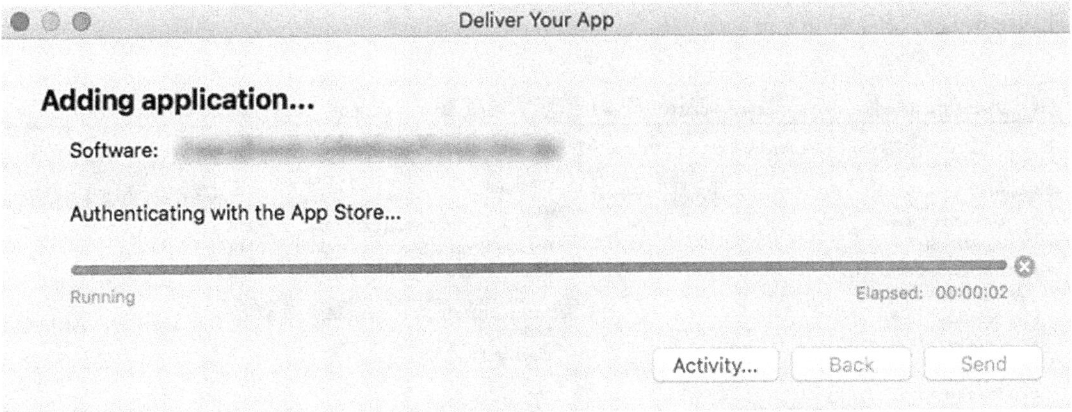

Figure 6-11. *The Application Loader performs some checks and uploads our app*

When the Application Loader is finished, our app is successfully uploaded to iTunesConnect. At this point we can use the iTunesConnect portal to link our uploaded app to a new app version in the AppStore and submit it for review. As soon as Apple has approved it we have successfully published our app to the AppStore!

Signing and Publishing on Android

This section will describe the entire process from creating a build up until publishing that build to the Play Store. Most of these steps are similar to the ones taken for iOS, but we describe the complete process for the sake of clarity. In these samples we will be using Visual Studio for Mac, but the same experience is available on Visual Studio for Windows. Some of the screens might look slightly different from the screenshots in the Windows version.

Archive for Publishing

The first step in creating an app binary that we can deploy to the Play Store is to build our application in Release mode. This ensures that all of our debug code is stripped from the application and other optimizations are performed. However, this step does not yet produce an APK file.

To get an APK file that we can use for publishing, we need to *archive* our release build. This can be done by choosing Build ➤ Archive for Publishing, as shown in Figure 6-12.

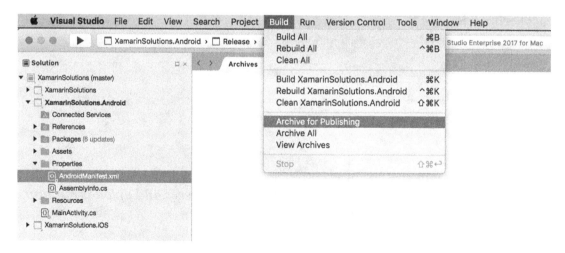

Figure 6-12. *Archiving our Android release build for publishing*

This process builds our project and bundles the application into an archive file. When the archiving process is done the Archive Manager will be shown (see Figure 6-13). This is where we can manage all of our created archives. We can add comments to each of these archives so we can identify the different archived versions of the app.

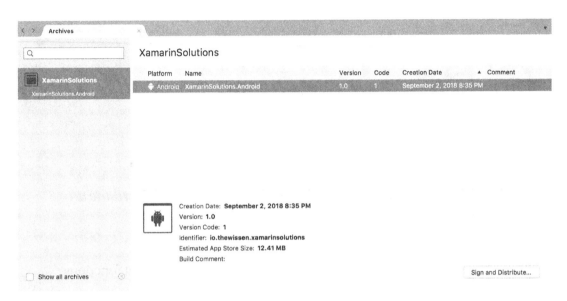

Figure 6-13. *The Archive Manager holding a single Android archived build*

Creating a Certificate

When we've successfully created an archive, we can start signing and publishing it. To sign our application, we first need to create a signing identity and a signing certificate before we can continue. To do so we need to click the Sign and Distribute button in the Archive Manager. We are then presented with a dialog giving us two options, as shown in Figure 6-14.

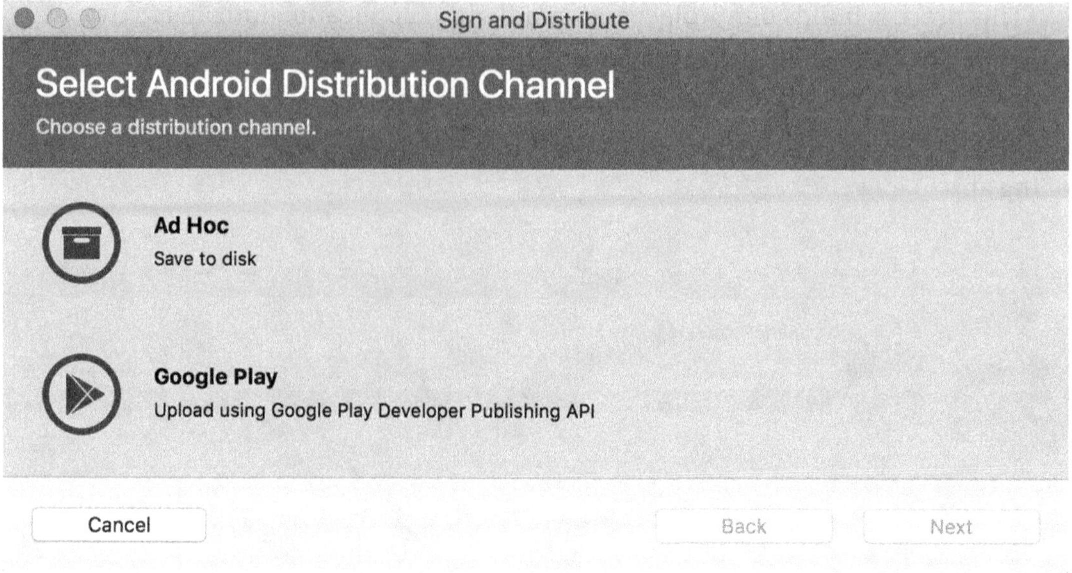

Figure 6-14. *The available choices when wanting to sign and distribute an Android archive*

These two types of distribution channels have significantly different functions.

- *AdHoc*—This option saves a signed APK to disk which we can then sideload onto Android devices. This is a simple way to create an APK for testing and distribution to your testers.

- *Google Play*—Publishes the signed APK to Google Play. This is the main distribution channel, so publish it there when you want to distribute a new production version.

To quickly create a certificate, we choose the AdHoc option. This will lead us to the Signing Identity page, as shown in Figure 6-15. The signing key is the same thing as the certificate. From this screen we can import an existing signing key or create a new one. Let's proceed by clicking the Create a New Key button.

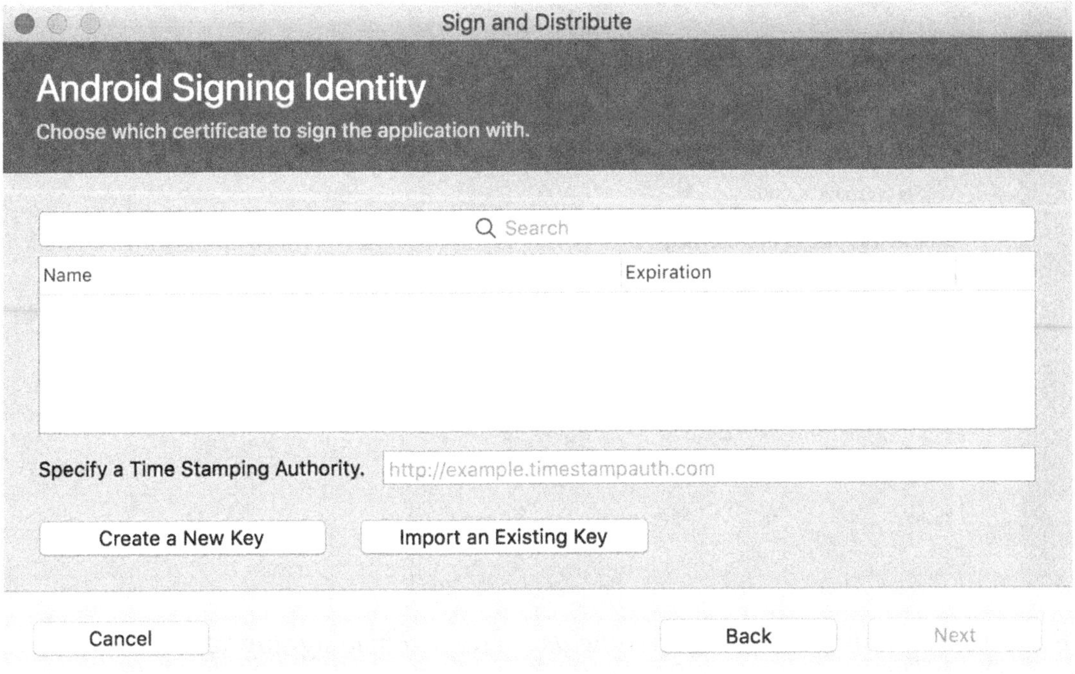

Figure 6-15. *The Signing Identity dialog where we can create or import a signing key*

A dialog to create a new certificate will popup, requiring us to provide some additional information. Figure 6-16 shows the kind of information we need to provide here. When everything is filled in, we click the Create button.

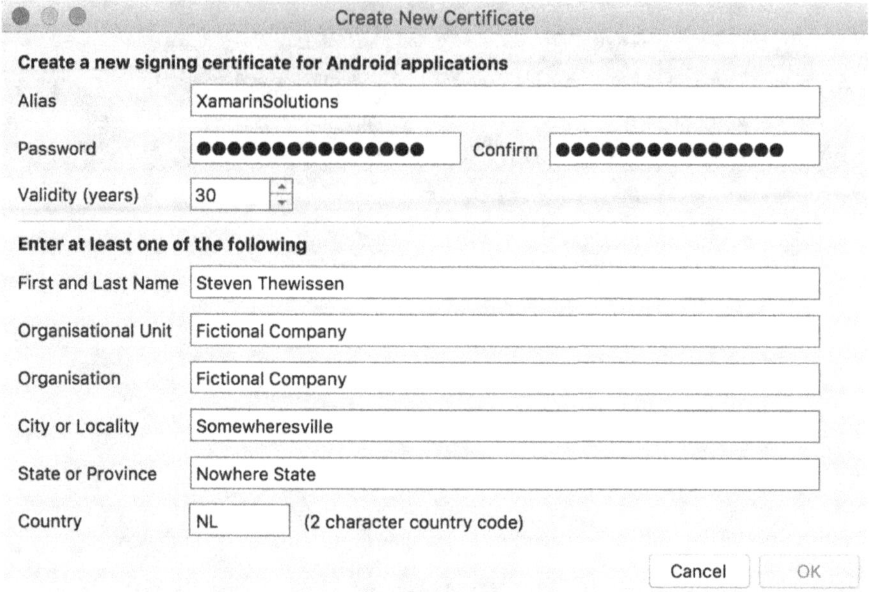

Figure 6-16. *Filling in the required fields to create a new signing key*

After filling in the form, a keystore file is generated. We have to make sure to back up this keystore file and the password in a safe location. This information is not stored within the solution, so if we lose our keystore file, we will be unable to sign the app with the same certificate as previous versions. Signing our app with a different certificate means we cannot use that APK file to update an existing version of our app in the Play Store.

Signing and Publishing APK File

After we've created the signing key, it will show up in the overview of our signing keys. Selecting it and clicking the Next button shows a screen indicating that we're ready to start the signing and publishing process. Clickingthe Publish button creates a signed APK file at the location of our choosing. See Figure 6-17.

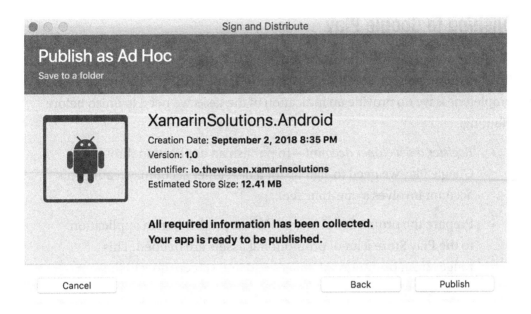

Figure 6-17. *The screen telling us that we're ready to start publishing our APK file*

When choosing the location of our APK file, we also need to provide the password of the certificate we just created. If the process completes successfully we see a screen indicating that we're done. This also gives us the option to quickly navigate to our newly created APK file. See Figure 6-18.

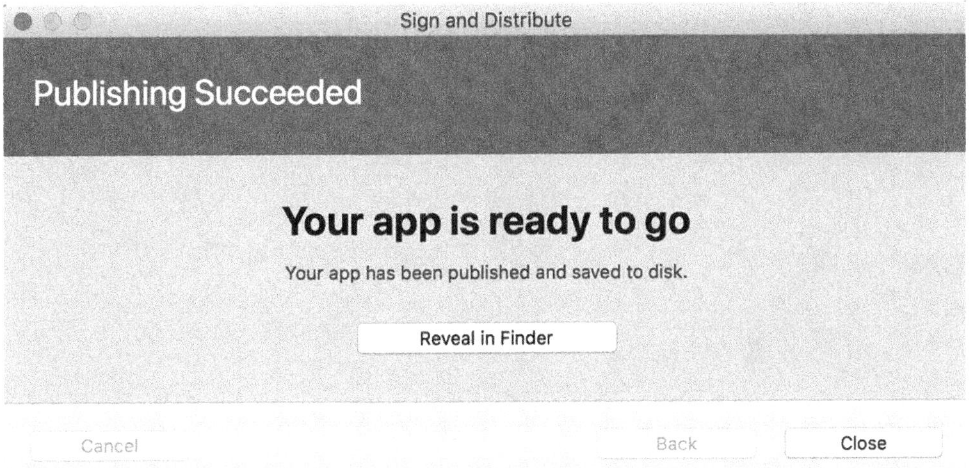

Figure 6-18. *The screen indicating that we've successfully created a signed APK file*

Publishing to Google Play

To distribute our application through Google Play, we need to fulfill a few prerequisites. Completing these prerequisites is not within the scope of this book, but for the sake of completeness we do provide an indication of the tasks we need to finish before distributing:

- *Register a developer account*—To publish an application through Google Play we need to sign up for a developer account. Creating this account involves a one-time fee.

- Prepare the promotional assets—When publishing an application to the Play Store a lot of promotional assets are needed. This ranges from promotional images and app screenshots to the app description text.

We already talked about the publishing process in the previous sections. To create a distribution that is suitable for Google Play, we need to choose the Google Play option shown in Figure 6-14. We are then presented with the Google Play API Account dialog that prompts us to provide the Client ID and Client secret. These provide Visual Studio with API access to our Google Play Developer account. See Figure 6-19.

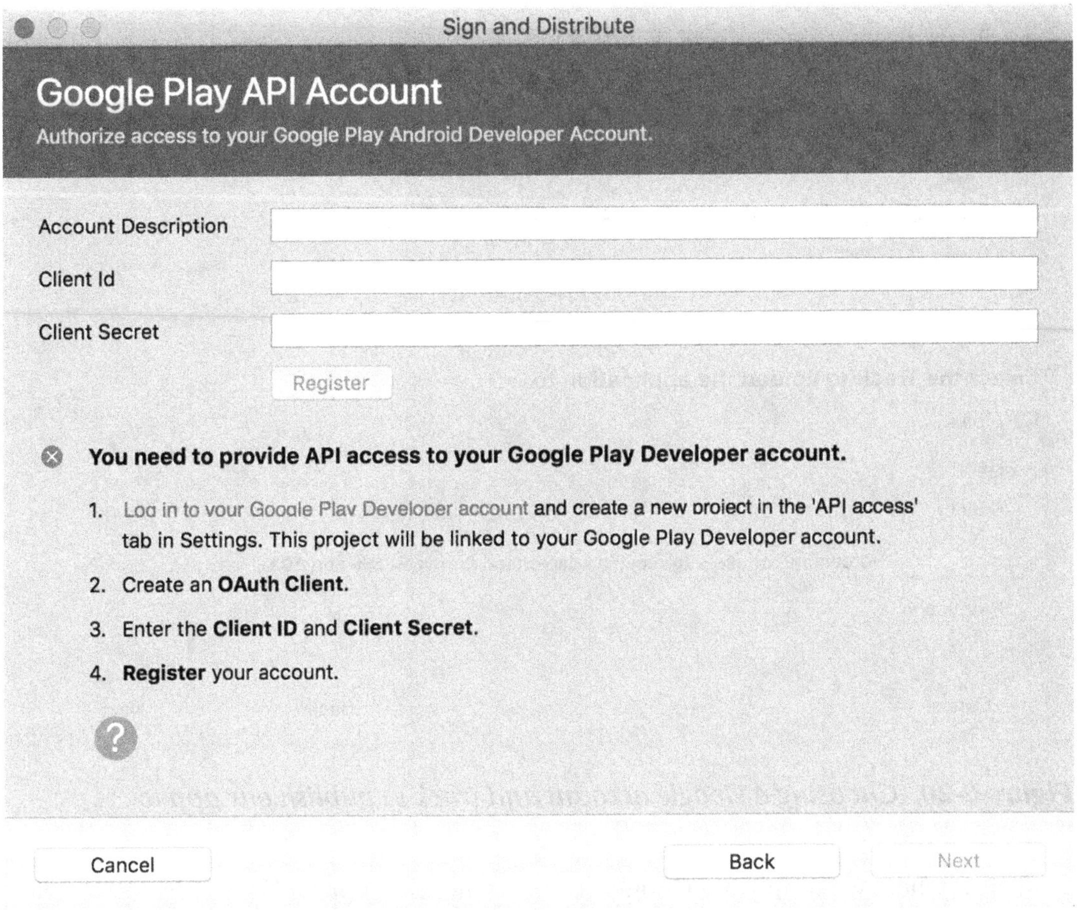

Figure 6-19. *Connecting our Google Play account to Visual Studio for Mac*

This dialog also provides information on how we can create a client ID and secret if we don't have them yet. It is therefore not described in more detail in this book. When filling in a valid client ID and secret, we can click Next and are presented with the Google Play Account dialog, as shown in Figure 6-20.

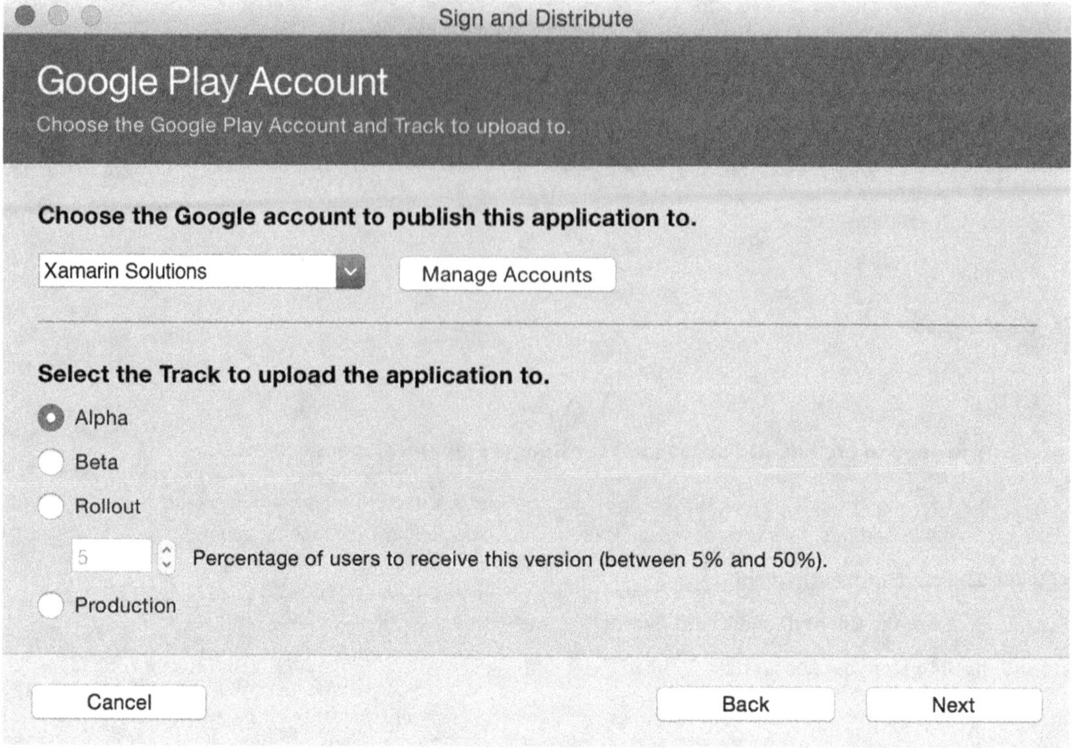

Figure 6-20. *Choosing a Google account and track to publish our app to*

This is where we supply our Google account where the app will be published to. We also have the option to choose one of four available tracks:

- *Alpha*—Use this option when a very early build needs to be made available to a small group of testers.

- *Beta*—Use this option when an early version of the app needs to be distributed to a bigger group of testers.

- *Roll out*—Use this option when we want to rollout an updated version of our app to a specific percentage of users. This enables us to rollout to, for example, 10% of all of our users and slowly increase the percentage of users receiving the new version.

- *Production*—Use this option when we're ready to roll out a new app version to all of our users enabling them to download it from the Google Play Store.

After choosing the track we want to publish to, we can click Next to continue. The steps after selecting our track are identical to the steps we described for an Ad Hoc distribution earlier in this section; creating a signing key and signing the build.

Contributing to Xamarin.Forms

There are two aspects to contributing to an open source project such as Xamarin.Forms. One is come to terms with your own expertise, to give yourself some credit, and to realize that the current contributors are human just like you are. Then you can begin the practical work, and that work starts by creating your own fork of the project to use as a development bed to create and test those features that you wish to contribute back to the project.

The Human Side

I (Gerald) have always been a bit reluctant to contribute to big awesome projects like Xamarin.Forms. The people working on those kinds of projects must be half-gods, right? They do all the awesome stuff, they are always right, are much smarter than me, what on Earth could I contribute to that?

I don't know about you, but that is basically what I used to think when pondering about contributing to a big opensource project. As it turns out, it wasn't as scary as I thought. Of course, I can't promise that the following will be true for all projects, but it is for Xamarin.Forms.

At some point, a couple of people from the Xamarin community got together to pick up a lot of small issues that we're lying around on the repository. Those issues known as the "F100" issues or F100 project. This project was targeting a hundred "papercut" issues. Issues that should have been features in Forms long-time ago, everyone is a bit annoyed by them, but now they are finally going to be implemented. To kickstart this, the people from the community I mentioned earlier, started an initiative later known as the community sprint.

We took a lot of these F100 issues that could easily—or not so easily—be implemented and did just that: implement them. I don't know the exact number, but a lot of those small issues have been picked up and implemented by now.

Adding a maximum length to an `Entry` and `Editor` control was the first contribution I made. It was small, but taught me a lot. It helped me find my way around the codebase. I took a good look at how similar properties were implemented and based my own code on that. After feeling confident enough and testing it on different platforms, I opened a PR and crossed my fingers. Luckily, the folks over at Xamarin are very kind and patient. They had some tips and pointers, but soon after that the PR got approved and merged.

Don't be bummed out by any comments that they might have. They are not trying to be better than you, they just have a lot of experience working on this product and know where the focus is. Also, they know their way around the codebase, so they might have more knowledge on how to implement something in a better way. That is basically something I had to realize for myself: see this as a learning experience. Just start somewhere and see where it takes you. It doesn't matter if it is not right the first time, you will do better next time.

Let's have a look at some more practical stuff to get you started.

How to Get Started

The first thing you want to do is create a fork of the Xamarin.Forms repository that you can find at `https://github.com/xamarin/Xamarin.Forms`. Getting everything to build shouldn't be too hard; when you are working with Xamarin already, all prerequisites should already be installed. Then, you start coding!

For the Xamarin.Forms repository everyone follows the .NET Foundation coding style. The guidelines can be found in this documentation page: `https://github.com/dotnet/corefx/blob/master/Documentation/coding-guidelines/coding-style.md`. There are two exceptions:

- We do not use the `private` keyword as it is the default accessibility level in C#.

- We use hard tabs over spaces.

Make sure to follow these guidelines, or else your PR will not be accepted. Of course, you will need something to fix or implement. This can be something you came up with yourself or something that is in the issues list of the project on GitHub.

In the former case, it might be a good idea to open an issue first. Let the guys over at Xamarin know what you're up to and let them weigh in on it. It might be something that they envision differently. It would be a shame if you put in a lot of effort and the team doesn't see the need to merge your carefully constructed code.

When picking an issue from the list, make sure you understand what is expected and no one else is working on it already. Also, just like before, make a comment and ask for clarification or elaborate on your plans.

When you've got something that is right for you, start implementing! This is the fun part. Writing code and thinking about how to make stuff work. There is a sample app project in the repository that you can use to test out your new fix or feature. Focus on iOS and Android first, if you can make it work for (all) other platforms as well, that is great! If not, maybe someone else can enrich your code further or do it at a later stage. You might encounter features that only make sense for a single platform, which means it doesn't make sense to implement it for the other platforms.

Testing for multiple platforms can also be problematic. I primarily use a Mac for development. This means Android and iOS are no problem at all, but Tizen or UWP are a bit harder to work with. You might lack the tools or environment to properly test these. For instance, UWP is relatively easy to work with by getting your hands on a Windows machine or VM. Tizen can also be done on Windows but needs special SDKs and emulators. While it can be a tough cookie to crack, it is worth it. I found it pretty rewarding being able to implement a new feature across *all* supported platforms.

When you are all done coding, don't forget about testing! Depending on how big of a change you are implementing, make sure to write unit tests and/or automated UI tests that verify your new code works. If, for some reason you skip this, make sure to state the reason in your PR.

When all the hard work is done according to you, head over to GitHub and create a PR on the Xamarin.Forms repository. Make sure you fill out the PR template to the best of your knowledge and submit it. From there you will have to wait for feedback from the team.

Initial feedback usually comes pretty fast, but before it will actually be merged it can take some time. Not sure what exactly happens behind the scenes, but they won't forget about you.

Tip   A very good writeup on the whole process has been done by Adam Pedley. In this blogpost, he describes some more in-depth details of the process. You can find it on his website: `https://xamarinhelp.com/contributing-xamarin-forms/`.

If you're like me and unsure how to begin, just begin. Make sure you understand what is asked of you, pull down the code and see if you can make something work. If you then decide you can't or don't want to do it, then don't. Maybe it's just not for you, or maybe it's not the right time. But I can tell you, it's pretty cool to see your feature on the release notes.

Do not be discouraged by your code not being merged directly or receiving some feedback. Remember that thousands of people are depending on this framework to work right, so the quality and performance has to be high, always.

Contributing doesn't have to mean adding code. You can also contribute by writing documentation, opening an issue with a great idea, localize things, etc. Basically, anything that someone else can benefit from one way or another.

Summary

In this chapter we aimed to tackle some of the more advanced topics that Xamarin. Forms developers come across regularly. We looked at converting our shared code from a Portable Class Library to .NET Standard to make our app more future-proof. All of your new projects should be .NET Standard from the start. We also looked at using an icon font for our images and how the built-in linker helps us reduce the file size of our binaries. Finally, we looked at how we can provision, sign, and publish our mobile application to a physical device and the App Store or Google Play.

Finally, we have given you some insights on contributing to Xamarin.Forms. Not a very technical story, but hopefully it can inspire you to have a look at the repository yourself and maybe even start contributing.

With this chapter we have also reached the end of this book. We hope you found a lot of useful content and you can be on your way with creating amazing Xamarin.Forms apps yourself. Thank you so much for buying and reading our book. If you have any questions or any other remarks, do not hesitate to reach out.

Index

© Gerald Versluis and Steven Thewissen 2019
G. Versluis and S. Thewissen, *Xamarin.Forms Solutions*, https://doi.org/10.1007/978-1-4842-4134-9

Printed in the United States
By Bookmasters